Music and song are central to modern culture, from social movements to cultural change. Building on their studies of sixties culture and the theory of cognitive praxis, Ron Eyerman and Andrew Jamison examine the mobilization of cultural traditions and the formulation of new collective identities through the music of activism. They combine a sophisticated theoretical argument with historical-empirical studies of nineteenth-century populists and twentieth-century labor and ethnic movements, focusing on the interrelations between music and social movements in the United States and the transfer of those experiences to Europe. Specific chapters examine folk and country music, black music, music of the 1960s movements, and music of the Swedish progressive movement. This highly readable book is among the first to link the political sociology of social movements to cultural theory.

Music and social movements

Cambridge Cultural Social Studies

Series editors: JEFFREY C. ALEXANDER, *Department of Sociology, University of California, Los Angeles*, and STEVEN SEIDMAN, *Department of Sociology, University at Albany, State University of New York*

Music and social movements

Mobilizing traditions in the twentieth century

Ron Eyerman
Uppsala University and the Center for Cultural Research, Vaexjoe University College, Sweden

and

Andrew Jamison
Aalborg University, Denmark

CAMBRIDGE
UNIVERSITY PRESS

PUBLISHED BY THE PRESS SYNDICATE OF THE UNIVERSITY OF CAMBRIDGE
The Pitt Building, Trumpington Street, Cambridge CB2 1RP, United Kingdom

CAMBRIDGE UNIVERSITY PRESS
The Edinburgh Building, Cambridge CB2 2RU, United Kingdom
40 West 20th Street, New York, NY 10011-4211, USA
10 Stamford Road, Oakleigh, Melbourne 3166, Australia

First published 1998

Printed in the United Kingdom at the University Press, Cambridge

Typeset in Times 10/12½ pt   [SE]

A catalogue record for this book is available from the British Library

Library of Congress cataloguing in publication data

Eyerman, Ron.
   Music and social movements : mobilizing traditions in the
twentieth century / Ron Eyerman and Andrew Jamison.
     p. cm. – (Cambridge cultural social studies)
   Includes bibliographical references.
   ISBN 0 521 62045 7 (hb) – ISBN 0 521 62966 7 (pb)
   1. Music and society. 2. Social movements – History – 20th century.
3. Political sociology – History – 20th century. 4. Popular culture –
History – 20th century. I. Jamison, Andrew. II. Title.
III. Series
ML3795.E98   1998
306.4'84 – dc21   97-25752 CIP
MN

ISBN 0 521 62045 7 hardback
ISBN 0 521 62966 7 paperback

In memory of Carl Sandburg, Langston Hughes, Janis Joplin, and Phil Ochs

Links on a chain

Contents

Acknowledgments

The writing of this book has been a truly collective experience, and there are many to thank. To begin with, the Swedish Research Council for the Humanities and Social Sciences has for a third time been generous in its support for our collaborative research, and we would like to express our appreciation. The editors of the Council's popular science journal, *Tvärsnitt*, Kjell Jonsson and Martin Kylhammar, have helped us reach a Swedish public with some of our ruminations about music and movements, more specifically, portions of chapters 5 and 6. A preliminary version of chapter 5 has also appeared in the Sage journal, *Media, Culture, and Society*, and is available as a chapter in McGraw Hill's sociology textbook, edited by Craig Calhoun. Thank you all for letting us reconstitute some of those thoughts here.

Along the way to publication, we sought out knowledge and advice about music and social movements from many sources. We were inspired by a number of papers presented at the meetings of the American Musicological Society in New York in October 1995, especially in the sessions organized by the Center for Black Music Research, whose library in Chicago we found a valuable stop on one of our trips to the States. Just before delivering the manuscript for publication, we took part in a conference in Santa Barbara, California, on "Social Movements and Music," organized by Dick Flacks. The discussions there with many leading scholars and performers provided the final kick we needed to bring the book to completion. Dick deserves special thanks for his encouragement and advice through the years, and, not least, for inviting us to give a seminar for his graduate students on a visit to California in May 1996 – and letting us attend his radio program on the "Culture of Protest" and listen to some of his vast record collection.

Many other people have helped, by singing along and listening to our presentations at conferences or seminars in Lund, Aalborg, Uppsala, Berlin, Bielefeld, Crete, and various other places. Those who have been especially important are Izzy Young, Johan Fornäs, Scott Baretta, Aant Elzinga, Arni Sverrisson, Mickey Flacks, Emily Jamison Gromark, Magnus Ring, and Jeff Alexander (whose series we are pleased to contribute to), and, as always, Johanna Esseveld and Margareta Gromark. To paraphrase Bob Dylan, you have been in our dream by helping it become real.

For permission to reproduce copyrighted material, we thank Harcourt Brace and Company for the quotations from *The People, Yes* and *Chicago Poems* by Carl Sandburg; Random House for the poems *Youth* and *I too hear America Singing* by Langston Hughes; Leif Nylen for the excerpt from his song, *Staten och kapitalet*; Sincere Management for the excerpt from *I Dreamed I Saw Phil Ochs Last Night* by Billy Bragg; and United Stage Publishing for the excerpt from *Victor Jara* by Mikael Wiehe.

Introduction

In April 1995, we attended a memorial celebration for Ralph Rinzler, a central musical activist in the 1960s social movements, at the Highlander Center, outside Knoxville, Tennessee, where Pete Seeger and Bernice Johnson Reagon and many others who had known Rinzler sang their songs of union organizing and civil rights struggle. Appropriately enough, it was there that the ideas in this book suddenly began to take form. Seeing and listening to Seeger and Reagon, along with "Doc" Watson, Mike and Peggy Seeger, Eric Weissberg, Jim Rooney, Hazel Dickens, and so many others, at the Highlander Center helped us to formulate the central arguments in this book. We saw, and felt, how songs could conjure up long-lost social movements, and how music could provide an important vehicle for the diffusion of movement ideas into the broader culture.

It was at Highlander, which, since the 1930s, has contributed so much to so many political movements, that the main point of this book became clear, namely that social movements are not merely political activities. Perhaps even more importantly, they provide spaces for cultural growth and experimentation, for the mixing of musical and other artistic genres, and for the infusion of new kinds of meaning into music. At Highlander, we saw some of the "results" of the movements of the 1960s, and the enormous influence that the mixing of music and politics had come to have on the popular culture. Out of the efforts of Ralph Rinzler and other "movement" intellectuals, bluegrass, gospel, folk music, even rock and jazz had been substantially reconstituted. At a time when the movements of the 1960s no longer have any meaningful political influence, the artists on the stage were living testimony to the cultural power that the sixties had harnessed and spread on into the broader society.

The central social process is what we term in this book the *mobilization of tradition*: in social movements, musical and other kinds of cultural traditions are made and remade, and after the movements fade away as political forces, the music remains as a memory and as a potential way to inspire new waves of mobilization. And perhaps no movement has been so important for this mobilization of tradition than the civil rights movement of the 1950s and 1960s, in which Reagon and Seeger and Rinzler played such an active role.

In a recent book, Robert Cantwell has offered a very different way of seeing the music of the 1960s (Cantwell 1996). Like many other cultural and musical historians, Cantwell stresses the apolitical nature of the music of the sixties, the generational longing that first led young people to folk music and later to rock, the spiritual vacuum that inspired the so-called "folk revival" and the counterculture. This nostalgia for a better, more innocent time "when we were good" is widespread in contemporary society, both among sympathizers like Cantwell and among "reborn" conservatives like David Horowitz – but, whether friend or foe, the love-it-or-hate-it relation to that tumultous decade tends to miss, or at least downplay, some fundamentally important connections between culture and politics, which continue to represent the "sixties" in the popular consciousness.

For Cantwell, the Kingston Trio and their hit song "Tom Dooley" symbolize the period, and he begins his book by tracing the development of that song during the various waves of folk revivals in the twentieth century. While Cantwell's account fascinates in its passion and enthusiasm – and we will be referring to it on several occasions in the pages that follow – it ultimately frustrates in its separation of the folk revival from the political movements that were taking place at the same time. The civil rights movement is mentioned, as are the antiwar and student movements, but they are not central to his story. For us, however, the central meaning of the 1960s was the visionary, collective project of the civil rights, student, and antiwar movements, and their composite program of political and cultural liberation: direct democracy, personalized politics, racial integration and equality, and respect for other cultures. And it is the songs of those movements – and of the singers, musicians, composers, and other artists who contributed their talents to them – that continue, throughout the world, to represent the spirit of the 1960s rather than the largely forgotten folk songs of the folk revival.

The evolution of the song, "We Shall Overcome," which more than any other expresses the project of the sixties, provides an instructive example of the mobilization of tradition in social movements, showing how traditions can link social movements, providing a river of embodied ideas and images between generations of activists. That song, which began as a spiritual, was picked up by the labor movement and, through contact between labor movement activists and civil rights activists at the Highlander Center, was transformed into the anthem of the civil rights movement and since then has found new "uses" in many other movements around the world.

A brief look at the history of that song can well set the stage for the pages that follow. "We Shall Overcome" emerged out of the collective song tradition created by African slaves in the United States. There was a gospel song, "I'll Be All Right," which was known in the late nineteenth century and sung among African-Americans in religious services in the South. A similar song appeared in written form in 1901 as "I'll Overcome Some Day" with a more European-style melody and slightly different words. Written by Charles Tindley, a black reverend in Philadelphia, it would be published along with other "modernized" spirituals in sheet music form in the first decades of the century, when spirituals achieved a degree of popularity not only as church music, but also as concert music. It was the older, more traditional song that survived in the collective memory, however, and that was later adapted into a song of labor activism. A major shift occurred in the 1940s when the song was taken up by the black Tobacco Workers Union as part of its mobilizing campaigns during labor conflicts in the South. The title was changed to "We Will Overcome." The collective pronoun replaced the singular, reflecting a shift in the locus of redemption, from sacred to secular, or at least from the individual to the group. And the tempo was slowed down, which helped to give the song a greater feeling of dignity and significance (Seeger 1993: 32–35).

In 1947 a second major shift occurred as the song was transformed into a white union organizing tool at the Highlander Center. Zilphia Horton, the music director at Highlander, had heard the song being sung among black workers, and it soon became one of her favorites and was taught and sung in the cultural programs that she had initiated at Highlander. Symbolically, the title was altered to the more grammatically correct "We *Shall* Overcome," probably by the Harvard dropout Pete Seeger, then active at the Center, which served as an institutional base in the struggle to keep the labor movement alive in the extremely hostile rural South. In his own rendition of the transformation of "We Shall Overcome" from spiritual to civil rights anthem, Pete Seeger has written, "No one is certain who changed 'will' to 'shall.' It could have been me with my Harvard education. But Septima Clarke, a Charleston schoolteacher (who was director of education at Highlander and after the Civil Rights Movement was elected year after year to the Charleston, S.C., Board of Education), always preferred 'shall.' It sings better" (1993: 34).

It was at the Highlander Center, which not only was one of the very few activist educational institutions in the United States, but also one of the even fewer to recognize the value of music to social movements, that the song was eventually passed back to blacks and to the civil rights movement. In 1959 at the end of a workshop at Highlander the local police burst in, and somebody started to hum "We Shall Overcome." In the heat of the moment, a young female high school student from Montgomery, Alabama, began to sing a new verse, "We are not afraid," and, according to Bernice Johnson Reagon, this helped give the song "new life and force." It soon became what Reagon calls the "theme song of the Movement, it was used wherever Movement activities were carried out" (1975: 82–83).

From Highlander, it was carried into the streets and jailhouses of the South, and of course its form of presentation was modified and what Reagon calls its "range of usage" expanded in the process. Eventually recorded by popular folksingers like Joan Baez and Peter, Paul, and Mary, the song has become part of a global culture of dissent and is usually sung in a ritualized way, as a sing-along, with the audience linking arms as they sing. In the United States, the traditional call-and-response technique of African-American musical culture is also usually used. In this style the leader, such as Pete Seeger in one of many live recorded versions, "calls" a verse and the audience responds with the well-known chorus.

At the Rinzler Memorial celebration, it was Bernice Johnson Reagon who led us in singing "We Shall Overcome." We sang it SNCC-style, the way the activists in the Student Non-violent Coordinating Committee sang it in the 1960s: arms crossed and joined, swaying back and forth, and with a caller – Reagon herself, as she was on so many occasions in the 1960s, when as a college student, she brought her magnificent voice into the civil rights movement. Intriguingly, Reagon was joined on the stage by many of the stars of contemporary country music, usually considered apolitical or even conservative. In the 1960s, Ralph Rinzler had been one of many musicians who had been led to folk music for both musical and political reasons, and he had, like so many others, seen the connections between tradition and dissent, between oldtime musics and contemporary political struggles. Indeed, it can be suggested that the resurrection of bluegrass music, as well as many other traditional musics, was inspired by the civil rights movement, and its actualization of history, its linking of the past with the present.

In any case, in April 1995, we saw the various strands of the 1960s "mobilization of tradition" gathered together on one stage. This book is an attempt to place the experience of that weekend into a theoretical and historical context, and, in particular, to show how the combination of music and politics that takes place in social movements is an important, if often overlooked, source of cultural transformation.

In this book, chapter 1 recapitulates the cognitive approach, and traces recent developments in social movement theory. We discuss the current "cultural turn" in sociology, while noting the continuing separation between those who concern themselves with political movements and those who study culture and its various shades of movement. The following chapter places our effort in relation to the ongoing debates about modernity and tradition. We present an alternative interpretation of traditions, and of their underlying rationalities, as a way to overcome the neglect that social theorists have shown in the contemporary fascination with traditional knowledge, ways of life, and music.

The next three chapters are substantive analyses of the mobilization of music, and the making and remaking of musical traditions, within social movements. We focus first on the folk musics of the United States, tracing them back to the country's multiethnic inheritance and, more specifically, to the populist movements of the late nineteenth century, which, we claim, provide the historical subsoil out of which so much of twentieth-century popular music has grown. The following chapter examines the movements of black music, characterizing an essential tension in African-American musical traditions between secular and sacred, highbrow and lowbrow, commercial and non-commercial. The movements of cultural nationalism in the 1920s and the civil rights movement of the 1950s and 1960s are seen as central moments in the resolution of these tensions, and in the subsequent reconstitution of black music, which now, as rap music, is having once again fundamental repercussions on global culture. Chapter 5 focuses on the 1960s. Here we analyze the changing relations between politics and music – from the reborn interest in folk music in the first half of the decade to the cataclysms of the so-called counterculture, which both mixed black and white musical traditions and articulated a new generational consciousness. Our reading of the 1960s stresses the movement roots of rock music, which unfortunately have not attracted the attention they deserve. Our chapter thus offers an alternative explanation of the contribution that the movements of the 1960s have made to world culture.

Chapter 6 attempts to bring the story up to date, by focusing on the diffusion of rock music from the sixties to the nineties. We use the case of Sweden as an illustrative example of the contemporary contradiction between a global commercial music industry, on the one hand, drawing the rest of the world under its control, and the rise of alternative folk, or roots, musics, on the other, which oppose but are often integrated into the commercial realm. In Sweden, this contradiction has been particularly visible, and was mediated, in the 1970s, through an explicit "progressive music movement." Our concluding chapter recounts the arguments, and seeks to connect our material to cultural theory.

1

On social movements and culture

The new sensibility has become a political factor. This event, which may well indicate a turning point in the evolution of contemporary societies, demands that critical theory incorporate the new dimension into its concepts, project its implications for the possible construction of a free society.   Herbert Marcuse, *An Essay on Liberation* (1969: 23)

Social movements and cultural transformation

Social movements are interpreted in this book as central moments in the reconstitution of culture. In the creative turmoil that is unleashed within social movements, modes of cultural action are redefined and given new meaning as sources of collective identity. For brief, intensive moments, the habitual behavior and underlying values of society are thrown open for debate and reflection, and, as the movements fade from the political center stage, their cultural effects seep into the social lifeblood in often unintended and circuitous ways.

It is our contention that both the culture of everyday life – the values, mores, and habits that form the basis of social behavior – and the "art worlds" of cultural expression are deeply affected by the innovative activities, the exemplary cultural actions, that take place in social movements. In the 1960s, Herbert Marcuse emphasized the aesthetic dimension of the movements of the time, suggesting that it was primarily in art and music that social movements "re-membered" traditions of resistance and critique (Marcuse 1969). More recently, Richard Flacks, in his analysis of the American "tradition of the Left," has indicated how social movements have often been more important as cultural than as political actors (Flacks 1988). This book continues along the lines staked out by Marcuse and

Flacks by offering a theoretically informed reflection on the relations between social movements and culture.

Our claim is that, by combining culture and politics, social movements serve to reconstitute both, providing a broader political and historical context for cultural expression, and offering, in turn, the resources of culture – traditions, music, artistic expression – to the action repertoires of political struggle. Cultural traditions are mobilized and reformulated in social movements, and this mobilization and reconstruction of tradition is central, we contend, to what social movements are, and to what they signify for social and cultural change.

These processes have generally been neglected in social theory and in cultural studies, where responsibility for change is usually attributed either to anonymous, universal forces, such as modernization, capitalism, or imperialism, or to charismatic leaders and powerful individuals. This book argues, in opposition to these dominant approaches, that the collective identity formation that takes place in social movements is a central catalyst of broader changes in values, ideas, and ways of life. We intend to give social movements the recognition they deserve as key agents of cultural transformation.

In the following chapters, we will consider the culturally transforming aspects of social movements primarily in relation to music. Music and song have been important in the formation, and remembrance, of a wide range of social movements, but these musical components of collective identity have seldom been examined explicitly in the social movement, or broader sociological, literature. By focusing on the interaction of music and social movements, we want to highlight a central, even formative aspect of cultural transformation. And we want to offer a new kind of contextual understanding for students of popular music and culture.

We conceive of these relations between culture and politics, between music and movements, as collective learning processes, in continuation of what we have previously characterized as a cognitive approach to social movements. In our previous work, we have sought to identify the knowledge-producing activities that are carried out within social movements, and have attempted to indicate how this "cognitive praxis" has affected scientific research programs and professional intellectual identities. Social movements have provided contexts for the politicization of knowledge, and the effects have often been profound on scientific theorizing, disciplinary identities, and even technological developmental trajectories (Eyerman and Jamison 1991). The aim of this book is to redirect the cognitive approach to music and to consider musical expression in social movements as a kind of cognitive praxis.

The labor movement, the civil rights movement, the antiwar movement, and the feminist and environmental movements have all largely disappeared as living political forces in our societies, but they remain alive, we contend, in the collective memory. These and other social movements have all been more than merely political actors; their significance has been also – in many ways even more so – cultural (Darnovsky, Epstein, and Flacks 1995). Reducing them to politics, as most students of social movements tend to do, is to ignore a great deal of what social movements actually represent. In essence, it is to relegate them to the dustbin of history, to a nostalgic activism that at best can serve to inspire new politics, but all too often evokes little academic or political interest. The attempts, for example, by Doug McAdam (1988), to revive the spirit of the civil rights movement, and by Jack Whalen and Richard Flacks (1989) to trace the impact of the "sixties generation" through empirical analysis of the life histories of activists have unfortunately fallen victim to changing political and academic fashion. The other tendency typically followed in cultural studies and the humanities, namely to limit attention to artistic or literary movements, frequently downplays the political basis, or underlying motivation, for many cultural innovators. Among sociologists like Howard Becker (1982) and Diana Crane (1987), for example, artistic creation is placed in social contexts of "art worlds" or "avant-garde movements," but the broader links to politics and social movements are barely noticed. The political movements have thus generated one sort of academic literature, while the cultural movements have generated very many others, subdivided and differentiated along genre, disciplinary, and national lines. It sometimes seems as if politics and culture were pursued on different planets.

The few analysts who have tried to link the two have provided us with some important starting points. Alberto Melucci, following in the tradition of Alain Touraine, has long stressed the centrality of the cultural aspects of social movements, as did earlier students of "collective behavior" (see Melucci 1989). For Melucci, movements are characterized as a kind of symbolic action, by which new forms of collective identity are created. The emphasis is on the psychological attributes of identity formation, on the meanings that individuals derive from participation in movements, and the results of movements are seen as codes or signs that challenge the dominant political order. It is an impressive sociological theory that Melucci presents in his most recent work, a major achievement in linking structure and action, and in infusing meaning into the study of social movements (Melucci 1996). And yet the actual cultural work that is carried out in social movements is given little attention. By viewing social movements through the deductive, or rationalist, lens of what C. Wright Mills once called "grand" sociological theory (Mills 1959), Melucci unintentionally transforms social movements into abstract concepts: into fields, arenas, forms, logics, frames, and symbols.

The work of R. Serge Denisoff, and, more recently, Ray Pratt, provides us with another point of departure (Denisoff 1972, Pratt 1990). Here the emphasis is on the cultural work of social movements themselves, the songs and the singers, to be precise. Like Crane and Becker in the world of art, the sociologist in this case is a descriptive categorizer of reality, giving particular songs and singers social functions or roles, and thus practicing a form of what Mills termed "abstracted empiricism." The many other students of musical and cultural movements who have provided so much of the "data" for our effort here are not to be faulted for neglecting the cultural activity that takes place in social movements. The problem is rather that the empirical material is separated out from broader patterns and conceptions of social change, and, indeed, separated from other domains of social life, becoming part of a sociological subfield, the sociology of music, art, or culture.

Our effort attempts to find a middle ground between grand theory and abstracted empiricism. Like Melucci, we seek to link politics and culture, but we want to lower the level of abstraction. Rather than imposing a language of discourse and coding onto the substance of social movements, we want to extract the cultural aspects from real social movement activity. Rather than constructing a grand sociological theory of social movements, we want to link social movement theory to cultural studies. By considering the cultural aspects of social movements as cognitive praxis, and thus viewing them through the lens of a critical theory of knowledge, we seek to avoid the opposite danger of abstracted empiricism. Our examples are, as it were, "theory laden"; they are selected to answer a theoretical question, namely how do social movements contribute to processes of cognitive and cultural transformation?

We have earlier argued that social movements are important sources of knowledge production, both scientific and non-scientific, and that it is, in large measure, through the knowledge interests of social movements that paradigmatic, or cosmological, assumptions about reality, as well as scientific approaches to nature and technology, are given new substantive content. Social movements provide an important context for at least some of the scientific revolutions, the formulation of new scientific paradigms, that Thomas Kuhn brought to widespread attention in the 1960s (Kuhn 1970). In our day, feminist theory and women's studies, African-American studies, and the wide range of environmental sciences and social ecological theories have been strongly shaped by the cognitive intervention of social movements. These social movements, like the labor movement in the past, have also provided new career opportunities, as well as training grounds for the testing of new ideas, which have later been translated into professional activities by academics and other intellectuals.

In this book, we want to extend our approach by examining the ways in which social movements contribute to processes of cultural transformation, particularly in relation to music. On the one hand, social movements challenge dominant categories of artistic merit by making conscious – and problematic – the taken-for-granted frameworks of evaluation and judgment. This they do on a discursive level as well as in performance practices, by experimenting with new aesthetic principles and creating new collective rituals. On the other hand, social movements utilize the media of artistic expression for communicating with the larger society and, by so doing, often serve to (re)politicize popular culture and entertainment. In music, art, and literature, social movements periodically provide an important source of renewal and rejuvenation, by implanting new meanings and reconstituting established aesthetic forms and genres. In more general terms, through their impact on popular culture, mores, and tastes, social movements lead to a reconstruction of processes of social interaction and collective identity formation.

Political movements or cultural movements?

These cultural political activities are not necessarily progressive nor need they always be morally commendable. In the twentieth century, traditions have been mobilized by movements with a wide range of political agendas, from the fascist and communist movements of the interwar years through the new social movements of the 1960s and on to the movements of ethnic nationalism of the 1980s and 1990s. The cultural work of many of these social movements has been regressive, if not reactionary, in that the selective transformation of tradition has often been aggressively directed toward the non-privileged others, those who have fallen outside the culturally defined categories of acceptance. The "reactionary modernism" of the Nazis, as well as the religious intolerance that is to be found in many contemporary forms of fundamentalism, is derived from mobilizing cultural traditions for political purposes in ways that are directly comparable to the "progressive" movements that we take up in this book – movements, we admit, with which we share a basic sympathy.

Whether progressive or reactionary, what is at work in almost all social movements, we would claim, is an active reworking of cultural resources, both an inventive, creative work of artistic experimentation and a critical, reflective work of evaluation. And it is the cultural effects that often live on; it is through songs, art, and literature – and as ritualized practices and evaluative criteria – that social movements retain their presence in the collective memory in the absence of the particular political platforms and struggles that first brought them into being.

In actual social movements, this cultural work is often subsumed to more immediate political tasks, and is seldom examined in an explicit way, either by activists or observers. Indeed, many activists are at pains to distinguish the political from the cultural in social movement activity. And, partly as a result of this separation, social movements are usually discussed and interpreted in political terms: ideologies, tactics, issues, campaigns, strategies, organizations. The dominant interpretative frameworks portray movements as instrumental actors, channeling material, human, and organizational resources into political struggles. What is of interest is the effectiveness with which social movements are able to achieve their political goals, while most analysts pay little attention to the deeper and more longlasting impact that social movements have on processes of cultural transformation. While movement "cultures" have come to be taken more seriously in recent years, there is still little attempt to focus analysis directly on the cultural work that is actually done in social movements (Johnston and Klandermans 1995).

For many empirical researchers of social movements, culture is viewed as a "frame" that structures the "real" movement of political activity, while for theorists like Alberto Melucci social movements are, as it were, reduced to a semiotic culture of codes and symbolic meanings. Our ambition here is not to belittle either contribution, but rather to focus on the essential tension between the political and the cultural, which, we suggest, is crucial for our understanding of social change. Such a focus can also provide a valuable corrective to the emphasis on discourse and language that characterizes so much of the ongoing debates about modernity.

Most of the literature on the "postmodern condition" focuses on texts, either actual literary products or the dialogic practices that can be read into social interactions. Society is treated, for the most part, as a web of discourses, and the emphasis is placed on the construction of identity and meaning through various forms of written articulation. The text, however, whether it be a book or a "social text," is usually treated as a thing in itself, decontextualized and disembodied. This often makes for fascinating analyses of particular cultural representations, and has led to the production of an entire new methodological arsenal for extracting the essence out of an exemplary document; but all too often the deeper structures of social and cultural change are left unexamined. The importance of history, and especially the role of collective action and social movements in reconstructing the contexts in which all texts are made and remade, is bracketed out. In order to concentrate on the specificity of texts, the generality of contexts is dismissed. We do not want to resurrect the "structuralist" theories that the postmodernists have challenged, but we do contend that there are very serious limitations in the attempts to read society in textual terms.

While there exists a vast number of accounts by historians of art, music, and literature on the cultural activities of political movements, most remain curiously underutilized by students of social movements. All too often, these accounts are written in the idioms of cultural history, where aesthetic considerations take precedence over social understanding. There are exceptions, to be sure, but it can be claimed that the voluminous writings about the relations between communist, fascist, and Nazi movements and culture have not had a great deal of impact on our understanding of social movements. There are exciting studies about the artists of the Bolshevik Revolution and the Weimar Republic, and there are fascinating portrayals of the use of art and performance rituals of left- and right-wing movements of the interwar period. Biographies provide detailed accounts of the involvement of many leading artists, musicians, and writers in political campaigns – from the resistance movements of the 1930s and 1940s to the civil rights and antiwar movements of the 1960s.

For our purposes, these accounts open up a rich field for sociological analysis. On the one hand, they point to the crucial importance of political commitment in much artistic production. So many of the leading artists, writers, and composer/musicians of the twentieth century have been involved, at formative periods of their lives, in political movements. This does not mean that the monumental artistic achievements of Picasso, Kollwitz, Rivera, Gorky, Brecht, Sartre, Weill, Copland, Bernstein, Baez, Dylan, and all the others can be reduced to their political involvements. But it does suggest that, without having taken active part in social movements, these individuals would have produced very different works. And, in most cases, movement involvement remained central to their artistic production. Their engagement was objectified in their art, and the movement thus came to be embodied in them. When the movements in which they had been involved were no longer active, the ideas and ideals of the movements lived on in their art. And, in many cases, they served to inspire new movements by helping to keep the older movements alive in the collective memory.

On the other hand, the detailed accounts of the relations between cultural expression and politics provide exemplification for expanding our cognitive approach into the realm of culture. What we have previously called cognitive praxis and movement intellectuals can be seen, with the help of this material, to encompass cultural practices of both anthropological and aesthetic varieties. Movements are seen to be the breeding ground for new kinds of ritualized behavior, as well as for artistic, musical, and literary experimentation. For example, Temma Kaplan's recent book on the interplay between art and politics in Barcelona at the turn of the century shows how participants in the Catalan national movement carried out a range of cultural activities, and how artists like the young Pablo Picasso served as movement artists in articulating the identity of the movement (Kaplan 1992). Closer to the concerns of this book, Robbie Lieberman's study of "people's songs" in the United States between the years 1930 and 1950 shows how the socialist movement provided a context for the making of American folk music. It was as part of a social movement that Pete Seeger, Woody Guthrie, Alan Lomax, Leadbelly, Burl Ives, and so many others brought folk songs into the popular culture (Lieberman 1995). Similarly, Bernice Johnson Reagon's doctoral dissertation on the songs of the civil rights movement shows how activists mobilized the traditions of black and white folk and popular music in pursuing their political goals (Reagon 1975). In both cases, the cognitive praxis of social movements has had, as we shall see in coming chapters, a major impact on musical taste and popular culture throughout the world.

Many cultural historians, and historians of music, art, and literature have begun to look more closely at the social contexts within which culture is created and produced. We now have a vast literature of studies of particular cultural and artistic "worlds," ranging from the galleries of Soho to the Grand Ole Opry in Nashville, or from the writers of the Harlem "renaissance" of the 1920s to the pop musicians of contemporary Africa. And there is, among the biographers of artists and musicians, a noticeable effort to socialize the subject, to see the individual artist as not merely expressing his or her own personality, but rather to see Duke Ellington, Bob Dylan, Janis Joplin, or Jimi Hendrix, to name some of the characters who will appear later in this book, as representative figures, as symbols for their times. More generally, Robert Cantwell's recent study on the "folk revival" (Cantwell 1996) and a range of other materials – from CD boxes to auto-biographical recollections – have brought the music of the 1960s back to life, and it has become obvious that many of the musical innovations of the times were intimately and intricately connected to the political campaigns and struggles that were taking place. The music and the politics fed into one another in complex and variegated ways, providing what Marcuse at the time termed a new sensibility, planting many of the seeds for today's "global" youth culture.

Unfortunately, this work has had little apparent influence on the sociology of social movements. Partly, this is due to a difference in focus: for most social movement theorists and other sociologists, culture is something that forms or "frames" social movements and other social activities as a set of (external) conditioning factors, while for the students of culture it is social movements or environments that provide the external contexts or conditions that shape the primary objects of analysis, art, music, literature, and their creators. The one talks of a movement culture or a cultural frame for movement activities and campaigns, while the other refers to the social background that is embodied in, or has helped to shape, the individual artist or group. The difference, we might say, concerns what is influencing what, the direction of conditioning. Even more importantly, there seems to be a fundamental difference in language, methods, and theoretical orientation. Sociologists and humanists are subjected to different processes of academic socialization, and are seldom given an opportunity to interact, or even read or hear about each other's works.

Our approach seeks to synthesize social movement theory and cultural studies by using the texts and contexts of popular music as illustrative material. In the twentieth century, a central component of the cultural work of social movements has been music and song, or what Houston Baker, in speaking of African-American movements, calls "sounding": musical traditions have been given new life through social movements at the same time as social movements have often expressed their meaning and gained coherence through music (Baker 1987). And perhaps nowhere has the "role" of music been more important than in the United States, where social movements have often been less ideological and more emotive than in other countries. From the abolitionists through the populists in the nineteenth century and on to the labor and ethnic and "new" social movements of the twentieth century, music and song have helped to shape the imagery and the meaning of American social movements. It has been perhaps primarily through music and song that social movements have exerted their main influence on the wider American culture, as well as on the rest of the world. By focusing on the interrelations between music and social movements in the United States – and on the transfer of those experiences to Europe – we hope to disclose a central but neglected force in broader processes of cultural transformation.

The American experience, at one and the same time exceptional and universal, will provide our main empirical material for illustrating the central importance of social movements in the "mobilization of tradition." By a selective reworking of traditional cultural materials, modern societies periodically reinvent themselves, and popular music is increasingly one of the most significant arenas for this mobilization.

Sociology and culture

Sociological approaches to culture are typically divided between so-called Weberian and Durkheimian traditions. Max Weber and his more recent followers locate culture within human consciousness, as worldviews or cognitive frameworks through which actors organize sense impressions and interpret the world as meaningful. Weber assumed that it is through subjectively rooted categories that human beings impose frameworks of meaning on an otherwise meaningless world. It is by uncovering these frameworks that sociologists are able to explain as well as understand human action because, as Anne Swidler puts it, "culture shapes action by defining what people want and how they imagine they can get it" (1995: 25).

Weber distinguished ideal-typical categories of "ethos" – like the Protestant-based secularizing ethos in the West and the Confucian-based customary ethos in China – and of "action," like rational-instrumental, value-rational, and effectual, which the sociological observer can use to explain why individuals do what they do. Talcott Parsons, Jürgen Habermas, and other "grand" theorists follow a similar procedure in developing categories or types of action from the point of view of the sociological observer, without consideration of the individual actor. The interactionist perspective of Jonathan Turner adds to categorizations of the Weberian type the point of view of the actor. From the interactionist perspective, culture or meaning is emergent and ephemeral; it develops out of the situated interactions of individuals as a collective accomplishment. As such, it is fragile and must continually be reaffirmed. Turner discusses the categories which actors use to define a situation when monitoring their own behavior, that is, when pondering which is the proper response in a given situation: such as work/practical, ceremonial, or social. Defining or categorizing a situation is a useful, perhaps even a necessary, simplifying procedure for actors in a complicated social world. The focus is on the interaction of individuals, rather than on the individual as such.

Emile Durkheim located culture in the social practices which tied members of a society or social group to each other, in the objective "collective representations" or the subjective codes through which they were understood. Such collective representations, writes Swidler, "are not ideas developed by individuals or groups pursuing their interests. Rather, they are the vehicles of a fundamental process in which publicly shared symbols constitute social groups while they constrain and give form to individual consciousness" (1995: 26). Ceremonies or ritualized practices were vital in maintaining group solidarity in simpler or primitive societies, while in modern societies more organic forms of interaction, mediated through a complex social division of labor, were seen to link individuals together. Regardless of such evolutionary distinctions, the focus of the Durkheimian analysis of culture, as Jeffrey Alexander writes, "is on the structure and process of meaningful systems, which are taken to be universal regardless of historical time or place" (1990: 18).

Theoretical constructions like internalization and, more broadly, socialization have since been developed to help identify the mechanisms linking the internal and the external, the Weberian and the Durkheimian notions of culture, into one theoretical framework. Talcott Parsons' notion of "role" as the pre-formed container of societal values and norms which individuals acquire was formulated with just this purpose in mind. Parsons used the concept of "values" to signify both the collective representations which Durkheim talked about and the frameworks of meaning analyzed by Weber. Socialization is the process through which the already-existing values which constitute a culture are inculcated into individuals. At the same time, values are transformed into norms and rules – proscribed proper forms of reciprocal action – which individuals internalize as they are acculturated.

The influential cultural sociology of Pierre Bourdieu adopts something of a middle position with its emphasis on education and processes of habituation and distinction. For Bourdieu, culture has all but replaced society as the object of sociological concern; and, while no one can accuse Bourdieu of not taking culture seriously, his concepts are of relatively little use in trying to understand how cultures change, or how social movements conduct their cultural activity and contribute to cultural transformation. By focusing on the manifestations of culture, the longer-term processual emphasis tends to be neglected. Like the many anthropologists who try to get within the cultures they study in a densely detailed way, Bourdieu is able to disclose fascinating aspects of cultural activity and develop a sociology of culture. The crucial link to social movements, however, is largely missing from his work.

Following Durkheim more closely than Weber, Bourdieu replaces the concept of role with that of habitus, to emphasize the weight of historically formed patterns of action and codes of understanding on individuals. From his perspective, the concept of role is too tied to rules and norms which must be actively learned, rather than to more passively acquired habits. For all their differences, however, Bourdieu shares with Parsons (and many other cultural sociologists) an interest in explaining the reproduction of society, rather than its transformation, and concepts such as role and habitus are central to that aim. As such, culture is conceptualized as an anonymous, macro-level realm of values and customs or as a micro-level individualized identity of habits and norms. The crucial "levels" of mediation in between the macro and the micro – which is where social movements are to be found – are accordingly given much less attention than they deserve.

The cultural turn in social movement theory

As has been the case for sociology in general, a growing interest in culture can be noted among scholars of social movements in recent years. In the ongoing questioning of modernity that is taking place throughout the world, there has emerged a range of new "identity movements" which is bringing issues of ethnicity, race, sexuality, and personal expression out of the private sphere and into broader societal arenas. At the same time, deep-seated cultural traditions and systems of belief have been challenged by processes of globalization, and, as a result, there has been a rise of vocal and often aggressive nationalist and "traditionalist" movements. In many of these social movements, the classical activity of political campaigning has been subordinated to a range of cultural or symbolic practices – from women wearing veils to the rediscovery of traditional forms of art, music, and religious ritual. Questions of meaning, belief, value, and identity have seemingly become more important than the political pursuit of power and the achievement of practical economic improvements. Many of the new social movements are actually practicing a new kind of cultural politics, where the main concern is to change values rather than to gain particular political results.

Culture has been brought into the sociology of social movements in recent years primarily through the idiom of "framing" by which social movement activity is subjected to a form of discourse analysis (see Hunt, Benford, and Snow 1994). A series of processes are defined – frame alignment, articulation, amplification, etc. – which are meant to give structure to the ideational activity that takes place in social movements. In the analysis of particular movements, a broader, more anthropological concept of "movement culture" has also begun to be used, particularly among analysts of women's movements and organizations (Taylor and Whittier 1995). In this perspective, social movements are seen as being formed within and, in turn, helping to re-form broader domains of social life. Particular feminist movements, for example, are seen to be part of an emergent feminist culture, with values and practices that are different from those of the dominant, masculine culture. As such, a wide range of approaches is emerging, influenced both by the so-called "linguistic turn" in philosophy and social and cultural theory, and by the importance that non-instrumental activities actually play within contemporary social movements.

The cultural turn in social movement theory can also be seen as an attempt to (re)connect European and American approaches, as a sort of positive byproduct of the globalization of academic work. When, in a now-classic article, Jean Cohen (1985) stylized two "paradigms" of social movement research, and then attempted to synthesize them, she was giving voice to processes which had been in motion since the end of the Second World War. The collective behaviorist tradition, which had dominated American research on social movements until the 1960s, had by the 1980s given way to the organizational analysis and rational choice approach of "resource mobilization" as the hegemonic leader in the field. This was matched on the other side of the Atlantic by a concern with interest mobilization and a focus on questions of power and domination. What all had in common was that social movement actors and organizations were approached from the outside, that is, as objects to be explained in terms of individual or collective strategies. The prime concern was the success or failure of movements, as measured through their longevity, power, and influence (see Eyerman and Jamison 1991).

The lack of concern with meaning by social movement theorists has now been increasingly recognized. What Jean Cohen helped identify as the "identity paradigm," which she associated with Habermas and Alain Touraine, and which has since been recast as new social movement theory by Alberto Melucci and others, has effectively challenged the hegemony of the resource mobilization approach. That this essentially European-based approach should be gaining ground represents a sort of coup for European sociology in what has been an American field.

The recent interest among social movement theorists in culture can thus be seen as an attempt to meet the challenge of constructivism and post-modernism by referring to the "frames" in which social movements conduct their political campaigns (Tarrow 1994). Like the border around a painting, the frame structures the picture of reality that guides the movement actors in pursuing their goals. The so-called "master" frame is seen to provide an interpretation of the problem complex that the movement is operating in, something akin to what Marxist-oriented social scientists call ideology or what Weber meant by ethos. What is different in the new language of framing is the specificity of the analytical focus; like the post-structuralist text, the movement frame is dehistoricized as it is made available for sociological investigation. Framing points to particular problems, or issues, that particular movements respond to.

As an analytic device, the frame comes to the movement from the outside, and, of course, needs the social movement theorist for its construction. It is a method for studying social movements as discourses, as texts. It is a heuristic tool for the social scientist, not an active component of social movement activity, at least not in an unproblematic way. The actual historical process by which the "frame" comes into being, and the traditions of ideas which are drawn upon by movement activists are seldom discussed. From this perspective, the meanings – what Melucci calls the codes of interpretation and identification – that social movement actors bring to a situation are treated as matters of secondary importance to the exercise of power in bringing about social change. Furthermore, the ways in which these meanings affect both the process of collective identity formation within a movement and the ways in which social movements affect the wider culture of the society in which they emerge are left out of the explanatory strategies of social movement theorists and relegated to the students of culture. That the alteration of meaning, the struggle to define the situation, and the discursive practices that are carried out within social movements might themselves be a major aspect of power and social change has, with few exceptions, not been considered. In the language of framing, culture is conceptualized as a kind of superstructural appendage to the real work of social movements; it is viewed instrumentally, and as an external condition of social movement activity. As such, the challenge of constructivism is not so much countered as avoided.

In his 1994 presidential address to the American Sociological Association, William A. Gamson noted that "students of social movements emphasize the importance of collective action frames in inspiring and legitimating actions and campaigns" (1995: 13). While the emphasis remains on the imposition on actors of predetermined frameworks of analysis, if we broaden our understanding to include the creation and recreation of interpretive frameworks within social movements – what we have previously called cognitive praxis – and relate this to wider historical processes, a new grasp of the relations between culture and social movements becomes possible.

A major problem with many of the existing approaches is that they are at once too general and too specific. They are too general in that an underlying phenomenological starting point begins at the highest level of abstraction, where all human understanding can be said to be framed. This is the level at which Kant spoke about the basic "categories of all experience." From the most abstract, the social movement researcher tends to move directly to the most concrete, to the ways in which frames are imposed on specific movements and the manner in which individuals, for this is also an individual-focused approach, acquire them. In the paper already mentioned, Gamson discusses the ways in which mass media are central to the process of the construction of adversary frames. Todd Gitlin (1980) used a similar approach in his study of how media framing affected the general public's perception of the American "New Left" of the 1960s, as well as that movement's own self-understanding.

At this "I was framed" level, what tends to be ignored is all that falls between, specifically, the historical, or what can be called tradition. It is here that present framing interacts not with the basic structures of human experience, but with previously "framed" experience. Such framing is the result of both personal experience and the collective practices we associate with the concept of culture. Traditions are inherited ways of interpreting reality and giving meaning to experience; they are constitutive of collective memory and thus provide the underlying logical structure upon which all social activity is constructed. This lifts the level of analysis, not only out of the immediate situation, but also to the collective level. Erving Goffman, who first developed the language of framing as part of his dramaturgical approach to social analysis, was primarily interested in how individuals monitor their own actions, and the reception of his ideas by sociologists concerned with social movements has retained this individual orientation. The notion of collective framing then becomes a problem.

Of the few sociologists concerned with social movements to recognize the importance of the symbolic in the formation of collective identity, Francesco Alberoni and, more recently, Alberto Melucci stand out. Alberoni (1984) discusses the processual succession and degradation between social movement and institution with reference to the theories of Max Weber and Emile Durkheim. Alberoni calls attention to how actors within social movements, which in his terms begin with "the nascent state and ends with the reestablishment of everyday-institutional order" (1984: 221), tend to reinterpret the past in terms of present needs for mobilization in a process he calls "historicization." In its formative stage, or nascent state, a movement "questions anew every act and every decision and considers open to appraisal the decisions of legendary and historical figures . . . In historicizing the past, the nascent state also historicizes the present" (ibid.: 60–61). Alberoni offers the example of the Black Muslim movement in the United States, of which he writes, "the choice of the Islamic religion represented a search for a past which would clearly distinguish the new movement from the black Christian movements that had predominated until then . . . Thus both sides are responsible for the formation of cultural traditions" (ibid.: 243).

Culture as cognitive praxis

Our interest in the relations between social movements and culture can be thought of as an elaboration of what we have previously called the cognitive approach (Eyerman and Jamison 1991). The cognitive approach focuses attention on the construction of ideas within social movements, and on the role of movement intellectuals in articulating the collective identity of social movements. The cognitive approach views social movements primarily as knowledge producers, as social forces opening spaces for the production of new forms of knowledge. By focusing on the cognitive dimension, our more general aim was to make the content of social movement activity, rather than its form or organization, the central focus of analysis.

Three concepts are central to this approach: context, process, and knowledge interests. Social movements emerge in particular times and places; they are the products of specific socio-political conditions as well as of deeper and more long-term historical and cultural traditions. But, while being shaped by these broader contextual conditions, social movements temporarily transcend the specific situations from which they emerge; they create new contexts, new public spaces for addressing the particular problems of their time. They are not to be reduced to the organizations or institutions that they eventually become; what is central is their transience, their momentariness, their looseness. Social movements are processes in formation; they do not spring already formed to take their place on the stage of history. Rather, they can be conceived of as contingent and emergent spaces which are carved out of existent contexts; they are creative, or experimental, arenas for the practicing of new forms of social and cognitive action.

In these newly opened spaces, the articulation of a cognitive identity is, for us, a core process. Social movements are the carriers of one or another historical project, or vision; they articulate new "knowledge interests," integrating new cosmological, or worldview assumptions, with organizational innovations, and sometimes with new approaches to science. The different dimensions of knowledge interest, which we term cosmological, technical, and organizational, are combined into an integrated activity in the space carved out by an emergent social movement. This integration of its utopian vision, or cosmology, with specific practical activities and organizational forms provides a cognitive core to movement activity as the participants form their historical project or collective identity. This process of identity formation is called cognitive praxis and those actors who are most directly involved in its articulation movement intellectuals. Cognitive praxis, like the cognitive approach as a whole, calls attention to the creative role of consciousness and cognition in all human action, individual and collective.

In its original formulation, the American civil rights movement and European environmentalism were used to illustrate how social movements affected scientific research programs, as well as how movement activists moved between the academic and the political spheres. In this book we want to expand our analysis to take into account the even-broader significance that social movements have on processes of cultural transformation. By elucidating the relations between social movements and (musical) traditions, we want to broaden the range of the cognitive approach to encompass additional aspects of movement activity, which precondition and are in turn conditioned by cognitive praxis. Among these other aspects are the forms of habituation – the habits, mores, customs, and rituals of movements – as well as the symbolic representations which movements produce, and, in particular, the sounds and songs of movements. It is not only science or formal knowledge systems that are affected by social movements; in this book, we want to show some of the ways by which the deeper structures of feeling that provide cohesion to social formations are themselves periodically reinvented through social movements. And we want to focus not only on movement intellectuals but also on "movement artists" and those individuals who construct and organize the cultural activities of social movements.

Epistemologically, our notion of cognitive praxis derives from critical theory and is meant as an alternative to the notion of framing, in which actors either impose order on a chaotic world or internalize an already-existing reality through socialization. Cognitive praxis calls attention to the active creation of knowledge or consciousness in encountering the world. Within social movements, this process of encountering and coming to know is usually more conscious than in what is normally seen as socialization or acculturation, i.e., the process of social learning or transmitting culture from adult to child in family or school settings. Any "framing" or interpreting that takes place within a movement is a collective and interactive process of learning; both the frames and their content are reflexively constituted in a collective process. By definition, social movements break with the routines upon which "habitus" is constituted, but, of course, they are not entirely free from their influence. A movement culture is neither internal nor external, individual nor collective, but rather an active process of recombination.

Art in general and music in particular are here discussed as part of the cognitive praxis of social movements. Cognitive is used to mean both truth-bearing and knowledge-producing. Calling art cognitive is once again to rub against the grain of Kantian distinctions. If we follow the terminology of Habermas, it is also to rub against the whole edifice of modernity, a defining characteristic of which is that art becomes an autonomous sphere, free from political and religious domination, and allowed to follow its own internal rationality. In one sense this could certainly be hailed as liberation; in another, it can be seen as part of a tradition which Kant reinvented and modified from classical Greek philosophy, which relegated art to the third rank as a basis for human understanding. As part of a struggle for domination on the intellectual field, Plato led the charge to displace art, in the form of Homeric epic poetry, as the prime source of human knowledge, and to replace it with philosophy. This "expulsion," according to J. M. Bernstein, "constitute[s] modernity even more emphatically than . . . Plato's philosophical utopia" (1992: 1). In viewing music as cognitive, we aim to reassert its knowledge-bearing, identity-giving qualities.

To the categories of action discussed by sociologists we wish to add the concept of exemplary action. As represented or articulated in the cognitive praxis of social movements, exemplary action can be thought of as a specification of the symbolic action discussed by Melucci and others. The exemplary action of cognitive praxis is symbolic in several senses; but it is also "more" than merely symbolic. As real cultural representations – art, literature, songs – it is artefactual and material, as well. What we are attempting to capture with the term is the exemplary use of music and art in social movements, the various ways in which songs and singers can serve a function akin to the exemplary works that Thomas Kuhn characterized as being central to scientific revolutions: the paradigm-constituting entities that serve to realign scientific thinking and that represent ideal examples of fundamentally innovative scientific work (Kuhn 1970). The difference between culture and science, however, is that the exemplary action of music and art is lived as well as thought: it is cognitive, but it also draws on more emotive aspects of human consciousness. As cultural expression, exemplary action is self-revealing and thus a symbolic representation of the individual and the collective which are the movement. It is symbolic in that it symbolizes all the movement stands for, what is seen as virtuous and what is seen as evil. In the age of symbols, an age of electronic media and the transmission of virtual images, the exemplary action of a movement can serve an educative function for many more than the participants and their immediate public. This exemplary action can also be recorded, in film, words, and music, and thus given more than the fleeting presence which for Hannah Arendt characterized the exemplary action of the Greek polis, one of the sources of our conceptualization (see Jamison and Eyerman 1994: 46–50).

In this light, art and music – culture – are forms of both knowledge and action, part of the frameworks of interpretation and representation produced within social movements and through which they influence the broader societal culture. As such, they are much more than functional devices for recruitment or resources to be mobilized. It is not our intention to deny that there are instrumental uses of music in social movements and elsewhere, but, to the extent that social movements are able to transcend these instrumental (and commercial) usages, music as exemplary action becomes possible.

As cognitive praxis, music and other forms of cultural activity contribute to the ideas that movements offer and create in opposition to the existing social and cultural order. Perhaps more effectively than any other form of expression, music also recalls a meaning that lies outside and beyond the self. In that sense it can be utopian and premodern. In saying this we do not mean to imply that such truth-bearing is inherent in music, part of some transcendent and metaphysical fundament. Our argument is more modest in that we restrict our claim to music in relation to social movements.

In social movements, even mass-produced popular music can take on a truth-bearing significance. As we will suggest in a later chapter, in the context of the social movements of the 1960s, American folk-inspired rock music became a major source of knowledge about the world and their own place in it for millions of youth around the globe. In terms of classical aesthetic theory, this music may not have been beautiful and awe-inspiring and, in that sense, not real art, but it clearly has had a truth-bearing role. On the other hand, music that was beautiful and more like "real" art in the terms of aesthetic theory, like classical music, did not, for many of those involved in this movement in any case, carry any truth-bearing meanings. It was the movement context that made this process possible, not the music itself. In that context, singer-songwriters like Bob Dylan and Phil Ochs created songs with wider meaning than perhaps even they had intended. In the case of Dylan, it was not long before he rejected the role being given him and his music by the movement. He preferred the more traditional role of artist and performer to "truth-bearer." Ochs turned just the other way. He could not live without that role, and committed suicide rather than face life in the more normal, routine sense.

One more qualification is perhaps necessary. We do not claim that all movements use and provide music which is truth-bearing. Empirically this is not the case, although most social movements, especially those connected to nationalist and ethnic causes, do use and produce music of this sort. Saying this should also remind the reader of the fact that we are not claiming any necessarily "progressive" role for social movements or for music. While we would attest to being partisans of progressive social change, whatever that may mean specifically, we recognize that many social movements, especially today, are hardly progressive in any sense that we would acknowledge. But social movements do create a situation, a context, where music can recover at least some of its ancient, truth-bearing role. Our aim in the pages that follow is to provide substantive exemplification of these claims.

2

Taking traditions seriously

> It is sometimes observed, by those who have looked into particular *traditions*, that it only takes two generations to make anything *traditional*: naturally enough, since that is the sense of *tradition* as active process. But the word moves again and again toward *age-old* and toward ceremony, duty and respect. Considering only how much has been handed down to us, and how various it actually is, this, in its own way, is both a betrayal and a surrender.
> Raymond Williams, *Keywords* (1976: 269)

What is tradition?

For sociologists, tradition has generally been seen as a barrier to social change; traditions are what "progressive" social movements are against. Traditions have tended to be viewed as habitual forms of behavior, legacies of the past that impede innovation and hold back progress. In social theory, as well as in progressive political ideologies, traditions have been characterized as conservative, even reactionary, ways of life that the forces of modernity have set out to transcend. The so-called project of modernity and its corresponding forms of rationality have thus often been portrayed as a battle against the past, a future-oriented struggle to free society from the constraints of cultural tradition.

As Anthony Giddens has recently argued, tradition is characterized by a "formulaic notion of truth" connected to magical rituals. Knowledge is not derived from experience or experimental observation, but from belief and magic. In traditional societies, Giddens contends, authority rests with the guardians of these mysterious truths, "be they elders, healers, magicians, or religious functionaries" (Giddens 1994: 65). One of the achievements of modernity has been to replace this ultimate authority – this recourse to tradition – by the objective methods of science. In modern societies, truth is determined by scientific procedures, or, as Giddens puts it, "science was invested with the authority of a final court of appeal" (ibid.: 87). One of the things that Giddens, and many other sociologists, finds so disturbing in the contemporary world is that the authority of science has been undermined, without any viable replacement coming to the fore, thus leaving room for the resurgence of traditionalism.

Through the paradigmatic lens of modernist ideology, tradition and modernity are seen as polar opposites, and it is thus difficult for the modernist to find anything of value or importance in the contemporary fascination with traditional music, arts, and ways of life more generally. The interest in traditions is all too easily seen as anti-modern traditionalism, and a challenge to the universal values and progressive achievements of modern societies. Our approach in this book is to characterize traditions less ideologically and somewhat more neutrally, and simply to think of traditions as beliefs and practices that are passed on from one generation to the next. As Edward Shils once put it, in tracing the history of the concept, tradition refers to the coexistence of past and present. "Tradition," Shils writes, "is whatever is persistent or recurrent through transmission" (1981: 16). It is the passing on, the collective remembrance, in short the conscious *process of diffusion*, that we see as being central to the notion of tradition, rather than the freezing of one tradition into a reified system of belief. This process of passing on of traditions can take many forms – from collection to invention – and traditions can be transmitted through ritualized practices, as well as through written texts.

We want to claim that it is the conscious articulation – the process of naming, defining, and making coherent – which distinguishes tradition from custom or habit, which are similar in that they all deal with recurrence. Custom, for us, refers to beliefs and practices which are less articulated than tradition, less durable and more short-lived, and thus more easily altered. Habits, on the other hand, refer to individualized forms of behavior and not to the ideas, beliefs, or practices of groups or entire societies. Traditions, even those of oral cultures, can be written about and talked about consciously, that is reflexively chosen, while habits and customs are routinized and generally taken for granted. As such, they can be practiced but not easily adopted.

Pierre Bourdieu's influential studies of education and taste are more concerned with habits than tradition in serving as a major force in the reproduction of social hierarchy (Bourdieu 1984). In his scheme, social practices and frameworks of evaluation are transmitted from one generation to the next through socialization processes which lie somewhere between conscious strategies and unconscious behavior. To capture this process of social reproduction, Bourdieu uses the term "habitus" rather than the more difficult term "tradition" (difficult, at least, for a Marxist-inspired cultural sociologist). Habitus is similar to tradition in that it entails embodied practices in addition to the transmission of patterns or frameworks determining criteria of taste. Bourdieu's habitus links expressed individual preferences – in art, music, food, etc. – not only to social categories, like status groups and classes, but also to the past, in his case to childhood socialization. Socialization, in turn, is historically rooted in structurally generated class cultures. On this reading, the concept of habitus, like the concept of tradition, calls attention to the significance of the past for the present. Like tradition, habitus is more than habit; both lie somewhere between the unconscious and the conscious, between the body and the mind, between behavior and action, and, most importantly for our purposes, between the past and the future.

Since Bourdieu is more interested in explaining social reproduction than in understanding social and cultural change, he makes no mention of social movements in developing the habitus concept. Indeed, throughout his writings, he displays little interest in analyzing under what conditions a habitus might change or, for that matter, form the basis of rebellion and thus social change at a societal level (Friedland 1995). However, armed with the notion, one can easily find examples of habitus in action within social movements, in demonstrations and meetings, in the performance of speeches, songs, and slogans, which serve to reconstitute the collective identity and to initiate new generations in traditions of protest and dissidence.

Within some national political cultures it is quite easy to identify a habitus of protest and rebellion – e.g., an American "tradition of the Left" (Flacks 1988) – as embodied in the ritualized practice of individuals and groups. Such practices help to personify the movement among individual activists, and serve to shape their preferences and tastes in much the same way that the conspicuous consumption of classical music or champagne reflects the reproductive strategies of certain segments of the middle class. Such a habitus can link generations, as was the case with the "red diaper babies," the children of Old Left parents, who were instrumental in the formation of the New Left in the United States in the early 1960s (Gitlin 1987). In this and many other cases which could be called upon, music and art have played an important role, as they have helped constitute the values and mores, the habitus or tradition of rebellion. Singing protest songs has been important in linking generations and in connecting movements, as have been certain artistic tastes and lifestyles.

The tradition provides rules, or regimens, that delimit the behavior of social actors. At the same time, however, traditions contain a good deal of the "resources" that make social action possible: actors renew themselves with the help of traditional materials. Tradition is thus double-edged. It is also, in our perspective, neither permanent nor changeless, but, on the contrary, continually being reformed, redefined, remade. Robert Cantwell provides an insightful illustration of this dual aspect of musical tradition in discussing Bill Monroe, the founder of bluegrass music in the United States. He writes:

Though bluegrass music, like other kinds of popular music, reflects the various social and commercial influences that worked upon it during its formative period, it stands securely upon a traditional foundation which, if we could somehow uncover it, would show itself to be as abstract as a grammar, and just as mysteriously linked on the one hand to the values of a culture and on the other to the structure of human thought . . . A traditional fiddler recalls the melodies he has heard around him, offering his own elaborations, combinations, and variations upon them; he finds that the circle of his memory intersects others', so that something independent reveals itself – the "tradition" – which compels his loyalty because it is apparently so much larger and more enduring than he his. What he has discovered, in fact, is sure evidence of an otherwise imperceptible interconnectedness in the human community, a community without which there would be no "tradition."

(Cantwell 1992: 16)

A tradition, for us, is a process of connecting a selected or "usable" past with the present – with ongoing, contemporary life. In music, and many other practical activities, as Cantwell suggests, the tradition can be considered a kind of grammar, or basic language, within which a particular song or piece of music is constructed. The musician, songwriter, or composer must first learn the notation and the melodic and rhythmic procedures of the tradition in order to make music; otherwise it could not be passed on. But, at the same time, artistic creation requires that those rules be broken, or at least amended, so that the tradition can be rejuvenated by adding something new to it, and by becoming embedded in an individual or collective performance. It is important to recognize, however, that there is a tension, or, better, an extremely fine line, between the dogmatic following of tradition, and, with it, the collection of the traditional, and the creative embodiment of tradition, or what might be termed innovation within tradition. But no artistic expression would be possible without a tradition to inform it, or enclose it.

The tradition to which one belongs is often an important source of personal identity; belonging to a particular musical (or other kind of) tradition distinguishes the practitioner – as well as the theorist or scholar – from others. The traditional identity makes it possible to participate in what Benedict Anderson has referred to as an "imagined community," which he associated with movements of nationalism, particularly in the colonies of

European imperialism (1991). A tradition is both real and imagined at the same time; indeed, it is the active identification with a tradition, the conjuring up, the imagining, that makes it real, that literally makes it come to life. In relation to music, traditions often involve collective rituals of one kind or another – concerts, festivals, or virtual variants thereof. And, as we shall see, these musical traditions can be a source of cultural creativity and change that is as "rational," if not more so, than the more formalized and socially legitimate forms of creativity and innovation, in, for example, science and technology. The rationality of musical and other cultural traditions is, however, non-scientific, or, at least, not merely scientific, in that emotive and spiritual elements of consciousness are combined with the scientifically objective. And the subjective identification, the collective memory, is often as important in giving the tradition meaning as the objectively observable representations of collective identity that are expressed through written and recorded songs and performance practices.

In our postmodern world, traditions have taken on a new significance with the breakdown of national and local communities, and participation in musical traditions, and other cultural traditions more generally, helps to satisfy the need for group belongingness. Like the clothes one wears or the slang one speaks, it is the music one plays and/or listens to that serves to define who one is. Equally important, however, is the growing tendency toward sectarian traditionalism, by which the identification with tradition serves to separate, and even segregate, groups of people from one another. Traditions in today's world are usually selected rather than imposed, and are often based on commonalities of age rather than the commonalities of place or location that have been so prevalent in the past. The selection of tradition has become ever more individualized and transitory, but it is still constrained by material and psychological factors. Not everyone can choose to belong to the same tradition (some are prohibitively expensive), nor would everyone want to: personality is not completely malleable. Indeed, the choice of tradition is as much an exclusionary process – defining the other – as an inclusive process of joining.

While the old allegiances of class, race, and gender still remain dominant, emergent traditions combining the dissenting alternatives of the past with the emerging hybrids of the present are increasingly competing for cultural hegemony. And the resilience of traditions has not escaped the attention of the marketers of popular culture, who have developed sophisticated strategies for constructing new kinds of artificial "traditions," musical and otherwise. As record-buying and concert-going have overtaken other entertainment forms in popularity and economic power, the continual renewal of musical traditions has become a lucrative enterprise. Politically, economically, and not least socially, traditions have become serious business. But sociologists, the children of modernism, have had difficulty taking traditions seriously. It has been left to the cultural theorists, the prophets of postmodernism, to reflect on the meanings of traditions and the knowledges, or rationalities, that they might or might not contain. Unfortunately, however, the postmodernists have often neglected the sociological dimensions, the contexts or the social bases, for the non-modern, narrative knowledges that they propound. Our effort here is meant to bring these competing discourses into closer contact with one another.

The dialectic of tradition

Traditions have become central to the "postmodern condition" of the late twentieth century (Lyotard 1984). Defined by the social theorists of modernity as residual traces of the past in the present, they have become, for many postmodernists, the seminal spaces within which the present is experienced and conceptualized. While what Jürgen Habermas has called the project of modernity involved the rejection, elimination, and eventual transcendence of tradition and the ambition to develop a set of universal values based on the precepts and methods of scientifically objective knowledge, the postmodern "project" implies a rediscovery of traditions and thus requires a reassessment of the particularist values – and alternative rationalities – that traditions contain. As Lyotard has put it, "scientific knowledge does not represent the totality of knowledge; it has always existed in addition to, and in competition and conflict with, another kind of knowledge, which I will call narrative in the interests of simplicity" (1984: 7). In our day, the questioning of the Modern tradition, with its overriding belief in scientific rationality and its concomitant faith in progress and evolution, has spread from the peripheral margins into the core institutions of contemporary society. At the end of the twentieth century, there is an ever more noticeable "eclipse of reason" and a growing disenchantment with, or at least ambivalence about, many of the achievements of modern technoscience. And as a result of this disenchantment, traditions, or what Lyotard and other postmodernists term narratives or narrative knowledge, have come to take on a new importance.

It is worth remembering that many of the traditions and traditional knowledges which are assuming importance in the period of late, or declining, modernity are themselves the creations of an earlier period of emergent modernity. In the course of industrialization, differentiated traditions were selectively constructed out of premodern ways of life in order to fill certain experiential lacunae in modern societies. Throughout the nineteenth century, critics of the emerging industrial order explored the past in order to resist and contain the coming of the future; they looked back to the Middle Ages, to antiquity, to the Renaissance for sources of inspiration, and for models of an alternative social, intellectual, or artistic practice. From Blake and Herder to Thoreau and Emerson and on to Morris and Nietzsche, the past was mobilized, in highly differentiated and variegated ways, as a counterforce to the onslaught of modernization. "Traditional" forms of production and expression and "traditional" criteria of beauty and truth were counterpoised to the abstract rationality and the universalistic claims of modern culture. There thus developed a curious double-edgedness, a dialectic of tradition and of the rationalities that traditions represent.

By the early twentieth century, entire fields of scholarship and domains of artistic and industrial practice had emerged to carry particular types of traditional knowledge into the modern world. The "arts and crafts" movement in England combined a modernist interest in innovation and industrial design with experimentation in premodern aesthetic practices and principles. By so doing, old industries – book-making, ceramics, carpentry, apparel – were given new life and inspiration, as well as economic viability, from an imagined and selectively remembered past. The new sciences of anthropology and folklore, and many of the sub-fields of history, utilized the methods and language of modern science in order to bring an often-idealized past back to life and into the modern age. And, as Anthony Giddens has recognized, "tradition was called upon particularly in respect of the generation, or regeneration, of personal and collective identity . . . The "sense of community" of working-class neighborhoods, for example, took the form, in some part, of a reconstruction of tradition; as did nationalism on the level of the state" (1994: 95).

In the colonies of European imperialism, traditions were mobilized by western-trained intellectuals, like Gandhi and Ho Chi Minh, to contribute to the construction of movements of national independence and liberation. And here, as well, the "uses" of tradition were double-edged, dialectical. Gandhi's interest in handicrafts and Ho's interest in Vietnamese history were consciously grafted onto modern, western theories of revolution and revolt that both men learned in Europe. The past was remembered by changing it: tradition was mobilized in the struggle for a new society. Many European intellectuals were drawn to these and other non-western traditions in the interwar years; and there was, in Italian fascism as in German national socialism, an explicit fabrication of a mythical past, a national tradition, in order to mobilize social movements of "reactionary modernism" (Herf 1984).

At the end of the twentieth century, many of these traditions have been reinvigorated by new social movements. Environmentalists have drawn on the ideas of Thoreau and Gandhi in seeking to ameliorate the risks of modernity, and they have looked to Native American and other "primitive traditions" for alternative ways of interacting with nature. These movements have also explored non-western modes of medical and agricultural practice, and, particularly in countries like India, have helped to legitimate the acceptance of alternative knowledge traditions and belief systems (Jamison 1994). Perhaps most obviously, they have helped transform global culture into a mosaic of local traditions, and "roots" musics, in which pre-modern forms of expression are diffused with ultramodern means of communication (Hannerz 1992). At the same time, ethnic and nationalist movements are bringing reactionary rituals and symbolic traditions back to life. In many parts of the world, fundamentalist religious movements are revitalizing older systems of belief and they are indeed tragically returning to what Anthony Giddens has called a "formulaic notion of truth." As a result the hegemony of western modernism has been shaken, and the dominance of modern culture has been challenged by a variety of emergent "traditional cultures," which, as traditions, did not exist, at least not in their current form, until the twentieth century.

On a more general level, the idea of tradition, and the process of tradition making, can be considered constitutive of modernity itself: having a tradition in the sense of a collective memory has been a defining characteristic of the core institutions of modern societies. In the sciences, arts, literature, politics, even economics, there are significant, collectively defined "traditions," and much effort has been devoted to tracing the histories of those traditions. Even though the essence of the institutions is usually seen as transforming the particular tradition into something new, something modern, something universal, the traditions are recognized and not infrequently honored. The establishment of a traditional legacy, or canon, on which innovative activities are seen to be based, has been a central component of what might be termed the legitimation practices of modern institutions.

What has been termed reflexive modernity (Beck, Giddens, and Lash 1994) can be seen as an attempt, on the part of sociologists, to come to terms with the role of tradition in both critiquing and constructing modernity. Traditions are curious phenomena, in that they are both real and imaginary at the same time; a tradition exists, we might say, by being imagined, but what is constructed or conceived as tradition does have real meaning and substantive content for those who identify with it, or believe in its realness, its authenticity. There is a paradox at the core of traditional, or what

Lyotard terms narrative knowledge, the fact that it both looks back, or remembers, a long-lost past, and transforms, or reconstructs, often unintentionally, that which is being remembered or imagined, as it is being realized.

Because of the major role that traditions play in the contemporary world, as sources of collective identity, but also as sources of postmodern knowledge, it has become increasingly urgent to recognize this dialectic of tradition, in much the same way that an earlier generation of critical theorists recognized the "dialectic of enlightenment" (Horkheimer and Adorno [1944] 1972). Rather than seeking to transcend or oppose tradition, as so many sociologists want to do, we need to understand the importance of traditions in both questioning and defining contemporary reality. In the 1970s, the philosopher of science Paul Feyerabend called for a "free society" where all traditions of knowledge were tolerated and could coexist with one another (Feyerabend 1978). His vision was of a pluralism of rationalities, an anarchistic epistemology, in which there was no one western scientific tradition that was accorded a dominant position. Now, some twenty years later, the hold of modern scientific rationality has begun to be broken in practice, but much remains to be done in assessing the alternative forms of rationality and experience that traditions represent. Part of the difficulty has been the reluctance, on the part of sociologists, to examine knowledge-generating activities, or "cognitive praxis," outside the established knowledge-producing institutions.

In order to assess the rationality that is embodied in traditions, it is necessary to have a broad notion of rationality and reason itself. So much of contemporary sociology equates reason with (modern) science, and denies rationality to forms of cognition other than the officially sanctioned expertise of the scientists and engineers. In most contemporary sociological accounts, tradition is treated as a constant, and as an impediment to change, as something that is largely unconscious and taken for granted. Like social movements, traditions are not considered sources of new knowledge or seen to provide resources for creative expression. Tradition, for Giddens and Habermas, as for Marx and Weber before them, primarily represents the weight of the past on the present. As the cultural theorist Raymond Williams wrote in the 1970s:

The concept of tradition has been radically neglected in Marxist cultural thought. It is usually seen as at best a secondary factor, which may at most modify other and more decisive historical processes. This is not only because it is ordinarily diagnosed as superstructure, but also because "tradition" has been commonly understood as relatively inert, historicized segment of a social structure: tradition as the surviving past.   (Williams 1977: 115)

Even Jürgen Habermas, who is interested in social movements and social change, and who has, in many other ways, transcended Marxist categories and biases, tends to equate tradition with the past: the Greens, for example, are a "defensive" movement in his eyes in that they seek to revive traditional belief systems and attitudes to nature. As such, these social theorists have difficulty accepting the emergence of new traditions, since all traditions are, by definition, conservative and reactionary. In this respect, the weight of the modernist tradition bears down upon social theory and sociology in general. The taken-for-granted assumptions about – and positive identification with – science, modernity, rationality, and progress impede the development of an understanding of those social actors who question the assumptions of modernity. In their espousal of tradition, many of the social movements of the twentieth century have disavowed the "myth of progress" and are thus, at least indirectly, opposing the project of modernity itself. They are seeking to articulate alternative forms of knowledge and rationality, which are not merely regressive or "formulaic" but are often creative reworkings or mobilizations of traditional knowledges. In order to understand the significance of these social movements – and of their precursors on whose cognitive praxis they inevitably build – we cannot see tradition merely as the enemy of modernity: we must learn to take tradition seriously.

The role of ritual

By considering the mobilization of traditions in social movements as a kind of cognitive praxis or exemplary action, we want to indicate that traditions are more than texts which carry ideas; they also involve practical activities, forms of ritualized practice in and through which meaning and significance are embedded. Music, in particular, embodies tradition through the ritual of performance. It can empower, help create collective identity and a sense of movement in an emotional and almost physical sense. This is a force which is central to the idea and practice of social movement, and corresponds to what we have previously discussed as the organizational dimension of cognitive praxis.

Singing a song like "We Shall Overcome" at political demonstrations is a ritual event, just as singing "Solidarity Forever" or the "International" at union meetings or on the first of May has long been ritualized (not to mention the singing of the national anthem at the start of sporting events). Such preordained ceremonies serve to reunite and to remind participants of their place in a "movement" and also to locate them within a long-standing tradition of struggle and protest, or, as in the case of the national anthem, a tradition of national identity. The effect here is probably more ideological than utopian, in that it links back to the past rather than envisioning a not-yet-existent future. But collective singing rituals can also capture, in a brief, transient moment, a glimpse of, and a feeling for, a spiritual bonding which is both rational and emotive at one and the same time.

Anthropologists have long recognized that rituals are central to the construction of meaning. Ritual can be defined as "an action which dramatizes and re-enacts the shared mythology of a social group" (Small 1987: 75). In his study of vernacular music, Christopher Small has shown how African slaves in the United States created rituals which enabled the preservation of dignity, even "the celebration of identity" under conditions of great deprivation. For cultural and historical reasons, musical expression, song and dance, formed the central part of these rituals. What was accomplished and preserved through the ritual performance of music was the affirmation of unity in variety, a sense of community. "It was musicking and dancing, those twin rituals of affirmation, of exploration and celebration of relationships, with their unique power to weld together into a higher unity the contradictory experiences of sorrow, pain, hope, and despair" (ibid.: 87). On Small's account, it is this which gives black music its power and explains why other groups, in very different circumstances, can be so powerfully affected by it.

Like tradition, ritual has often been relegated by social theorists to the long-forgotten past, and to the so-called "primitive" societies of the present (for an exception among social movement researchers, see Taylor and Whittier 1995). Such a danger remains even in an analysis such as Small's cited above, if one sees in African-American music remnants of a "primitive" past, rather than a creatively remembered present. However, as recent research and theorizing in what has come to be called cultural studies has revealed, rituals are very much part of meaning construction even in the most modern or, if you will, postmodern social reality. Rituals, Durkheim argued, are central to the constitution of social solidarity and to the creation and maintenance of social order. Rituals perform a similar function in social movements, in the central process of the formation of a collective identity (Salomon 1996).

The meaning of ritual performance is not given, however, as a Durkheimian functional analysis might lead one to believe. In her study of the interplay between art and politics in turn-of-the-century Barcelona, Temma Kaplan (1992) reveals how the same rituals – popular street festivals – could serve two quite different political functions. "They [the festivals] could express or encourage local solidarity or internal struggle, celebration or opposition" (Kaplan 1992: 1). For the established political and religious institutions, these ritualized events were intended to reaffirm and legitimate their established power and authority. But such authorities could not control how the same events were interpreted and used by those who participated. In this case rituals that were intended to reaffirm authority actually contributed to the reverse, as the participants, including the group of rebellious artists of which the young Picasso was a part, used the occasions to promote alternative visions and group solidarities.

Drawing on the work of Victor Turner, Richard Schechner (1993) discusses ritual as a form of resistance and rebellion to established ideas and practices, rather than as an aspect of their reproduction. In relation to social movements, his analysis of "liminality" is especially important. The term is taken from Victor Turner (1969) and refers to states or periods of transition between ordered structures, in which actors "lose themselves" in ritualized performance. Such periods can themselves be more or less ordered and structured, like the festivals and carnivals studied by Kaplan, or the more spontaneous mass demonstrations choreographed by social movements. Schechner's examples of the latter include the antiwar marches in the United States in the 1960s and 1970s and the democracy movement in China as it surfaced in Tiananmen Square in 1989. As opposed to Kaplan's examples, where popular forces redefined an established ritual practice to their own ends, Schechner's are of movements creating the possibility to express both their rebellion and their (utopian) desire for freedom through ritualized performances: song, dance, nakedness and sexuality, and so on. In the space opened by the movement, established constraints can be cast off and "freedom" expressed. The ideals of the movement are thus objectified, embodied, and expressed in practices which can be seen, learned, and transmitted to others. In the age of global media this transmission can involve millions of people, and it can also take place extremely effectively through cultural expressions like music and song. What Herbert Marcuse in the 1960s referred to as a new sensibility, a "cultural revolution," has indeed affected the values and mores of late modern societies.

Where do traditions come from?

Traditions are usually defined according to time, region, or genre. There are thus, in relation to music, classical, romantic, and modern traditions; there are American, Indian, French, and Chinese traditions; and there are folk, jazz, blues, bluegrass, even rock music traditions. The important thing – for musicologists, historians, and folklorists alike, as well as for many practitioners and their audiences – seems to be to draw distinctions, to define boundaries, and to characterize the contours of one tradition in opposition to others.

But where do traditions come from? And why are some traditions periodically reorganized into new formations or configurations? Even more importantly, why do some traditions play a stronger role in cultural transformation than others? One way to answer these questions, we contend, is to locate the social contexts in which traditions are formed and identify the types of actors who form them. Traditions are not just out there waiting to be found; they have to be made by somebody. They must be based on some actual experiences – there must be a basis for a tradition – but the important thing is that a certain range of expressions be given a new interpretation, a new set of meanings, by some influential, or at least articulate, people. In other words, traditions have to be constructed; they have to be made by melding existing cultural materials into a new vision or idea of some kind. And in this making and remaking of tradition, we want to suggest that social movements play an important, even crucial, role.

The British historian Eric Hobsbawm (1983) has claimed that many traditions are "invented" post facto in order to give a false picture of the past, that traditions often provide an idealized or distorted version of reality that serves some political purpose. Thus certain elements of a Scottish tradition – the kilt, the Highland music – were invented as part of a nationalist movement in the nineteenth century; and, in another realm, Indian traditions, of philosophy, religion, and music, were invented by British colonists to help them control the native population. A tradition, according to this way of thinking, is thus a kind of false consciousness, or, to use a more current phrase, a virtual reality, which resembles certain features of an actual past, but which takes those features out of the context in which they existed and tries to make them timeless. As Hobsbawm writes, "The object and characteristic of 'traditions,' including invented ones, is invariance. The past, real or invented, to which they refer imposes fixed (normally formalized) practices, such as repetition" (1983: 2). Tradition, for Hobsbawm, is opposed to what he terms custom or customary behavior, which is the lived thing, the way of life that the invented tradition subsequently distorts.

To be sure, traditions are never to be found in a pristine form, waiting to be discovered and disseminated; and even though some folklorists and collectors have tried to be faithful to the authenticity of their materials, they have seldom, if ever, succeeded in actually preserving traditions as they found them, or, for that matter, in "reviving" lost traditions. Indeed, the notion of revival that is so widespread in discussions of folk music seems even more misleading than the notion of invention. For what is at work in periods of recombination or transformation is both more creative than revival and less creative than invention (Rosenberg 1993). It is more like a selective reworking of cultural resources, through which traditions get infused with new kinds of meaning. Musical traditions are thus made, and remade, in processes of mobilization; and, in the twentieth century, those processes have been closely linked to social and political movements.

In the making of traditions, certain elements of lived experience are emphasized over others. In the words of Raymond Williams:

What we have to see is not just "a tradition" but a *selective tradition*: an intentionally selective version of a shaping past and a pre-shaped present, which is then powerfully operative in the process of social and cultural definition and identification . . . From a whole possible area of past and present, in a particular culture, certain meanings and practices are selected for emphasis and certain other meanings and practices are neglected or excluded.   (Williams 1977: 115)

An important component of tradition making is what might be termed exploration: the terrain must be mapped, the resources mined, and the gold sifted from the sand. The explorers, or those who identify a tradition, always have an interest of their own, which can be theoretical, personal, commercial, or political. Some, who have lived within what they take to be a tradition, are most interested in saving a dying way of life from extinction. Identifying the defining elements of that culture is thus an act of preservation, and selection, in this case, can be based on highly individual criteria of evaluation. John Lomax chose to collect cowboy songs because, as a boy growing up in Texas, he had heard them sung, and he felt that they contained meanings about the more general experience of frontier life in the nineteenth century that was in danger of being lost (John Lomax 1947). Those who come to the "tradition" from outside often bring a more conscious theoretical interest to their exploration. In the late nineteenth century, Cecil Sharp, the pioneering folklorist, was looking for a continuation in the Appalachian Mountains of the Anglo-Irish ballad tradition in order to further his understanding of balladry as a musical genre. The songs he found were thus selected according to their relation to a canon of songs already collected – the Child ballads. The early explorers of rural "country" music often had commercial interests; they were mainly looking for talent that could be exploited in the new media of radio and records (Malone 1993).

Most traditions, however, are not made all at once. The exploration, the mapping of the terrain, is not enough; there is also a process of "systematization" when the raw materials of the first selection are filtered through another, more organized set of interests, be they academic, political, or commercial. In the case of the American folk tradition, systematization meant the combination of certain types of folk song into larger units of aggregation: cowboy songs and rural hillbilly music tended to be grouped together as country music, while sacred songs, work songs, and topical songs tended to be distinguished from one another and divided along racial and ideological lines. In the 1930s, these categorizations were further politicized, as new actors grew interested in folk music, and a new social movement context appropriated the emergent tradition of folk music to its own political purposes.

The social movements of the popular front era made folk song into a distinctive musical tradition, as well as bringing important elements of the African-American musical tradition into the broader American culture. It was primarily the new and old folk music that was created at that time that was diffused into the wider popular culture after the Second World War, and, interestingly enough, that music combined both white and black folk traditions. This diffusion process was largely the work of movement artists such as Pete Seeger, Huddie Ledbetter (Leadbelly), and Woody Guthrie, whose interest in folk music was motivated by a larger political project. Guthrie, Leadbelly, and Seeger would write a number of important songs, and Burl Ives and the Weavers (Seeger, Lee Hays, Ronnie Gilbert, and Fred Hellerman) would popularize a large number of songs that came to make up a kind of folk music canon and largely define the folk tradition in the postwar United States.

Many of those who take part in making, or constructing, traditions honestly believe that there can be something truly traditional, and that traditions should be preserved, as much as possible, in the form in which they are found. In relation to music, traditions and traditional music are often distinguished from commercially popular music, on the one hand, and from the classical music of "high culture," on the other. According to John and Alan Lomax, who, more than any other single individuals, have given American folk music public and scholarly visibility, the American folk song tradition is "quite distinct from popular song (made to sell and sell quickly) and cultivated art (made, so much of it, to conform to prestige patterns) . . . This is a truly democratic art, painting a portrait of a people, unmatched for honesty and validity in any other record" (Lomax and Lomax [1947] 1966: viii). The folk music canon that the Lomaxes have constructed out of traditional materials is the story of a people, and it should be told in the people's own, primarily anonymous, voice. Similarly, many of the leading activists of the New Negro movement in the 1910s and 1920s sought to distinguish a tradition of "sorrow songs" or spirituals from the commercial, or vulgarized, blues and jazz music. A tradition was constructed in order to distinguish an authentically popular music from a commercial culture industry.

"Traditionalists" like the Lomaxes tend to criticize, and at times angrily repudiate, those who would innovate within traditions, and, even worse, who would mix, or recombine, different traditions for the purpose of individual commercial gain. In this, as in so many other areas of social life, the preservationists compete with the modernizers in a sort of essential tension, without which cultural change would probably not be able to happen. For without the preservationists and their dedicated, often under-appreciated, work of collecting and recording, there would be little basis for the modernizing innovators' periodic mobilization and remaking of tradition; and without the challenge of the distorters and the popularizers, there would be less incentive for new waves of preservationists to go out and discover sources for making new traditions. Traditions, we want to suggest, are constructed and reconstructed through a continuing dialogue between the upholders of the past and the spokespeople for the future, between traditionalists and innovators.

Social movements and the mobilization of traditions

In the chapters that follow, we aim to show how social movements have provided both a context for the reworking of cultural materials into musical traditions and a legacy of ideas, symbols, and images upon which innovators within traditions have drawn in their artistic expression. Movements can be thought of as playing a catalytic role in the transformation of cultural preferences, mores, and values. They set off transformations; and they provide social spaces for experimentation that later diffuses into the larger society. There is a sense in which social movements are cultural laboratories, arenas for the creative work of deconstructing and recombining the materials, or resources, of traditions.

Part of our method will be to present the substantive content of the traditions that we discuss: their underlying philosophy and rationality. Here we will try to characterize the values, or central ideas, that are articulated and the ways in which those values are mobilized by social movements. We will also focus attention on the techniques of articulation, the particular artisanship or skills that are embodied in the tradition and through which the tradition is expressed. Like other narrative forms, the traditions that we will be discussing are primarily oral rather than written, and are often associated with particular narrative or "storytelling" techniques. In addition, there are performance skills that are made use of, as well as particular modes of organization. The tradition is thus a set of ideas as well as practices, and a good deal of its rationality is derived from the way in which theory and practice are combined in particular rituals or collective festivals.

Traditions are thus mobilized as a form of cognitive praxis, containing both a philosophy and a set of performance principles. In much the same way that scientific rationality is articulated through practices known as experiments, and is disseminated through reports, articles, books, etc., traditional rationality is articulated through performance practices and disseminated through stories, songs, and art. There is thus a comparability that has escaped many postmodernist thinkers, even if narrative, or traditional, rationality can by no means be reduced to a scientific rationality. There is similarity, but there is also difference. And to understand the distinction and to see the similarity and the difference is, we contend, an important step toward a real acceptance of the diversity of experience and the legitimacy of plural rationalities.

The mobilization of tradition that takes place within social movements can be thought of both as "pre-political" and as overtly political activity. By pre-political we mean the everyday processes of meaning construction, where musical and other traditions can be important sources of identification, as well as provide materials, or resources, for the "framing" of reality. They are thus a latent well of preexisting forms of social solidarity upon which political movements can draw. As Murray Edelman has written, "contrary to the usual assumption – which sees art as ancillary to the social scene, divorced from it, or, at best, reflective of it – art should be recognized as a major and integral part of the transaction that engenders political behavior" (1995: 2). Art, especially in what Walter Benjamin termed the age of mechanical reproduction, and which today has become electronic and global, provides a reservoir of images which inform political impulses and inspire politically motivated actions. Culture, in this sense, has been said to operate at "that level at which social groups develop distinct patterns of life, and give expressive form to their social and material life experience" (Clarke, Hall, Jefferson, and Roberts 1975: 10).

Many social movements bring older movements back to life by remembering the songs that were sung and the images that were drawn by giving them new meaning. This mobilization of tradition is part of what we have previously identified as the cosmological dimension of a social movement's cognitive praxis. The worldview assumptions, the underlying beliefs, are articulated as much through art and music as through more formalized written texts. In particular, singing and songs, as bearers of traditions, are powerful weapons in the hands of social movements. They contribute to the "structures of feeling" that Raymond Williams identified as central to cultural formations.

The mobilization of tradition also involves the more overt use of cultural artefacts, songs and art works for example, as tools for protest and the formation of collective identity. This overt cultural activity is directed at movement participants, as well as at the larger society, and each requires its own techniques of communication: the shaping of "internal" cohesion and commitment requires one kind of cultural expression, while the external dissemination of movement ideas and ideals requires another.

In his study of music and American left-wing movements, Serge Denisoff (1972) distinguished between types of "protest songs" based on their function in giving voice to dissent, which in part can be directly connected to social movements. The first type he called "magnetic," those songs which attract the non-participant to join the movement or reinforce the commitment level of adherents. The structure of these songs is such that they encourage participation, building around known and catchy melodies, repeating verses, simple chords, and offering a straightforward political message. Here the verbal elements – the singing and the text – are central, according to Denisoff, while the music is only secondary, a means to the message. In this regard, Denisoff's functional approach shows its limitations. For, as we shall see, it is often the seemingly simplest songs that evoke the strongest emotions, primarily because they are the bearers of musical tradition. Indeed, part of the power of many protest songs stems from their use of familiar tunes, both sacred and secular. And while no doubt serving as magnets, they also open channels of identification through which the past can become present. The second type Denisoff identified is the "rhetorical," which focuses attention on individual indignation and dissent, but offers no solution. Rhetorical songs place some emphasis on lyrics, but allow more space for musical sophistication and skill. It was such rhetorical songs, Denisoff argued, that were so popular in the 1960s, and which therefore had so little political "impact."

There is more to music and movements than can be captured within a functional perspective, such as Denisoff's, which focuses on the use made of music within already-existing movements. Music and song, we suggest, can maintain a movement even when it no longer has a visible presence in the form of organizations, leaders, and demonstrations, and can be a vital force in preparing the emergence of a new movement. Here the role and place of music needs to be interpreted through a broader framework in which tradition and ritual are understood as processes of identity and identification, as encoded and embodied forms of collective meaning and memory.

The various ways in which tradition provides resources for social movements can be illustrated through the historical role of music in African-American life. Beginning with the slave songs, music has provided African-Americans with a way of expressing and communicating under conditions of great oppression. While the distinction is a matter of controversy, in both their sacred and secular forms these songs carried a message of hope and transcendence through decades of struggle even after formal emancipation. It was these songs which formed the basis for the "freedom songs" which were so important during the civil rights movement in the 1950s and early 1960s.

There is an underlying tension in the tradition of black music between exclusion and inclusion, and between those who see in black music the source of a separate African-American identity and those who see black music as essentially a part, often the most important part, of American music (Floyd 1995). Rooted in the experience of slavery – a social relation based both on interdependence *and* domination – black music expresses the double consciousness of black people in the United States, belonging to but separated from the hegemonic American culture. This tension has manifested itself in the continuing conflict between the secular and the sacred, the popular and the elitist, the political and the artistic, the highbrow and the lowbrow in the history of black music (Southern 1983).

Within the space opened by the civil rights movement, this double-edged black music tradition could be successfully mobilized in pursuit of a common project. It was a short-lived yet powerful resolution of tension, which has had monumental importance for the development of American, and global, culture. For a brief moment in the late 1950s and early 1960s, the civil rights movement made it possible for black music to bring a new kind of truth into American society, a redemptive, visionary, even emancipatory truth. By momentarily resolving, or synthesizing, the contradictions and tensions inherent in their own condition – and their own music – African-Americans could hold up a mirror to American society, and show a path to what Martin Luther King, Jr., called the promised land. "We'll walk hand in hand," the song said: through integration, the United States could redeem itself, and, through black music, the United States could find its soul.

Bernice Johnson Reagon, who has both sung and written about the songs of the civil rights movement, has argued that "the songs of the slaves represented a body of data that remained present in the Black community to be used in future crisis situations" (1975: 38). The Negro spirituals, or slave songs, served as cultural resources that could be mobilized in the struggle for civil rights. This mobilization of tradition was a process of remembering, which included revision and reworking of old songs into new ones:

On many occasions, the new moved from the old in the midst of Movement activity. This evolutionary process was possible because the structure of the traditional material enabled it to function in contemporary settings. There was continuity with some traditional lyrics being changed for statements of the moment. These transformed songs were used in conjunction with older songs to convey the message that the struggle of Blacks had a long history.   (Reagon 1975: 96)

The freedom songs associated with the civil rights movement provide an illustration of how songs help mobilize protest and create group solidarity in specific situations. Bernice Johnson Reagon writes of its early stages: "music supplied the cohesiveness to the masses of people of the Montgomery Bus Boycott; it conveyed the essence and unity of their movement" (1975: 93). In the process, many traditional songs were transformed, such as "We Shall Overcome" and "We Shall Not Be Moved." Another older song, originally written as a Christian hymn, "Onward Christian Soldiers," became the most popular marching song within the movement context. In Reagon's words, "Out of the pressure and needs involved in maintaining group unity while working under intense hostility and physical opposition, the Sit-in Movement developed its culture. Music was the mainstay of that culture" (ibid.: 101). Mary King, active in the Student Non-violent Coordinating Committee (SNCC), the student arm of the civil rights movement in its early phase, wrote in her memoir *Freedom Song*, "the repertoire of 'freedom songs' [sung at demonstrations] had an unparalleled ability to evoke the moral power of the movement's goals, to arouse the spirit, comfort the afflicted, instill courage and commitment, and to unite disparate strangers into a 'band of brothers and sisters' and a 'circle of trust'" (1987: 23). In the following chapters, we will show how the traditions that were mobilized in the civil rights movement had themselves derived from earlier social movements in the 1920s and 1930s.

Music and cultural change

As the carrier of (past) traditions, music bears images and symbols which help frame (present) reality. Music represents many traditions, as it expresses a range of social forces and processes, local cultures, and, as we shall see, inevitable tensions between commercial and political interests. In that sense, music is central to what Gene Bluestein (1994) has called "poplore," the syncretic process through which modern cultures are formed. By proposing the term "poplore" rather than the backward-looking "folklore" Bluestein seeks to emphasize the positive role of folk traditions in the transformation of popular culture. Indeed, Bluestein's claim is that poplorists, such as Pete Seeger, Woody Guthrie, and the blues singer Robert Johnson, occupy an important place in American culture that is usually not recognized by folklorists or historians. Like Raymond Williams, Bluestein stresses the processual nature of tradition, and the ways in which a selective reworking of traditions is a central component of cultural change.

Because it is the bearer of many traditions, the images and symbols music gives rise to are open-ended, not closed and determinant. This is something which distinguishes music and song from ideology. As it is being defined here as carrier of images and symbols, the music of social movements resembles ideology. Ideology, which can be defined as a ready-formed system of interpretation, which explains why things are as they are, also is composed of images and symbols which provoke emotional response and which provide a basis for framing or interpreting reality (Eyerman 1981). The difference is that, while both encourage action through symbolic representation, ideology is more direct in what it does. Music suggests interpretation, ideology commands it. Ideology tells one what to think, how to interpret, and what to do; music is much more ambiguous and open-ended and like any art form contains a utopian element. Music, like art generally, opens experience to the potentialities of life, but it does not necessarily proscribe or even describe them. Admittedly, this can be a fine line and there is certainly a point where music becomes ideology or propaganda and ceases to be art. The two, however, can and should be distinguished.

The past is kept alive through culture, through art and music, but also through ritual and tradition. Social movements create a context in which the traditions carried through art become actualized, reinvented, and revitalized. There must, however, be some fit, some congruence, between the traditions carried in a particular song or piece of music, and the ideas and ideals of an emerging social movement. Just as not any political ideology will fit any social group or individual, not every type of music or song will fit any social movement. Musical traditions embody particular experiences and frameworks of meaning, and utopian images of possible futures, which limit their re-invention. It is hard to imagine country music, which emerged out of the everyday experience of a rural white working class, being used to mobilize a black protest movement. The small-town, rural "family values" such music often contains would much more likely be heard at a conservative white rally or public function. And this congruence works in the other direction as well. While the song "Swing Low, Sweet Chariot" can be sung by crowds at English sports events, it is hard to imagine the same for "We Shall Overcome," also derived from a slave song. While both have similar roots (and perhaps also similar "utopian images"), the latter has become part of the ritualized practice of a distinct political tradition; its singing at a sports event would most likely evoke feelings of anger and disgust, or at least of meaning out of place, if the intended effect was not meant to be ironic or agitating in a consciously political way.

The importance of what we have called a social movement's mobilization of tradition works on two levels. On the one hand, there is a deep-rooted, anthropological level at which reality is interpreted and experienced. Here traditions and rituals provide bridges between movements and generations. Traditions form part of a collective memory which carries ways of seeing and doing between past and present and between individuals across the generations. Rituals, symbolically pregnant performances, embody the ideas and orientations contained in traditions, providing also a structured link between movements and generations. Protest may very well occur in visible waves and cycles, but there are also invisible links between the waves. On the other hand, there is an artistic or aesthetic level, by which cultural expression transforms traditions into living sources of collective identity. Roger Friedland writes, "It is not a question of whether ideas matter, but when, how, and what do they materialize; and not whether matter idealizes, but when, how, and what it does" (1995: 34). Ideas and traditions of protest matter when social movements revitalize them. They can be revitalized in large measure because they have become objectified as cultural artefacts, in songs and music, as well as in other "symbolic" or intellectual representations. In the chapters that follow, we will trace these processes through the course of the twentieth century.

3

Making an alternative popular culture: from populism to the popular front

"The people is a myth, an abstraction."
And what myth would you put in place
  of the people?
And what abstraction would you exchange
  for this one?
And when has creative man not toiled
  deep in myth?
And who fights for a bellyful only and
  where is any name worth remembering
  for anything else than the human abstraction woven through it with invisible thongs?
"Precisely who and what is the people?"
Is this far off from asking what is grass?
  what is salt? what is the sea? what is
  loam?
What are seeds? what is a crop? why must
  mammals have milk soon as born or they
  perish?
And how did that alfalfaland governor
  mean it: "The common people is a mule
  that will do anything you say except
  stay hitched"?

Carl Sandburg, The People, Yes (1936)

Music and social movements in the United States

In contrast to the situation in most European countries, where cultural tastes and traditions have been dominated by the preferences of the bourgeoisie, American music, and cultural expression in general, has been strongly colored by the democratic values and the "exceptional" political and cultural experiences that have served to define the country's national identity. American culture has been essentially syncretic, whereby ways of life and forms of expression derived from different ethnic and national traditions have been combined into something new – what used to be called the "melting pot." The American political culture has been egalitarian in its underlying resistance to elitism and authoritarianism of all kinds, a characteristic feature that has not always been seen as positive by the proponents of modernity and the arbiters of taste. For while there has definitely been a strong commitment to democracy and equality, there have also been throughout American history strong strains of what Richard Hofstadter in the 1950s depicted as anti-intellectualism, and which many intellectuals in the twentieth century have decried as a vulgarized "mass culture" in the form of patriotic provincialism (Jamison and Eyerman 1994: 145–50).

Whether the results are praised or disdained, there can be no denying that modernity, considered either as a cultural formation or as a stage in social development, was constructed in the United States in large measure out of the confrontation of the immigrant, the slave, and the pioneer with a wild frontier. The resultant structures of feeling – of independence and freedom, but also of community and solidarity – were thus fundamentally different than those that emerged in Europe. In a hostile environment, far removed from civilization, the peculiarly American concept of the people was articulated by politicians and writers, and especially by social movements. What Americans have in common, and what forms a central ingredient in their collective memory, is a mythical belief in the power of the people, in their creativity, their intelligence, and their moral virtue. From the abolitionists to the creationists, American social movements have continually actualized and reinvented the myth of the people in their cognitive praxis. They have periodically challenged the "power elites" and their notions of culture, and they have created an alternative kind of popular culture, a folk culture, in which music, song, and dance have played a defining role.[1]

Since many of the people who came to the United States were illiterate, and a good many of them were slaves, the emergent culture that they forged out of the wilderness drew primarily on oral traditions. More conspicuously and actively than was the case in Europe, the message of modernity in the United States was transmitted through rhythmic forms of expression that could be communicated without, or at least in addition to, words. The Frenchman Alexis de Tocqueville, the Swede Frederica Bremer, and many of the other early visitors to the United States noted the central role that song and dance played as a source of cohesion for the black slaves as well as for many whites, especially those who had been influenced by the music of the slaves (Southern 1983). The uniqueness of American music has long been attributed to slavery, and the saving grace, or spiritual salvation, that music could provide for blacks on the southern plantations. The slave songs came to codify an experience that found its most appropriate expression in music, and it was in music more than anywhere else that the African legacy worked its way into the American consciousness (Floyd 1995). It has been in the mixing of that experience with those of other immigrant groups that a distinct American culture or range of cultures has emerged. Both the dominant commercial culture of Hollywood films and Tin Pan Alley and the alternative popular cultures of folk music, handicrafts, and folk art have reflected the "exceptional" nature of American history: its multiculturalism and its populism.

As in Europe, the development of what Lawrence Levine has called a cultural hierarchy did lead in the course of the nineteenth century to a "high-brow" culture where classical music had a pride of place, and where the idea of culture took on an exclusionary, elitist meaning (Levine 1988). The interesting thing about the United States, however, is that the highbrows looked to foreign models and exemplars, while the emerging "lowbrow," or popular, culture could make stronger claims for drawing on distinctively American sources of inspiration. The highbrow culture was the foreign influence while the popular culture, and in particular the hybridization of the music of the slaves with the transplanted folk musics of European immigrants, was the more authentically national culture. The attempts to create an American "classical" music suffered from an inferiority complex, which led to imitation rather than innovation, while the arbiters of musical taste looked down on the rich range of popular music that their countrymen produced and enjoyed (Tischler 1986). Unlike the situation in most European countries, an indigenous classical music did not develop in the United States until well into the twentieth century, and, by then, the influence from popular and/or folk music traditions was quite strong. The specifically American classical music of Aaron Copland, George Gershwin, Charles Ives, and Leonard Bernstein made a point of utilizing jazz, blues, gospel, and folk themes, as well as seeking, both institutionally and musically, to break down some of the barriers between the highbrow and lowbrow.

In the nineteenth century, the art music of the concert halls – what might be termed a classical tradition – did not attain the same degree of hegemony that it did in Europe, while commercial forms of popular entertainment – minstrelsy, in particular – became an important component in the making of American popular culture. In the words of Robert Toll, "The blend of Afro- and Euro-American musical and dance styles, which later became common in American popular culture, began on the frontier and was first given wide exposure by minstrels" (quoted in Bluestein 1994: 71). While the urban elites of the eastern cities looked to Europe, and tried to create a Eurocentric cultivated class, the so-called mass culture grew out of the rural consciousness of the western and southern regions, drawing heavily on the legacy of the frontier, and what Lewis Mumford once termed the "romanticism of the pioneer" (Mumford 1926). American culture involved the confrontation of the values of an old world with a wild and often raw natural environment. And, even more importantly perhaps, American music melded together various traditions from Africa and Europe in a number of distinctly American contextual settings, colored by what Gene Bluestein has termed "radical egalitarianism." American folk music has been characterized from the outset by respect for the worker, the slave, and ethnic diversity, and by a certain skepticism toward the Eurocentric, urban values of "civilization." It has been a music from below that has put into words and rhythms the range of disparate identities that make up the American peoples. As Bluestein puts it, "more than any other field, American music symbolizes the general development of American culture and its reliance on the vast resources of its ethnic inheritance" (Bluestein 1994: 58).

The populist heritage

Because of this distinctive historical background, it should not be surprising that the various genres of folk music that emerged in the rural United States should have had a much greater political, social, and economic significance in the twentieth-century United States than similar kinds of folk traditions have had in most European countries. In the relative absence, or at least weak social base, of older, competing cultural traditions – the United States, after all, had no aristocracy and no feudalism – popular forms of cultural expression could exert a greater influence on the development and definition of an American way of life than similar forms of popular entertainment could have in defining national identities in Europe. In Britain, for instance, folk music had all but disappeared by the time upper-class collectors came along to reinvent the tradition in distinctly conservative ways (Boyes 1993).

In the United States the various traditions of popular music have been tied, again more directly than in most European countries, to social movements. Particularly in the late nineteenth century, when waves of immigrants came to the United States speaking different languages and upholding different religious and political beliefs, music offered a crucial means of communication. The simple refrains of songs could be learned more easily than complicated written texts, and the rhythms of dance music could create a spirit of community when a common language was lacking. The active use of music and song by social movements was thus a natural outgrowth of the multilingual background of the American people. By the late nineteenth century, popular music, and especially what were beginning to be labeled folk songs, was already becoming a conscious ingredient of social movement activity. This is especially visible in the case of white folk music, which was very early on used by movements of social reform for getting the message out. The agrarian populist movement of the 1880s was one of the first to discover the power of song; songs like "The Farmer Is the Man" proclaimed the dignity of the small farmer and helped inspire the "moral community" of producers and artisans that populism envisioned. Another song of the period, "Big Rock Candy Mountain," simplified the message and became a part of the folk song tradition. The man who wrote it, Harry MacClintock (perhaps more famous for the hobo classic, "Hallelulah, I'm a Bum"), would, appropriately enough, be one of those who would be involved in collecting political folk songs in the *Little Red Songbooks* of the 1910s, when the Industrial Workers of the World came onto the scene.

The relations between populism and folk songs are interesting on several levels. There is already in the "movement culture" of agrarian populism the combination of different substantive components in particular song texts, as well as the mobilization of a range of traditions and rituals in the movement's collective manifestations. Songs like "The Farmer Is the Man" speak with pride of the farmer's competence and criticize the exploitative role of the bankers, while other songs that were popular among the populists identified with the outcast, the marginalized, the freedom-seeking. In terms of the contents, the music of the populist movement already proclaims the peculiarly democratic spirit of folk song that would manifest itself throughout the twentieth century (Greenway [1953] 1971). In part, this was because the songs were part of an existing way of life; there was an authenticity to them that was often missing from the more contrived, or invented, folk song "traditions" in many European countries. Unlike the ballads of a long-lost "imagined village" in the countryside that Cecil Sharp sought to establish as a folk music canon in England, many of the best-known American folk songs emerged amidst the actual lived, rural experiences of the late nineteenth-century United States – driving the cattle across the prairies, carving out an existence on a small farm, taking on the big city politicians and the railroad bosses, and eventually joining together in strikes and demonstrations. And, as a result of this closer, more intimate connection between (folk) music and life, the American folk song tradition, more directly than in Europe, could form part of the cognitive praxis of social movements – from agrarian populism to the multifaceted labor movement of the twentieth century. On the other hand, the populist movement of the late nineteenth century was also a meeting place – a public sphere – for various immigrant groups and religious traditions.

The cultural expressions of the movement, in its songs and dances, but also in its "camp meetings" and other rituals, reinvented the American myth of the people in a new historical context. By mobilizing the cultural resources of a rural South marked by defeat in the Civil War and colored by the participatory music-making of old-time religion, the populist movement helped create a music of protest and defiance, as well as a somewhat different music of longing and despair. Both would become important components of popular culture in the twentieth-century United States. Folk music, as well as the various genres of country and hillbilly music, would grow out of the unique mixtures of politics and culture that took place in the antebellum South (Malone 1993).

As a social movement, American populism emerged in the southwest in the late 1870s. Centered first in Texas, it organized the interests and altered the worldviews of small farmers, many of whom had migrated from the Deep South to escape the share-cropping and crop lien system that came into place after the Civil War (Goodwyn 1978). Begun as a self-help farmers' alliance concerned with building large-scale cooperatives to counter the corporations and trusts which ruled their lives from afar, populism took shape as a radical social movement in the 1880s, and became institutionalized as the "People's Party" in 1892, before effectively taking over the Democratic Party, at least in the presidential campaigns of William Jennings Bryan (Kazin 1995). According to Lawrence Goodwyn, the populist movement, like all social movements, created a context for "redefining the situation" at both a personal and a collective level. Populist writers and leaders provided a set of ideas and images that characterized a movement culture. There were the more theoretical formulations of Henry George and Edward Bellamy, as well as the slogans and speeches of Bryan and other populist politicians. And there were songs and plays and stories that were produced, as well, all of which were used to challenge the mentality of subordination imposed on small farmers of the South and Midwest by the dominant, urban culture of the northeastern elites. The small American farmer was the victim not only of absentee bankers and trusts and of the unseen forces of the market, but also of the self-image given him through the dominant culture. Like all exploited and subordinate groups, the small farmer was supposed to accept his fate, as natural and pre-ordained. The role of the movement was to empower the farmer and the artisan, through offering a positive notion of his role and place in society.

In this regard, songs like "The Farmer Is the Man" were as important as the Grange and other self-help organizations created by the movement.

Twentieth-century populisms: country music and the Wobblies

Michael Kazin has recently noted that the "populist persuasion" bifurcated at the turn of the century into secular and religious streams:

In the early twentieth century, there was a parting of the ways. During the Progressive era, small farmers ceased to have the enthusiasm or the numbers to lead a national insurgency. But two other groups with dissimilar goals did: wage earners and evangelical churchgoers. A rising labor movement, including many socialists, articulated a narrowed version of the ethic that linked political virtue with manual work. It was now unions, they argued, that best represented the "average man." And a religious vocabulary had to be avoided, lest it divide labor's heterogeneous ranks. At the same time, middle-class Protestant women and ministers were mounting a righteous crusade against "the liquor trust," inevitably clashing with workers and immigrants who had no animus against the saloon.   (Kazin 1995: 4)

This parting of the ways between a secular labor movement on the one hand and a spiritual, or religious, movement on the other is directly relevant for the emergence of an alternative popular culture. Where the labor movement provided a context for the further development of political songs and for a broader tradition of political radicalism and dissent, the religious movements provided contexts, and cultural resources, for the development of country music. The labor movement incorporated elements derived from the ethnic cultures of immigrant groups into its songs, while religious movements often drew on the "camp-meeting" revivalist culture of the rural South, and its various forms of song and dance. The progressive political ideals of populism, which gave voice to the dreams and ideals of the small producer and which championed direct participatory democracy, were transformed, in the idiom of country music, into a moralistic, often reactionary, anti-modernism.

American country music emerged as a distinct tradition in the 1920s, when, spurred by an unexpected interest in barn dancing, nationally based recording companies sent agents and scouts to rural areas in search of new talent. As Bill Malone puts it, "the music that is now described as 'country' was called into existence in the early 1920s by those powerful urban forces of technology, radio and recording. During that decade a disparate assemblage of fiddlers, banjo players, string bands, balladeers, yodelers, gospel singers, and other 'grassroots' performers for the first time began making phonograph records and radio broadcasts" (1993: 6). And as it became a commercially successful form of popular culture, the meanings of the music were transformed. As country music, the cultural expression became product-oriented and formulaic. Whatever "truth" the music subsequently contained was subordinated to the logic of the marketplace, to commercial rationality. Intriguingly, however, country music would periodically, throughout the twentieth century, provide resources for the cognitive praxis of social movements of both the Right and the Left. In the words of Curtis Ellison,

> Commercial country music was invented during a period of intense modernization in the twentieth-century American South . . . for seventy years, even with its complexity, this entertainment has maintained a distinctly personal tone and a sustained focus on domestic life. This persistence has achieved an impressive irony in American society: while the marketing of commercial country music and its trappings fully embrace modernity, the resulting popular culture community functions as an imaginative means for transcending the negative effects of modernity.
>
> (Ellison 1995: xvi–xvii)

When speaking of country music one must distinguish the varieties of local musical traditions – which were transmitted orally and performed privately, the range songs of mythical cowboys or the back-porch music of mountain folk – from the collections and performances of this music made in the early part of the twentieth century. These collections were necessarily selective and their unintended effect was to rationalize and standardize these "traditional musics." The creation of the distinct musical genre known as country music involved the written and recorded transcription of orally transmitted, locally based cultural forms into more universally accessible artefacts. Although based in a common religious heritage and rural lifestyle, the music of the American countryside was as diverse as the landscape itself; documentation and commercialization simplified as they categorized and transcribed.

Key actors in this transformation were folklorists and collectors like John Lomax, collector-performers like A. P. Carter and his singing group the Carter Family, and agents and talent scouts like Ralph Peer, who discovered them. Lomax prepared the first collection of "cowboy" songs for publication in 1910. The Carter Family made a series of recordings of "traditional mountain music" in the 1920s for Peer, a Victor Recording Company field agent, which have become standard performances of country music even as it is sung today. During the same sessions, Peer recorded the voice of Jimmy Rogers, who, along with the Carters, is often recognized as the originator of modern country music. Lomax transformed oral performance into written documents which could be transmitted and communicated over space and time; with the help of Ralph Peer, the Carters created a composition format and style of musical performance that could be listened to and copied over equally wide distances – and, most importantly, it could be consciously manufactured and reproduced.

While concepts like standardization and formula are certainly applica-

ble, they tend to hide the deeply emotional origins and impact of the performance style the Carters developed. As Robert Cantwell writes, "it was a
style of music that came psychologically, as well as emotionally, from the
heart . . . which perfectly embodied the universe of values for which the
Carter Family and their songs stood: the sanctity of home, hearth, and
mother's love, sexual innocence, the necessity of firm religion, the purity of
the grave, and the durable hope of a better world beyond it, whose earthly
colony was the church" (1992: 55). The meanings that these songs and their
performance expressed are very much akin to those of American populism.

The values country music represents through its songs have come to be
embodied in and through their ritual performance. Contemporary performances are staged and choreographed to emphasize community, family,
friends, and Christianity. Even large-scale highly commercial performances
attempt to create the mood of one big extended family. Country music has
its stars, of course – it wouldn't be American if it didn't – but one of the
charms, and also the marketing strategies, of country music is that the stars
are given a kind of down-home everyman character, dressed in the same
western clothes and affecting the same mannerisms as the members of the
audience. Country music performances are often staged to give the impression of large family gatherings. Even the names of the singers reflect this,
from the Carter Family and the Everly Brothers to Cousin Minnie Pearl
and Uncle Dave Mason. The annual Fan Fair in Nashville gathers together
the stars and their fans for a week-long campground get-together. The
result is to create the impression that country music is not just one musical
genre among many, still less a big business with billions of dollars at stake,
but rather a family affair, a close-knit community within a fragmented
society. In the famous terms of Friedrich Tönnies, the nineteenth-century
German sociologist, country music presents itself as a long-lost
Gemeinschaft (community) within the modern *Gesellschaft* (marketplace).

There is no more tradition-bound music to be found in the United States.
This does not mean that country music has not developed and changed over
the years or that there are no truly innovative performers; rather it means
that as public spectacle, as performance, country music is staged so as to
reinforce a sense of living in the past. This means that dutiful attention is
paid to the older songs and performers. Shows at the Grand Ole Opry, the
institutional as well as spiritual home of country music, are a careful mix
of old and new; performers from different generations often appear on the
stage at the same time. The effect is not only to create a sense of belonging
to a tradition, but also to give an almost religious feel to these country
music performances. Going to Nashville, to visit the Opry, and then on to
Memphis to visit Graceland, Elvis Presley's home, is undertaken as a

pilgrimage, which the true country fan must undertake at least once in his lifetime. Entering the Grand Ole Opry building, Curtis Ellison writes, gives the feeling of entering Mother Church, a spiritual temple, not a commercial establishment, and this feeling is reinforced during performances where traditional songs and acts give the sense of being in the presence of the saints and ancestors of the past.

When the labor movement began to take shape, a central component of its cognitive praxis was the bringing together, or recombination, of various sources – both foreign and domestic – into a collective identity. This was, however, a somewhat different identity than the populist movement had articulated and which affected country music as a glorification of the rural countryside; instead of the myth of the people living on the land, the labor movement constructed its cultural expression around the myth of the urban worker, and this was to be an extremely important shift in emphasis. The labor movement, particularly in many of its manifestations in the eastern part of the country, came to oppose populism as an ideological leftover from the days of the frontier, to be relegated, according to a Marxist theory imported from Europe, to the dustbin of history. Socialists and, after the Russian Revolution, communists saw themselves as belonging to the future, while the populist ideal of the "people" became associated with forces of reaction, which sought to recreate an idealized past. Within the labor movement, however, particularly in the western and midwestern states, the populist legacy continued to provide residual cultural resources, living on in the collective memory, perhaps especially in song and poetry, even while the new political organizations broke with the political or ideological programs of populism.

The IWW (Industrial Workers of the World), better known as the Wobblies, were especially important in the way that they made substantial use of songwriting and singing in conducting their political struggles. Not all movements generate new songs; most make do with what is available. But the Wobblies not only wrote songs, they produced songbooks and singing demonstrations. As John Reed wrote at the time, the Wobblies were a singing movement:

Remember, this is the only American working class movement which *sings*. Tremble then at the IWW, for a singing movement is not to be beaten . . . They love and revere their singers, too, in the IWW . . . I have met men carrying next their hearts, in the pocket of their working clothes, little bottles with some of Joe Hill's ashes in them.
(Reed [orig. 1918] in Stuart [1955] 1972: 216)

The IWW mobilized the materials of both folk and popular song for the purpose of propagating their highly utopian visions of a collective future.

The Wobblies and the wider labor movement of the early twentieth century provided a public space for the various immigrant communities to meet and interact, and formulate a collective mission. The One Big Union that the Wobblies sang about symbolized an exemplary ambition to link together the destinies of the disparate working-class cultures. Instead of the separate ethnic identities that they had brought with them to the United States, the Wobblies offered immigrants a universal brotherhood of labor, and their songs became an important constituting component of an alternative popular culture. "Solidarity forever," the Wobblies sang (to the tune of "The Battle Hymn of the Republic"):

> When the Union's inspiration through workers' blood shall run,
> There can be no power greater
> Anywhere beneath the sun.
> Yet what force on earth is weaker
> Than the feeble strength of one?
> For the Union makes us strong.   (Ralph Chaplin, "Solidarity Forever")

The Swedish immigrant Joel Hägglund (or Joe Hill, as he called himself when he had settled in the United States) was perhaps the most active articulator of the IWW's cognitive praxis. His songs – and the story of his tragic life – have lived on in the collective memory even while the political struggles that shaped them, and to which they sought to contribute, have long since disappeared. The social movements of the so-called Progressive era in the first decades of the century, in the form of both the Wobblies and the American Socialist Party, were quickly spent as active political forces – the First World War and the rise of the corporate state saw to that – but their cultural expression lives on, and has inspired many subsequent social and cultural movements throughout the twentieth century. Woody Guthrie, Earl Robinson, Lee Hays, Pete Seeger, even Burl Ives, were inspired in the 1930s by the songs of Joe Hill and the other Wobblies. And in the 1960s, a slew of young singers and songwriters would reinvent the topical song once again as part of the civil rights and antiwar movements (Eyerman and Jamison 1995). It was only fitting that, at the end of the sixties, when politics and popular music had once again started to part company, Joan Baez would sing about Joe Hill at Woodstock. Or rather she would "dream she saw Joe Hill last night/Alive as you and me." The song she sang had been written as part of an earlier movement by Alfred Hayes and Earl Robinson in the 1930s. Joe Hill's execution for a murder he probably didn't commit was remembered in the 1930s as it would be remembered in the 1960s, and the example of Joe Hill, fashioning poetic politics to the melodies of the day, has been remembered and emulated as well:[2]

"The copper bosses killed you, Joe,
They shot you, Joe," says I.
"Takes more than guns to kill a man,"
Says Joe, "I didn't die,"
Says Joe, "I didn't die."

From San Diego up to Maine
In every mine and mill,
Where working men defend their lives
It's there you'll find Joe Hill.
It's there you'll find Joe Hill.

(Hayes/Robinson, "I Dreamed I Saw Joe Hill")

Joe Hill's songs, and the songs of the other Wobbly songwriters, sought to educate and empower at one and the same time. As cognitive praxis, the music of the Wobblies stood for a cosmology of brotherhood and solidarity, a participatory organizational dimension, and a technical ideal of topicality, immediacy, and directness. For Joe Hill, a song was much more effective than a political pamphlet:

A pamphlet, no matter how good, is never read but once, but a song is learned by heart and repeated over and over; and I maintain that if a person can put a few cold common sense facts in a song, and dress them up in a cloak of humor to take the dryness off of them he will succeed in reaching a great number of workers who are too unintelligent or too indifferent to read a pamphlet or an editorial on economic science.
(Joe Hill to the editor of *Solidarity*, December 1914, quoted from Reagon 1975: 54)

Unlike a political pamphlet or speech, Hill's songs tried to amuse the listener. An element of irony is there from the outset, distinguishing the politically motivated topical song, or a form of cultural practice, from ideology, a form of political practice. Even though Joe Hill on only two occasions wrote his own melodies, he nonetheless had an explicit ambition, as would so many topical songwriters to follow, to link the text to a rhythm, and to experiment poetically with rhyme, cadence, and alliteration. Most importantly, Hill's songs tell stories; they personalize political communication by bringing in the human component. Joe Hill's "Casey Jones" may be a social type, a caricature of a strike breaker, but he is also an individual. "The Rebel Girl" is similarly personal, taking a living example of a dedicated worker and turning her into a working-class heroine. Later, Woody Guthrie's "Dust Bowl Ballads" would also tell the stories of individual people, often the omniscient narrator, talking the blues, but also the fictional Tom Joad or an anonymous homeless hobo (e.g., "I Ain't Got No Home"). The point is that, in topical song, a literary mode of expression is put to political uses. It is a kind of hybrid between poetry and song, not reducible to either. What makes a topical song memorable is its mixing of the media, its recombination of art and politics.

Joe Hill is important not just because his song texts were clever and witty and continue to strike a meaningful chord in the late twentieth century when religion still offers "pie in the sky" for the poor and downtrodden to enjoy first when they die. By appropriating the materials of popular culture – both commercial and religious tunes – for the articulation of the collective identity of a social movement, Joe Hill helped to reinvent, and radicalize, the populist legacy. Cultural resources, and, in particular, the resources of the populist tradition, were recontextualized by Hill and the other Wobbly songwriters. In a way, the hegemonic culture was turned against itself, and the seeds for an alternative popular culture for the twentieth century were given new vitality.

All movements have a form of cultural expression, but the Wobblies, and especially Joe Hill, used topical, satirical song to get out their message. And it is perhaps mostly through Joe Hill's songs – "Pie in the Sky," "The Rebel Girl," "Casey Jones" – and the others included in the *Little Red Songbook* that the Wobblies live on in the collective memory. Radical songs did for white immigrant workers something similar to what the blues did for the blacks in the Mississippi Delta: you could laugh to the words, you could identify with the singer, you could sing along, even play along. Joe Hill's parodies of the Salvation Army songs were, like so much of the blues, expressions of collective experience, and, as such, they were part of a collective identity formation. Even more than the texts themselves, Joe Hill changed, or at least added something important to, American culture. He and the other IWW songwriters put rebellious feelings into words, and into words that anyone could understand.

Between movements: Lomax and Sandburg

On a more general level the tradition of American folk song can also be seen to have been inspired by the populist heritage. After the First World War, when progressive and socialist movements were largely overwhelmed by the forces of corporate expansion, individualism, and commercialism, it was a small number of individuals who served to keep alive, and codify, the emergent alternative popular culture that had been revitalized by the Wobblies and other socialist parties and organizations. As collectors, artists, writers, and performers, these "partisan intellectuals" carved out social spaces and created informal networks for cultural diffusion.

What John Lomax called "ballad-hunting" – his single-minded pursuit of folk songs among cowboys, farmers, workers, and prisoners – involved, like populism, a similar rejection of the European values of the eastern elites, and a similar glorification of the pioneering spirit to be found in the rural countryside. Like populism, folk songs sought to re-collect, to remember the frontier days, the wide, open spaces, or "home on the range," that Lomax identified in the cowboy songs that he was the first to collect and put into printed form. His *Cowboy Songs and Other Frontier Ballads* (1910) was an important early contribution to the making of a folk song tradition (Norm Cohen 1991). Lomax was apparently driven more by a personal mission of saving a heritage that was in danger of being lost than in propagating any explicitly political mission (John Lomax 1947). But there can be no denying that an anti-eastern populism inspired his dedicated exploration and lifelong collecting of American folk songs; Lomax wanted to uncover and disclose an alternative popular culture among the real people of the rural United States, a culture that he considered far richer and far more meaningful than the artificial and highly commercial popular culture taking shape in New York's Tin Pan Alley.

Lomax's collecting, and not least his own deeply felt renditions of many cowboy songs, were an important source of inspiration for the folk song activity of the writer Carl Sandburg (who published his own collection, *The American Songbag*, in 1927). Sandburg was a much more political writer than Lomax, identifying throughout his life with populist causes and beliefs; and his collection can be said to have begun a politicization process that was to become more conscious and explicit during the 1930s and 1940s. It also provided the first opportunity for Ruth Crawford (later Ruth Crawford Seeger) and other composers to learn to transcribe folk music. Lomax and Sandburg first met and traded songs when Lomax worked in Chicago just after the First World War, and they were perhaps the two most important "partisan intellectuals" who linked the populists of the nineteenth century to the people's songsters of the twentieth century. Lomax and his son, Alan, would be the main collectors of the folk song canon, and Sandburg's writings would provide a good deal of the substantive inspiration for the political songwriters of the 1930s and 1940s. In their politics, as well as in their general approach to popular culture, both Earl Robinson and Charles Seeger as well as Pete Seeger, Woody Guthrie, and Millard Lampell of the Almanac Singers (and, in our day, Bob Dylan) have all been twentieth-century populists of the Carl Sandburg variety rather than ideological communists.[3]

The down-to-earth, somewhat mythological belief in "the people" that was so central to Sandburg's poetry and overall philosophy of life (and so opposed to the Communist Party's dogmatic glorification of the worker) flows deep in folk music. Sandburg rejected communism, as he rejected most forms of organized politics. His politics was rather a twentieth-century version of American personalism, following Emerson, Thoreau, and Whitman in providing what might be considered a poetic representation of the populist tradition. And it can be argued that it was Sandburg's – and eventually John Steinbeck's – less ideological, more emotive form of populist politics, rather than an imported European tradition of Marxism, that has provided much of the "theoretical" underpinning to American folk music. The author of a six-volume biography of Abraham Lincoln, which won for him a Pulitzer Prize in 1940, Sandburg is perhaps most remembered today for his poetry, if he is remembered at all; but he was actually one of the very first to make phonograph recordings of folk songs. He sang in a highly personal way, and he played the guitar only rudimentarily, but he persisted, throughout his long life, in singing at his poetry readings, and in stressing and exemplifying the participatory nature of folk songs. It is the Sandburgian faith in the people, his strong sense of anti-elitism and radical egalitarianism, that one finds in so many folk songs. In many ways, Sandburg's books and his poems – especially the Lincoln biography and his collections, *Good Morning America* and *The People, Yes* – are the most conspicuous attempt in American literature to articulate a cosmology of populism in the twentieth century.

It is a curious and extremely ambiguous political philosophy, mixing common sense, proverbial knowledge, and an emotive egalitarianism into an often wordy and repetitive form of expression. Sandburg was throughout his life a controversial poet, never really acceptable to the arbiters of cultural taste but always popular at colleges and on the radio – and, toward the end of his life, on television, as well. Like the philosophy he preached, Sandburg was a uniquely personal presence in his performance practice; his folksy form of reading and singing offered a window on the past, a way of remembering how frontier life had been, what had made the country great, and especially what the country had stood for.

Sandburg and Lomax, in their different yet complementary ways, sought to contribute to the making of an alternative popular culture based on the legacy of populism. While Lomax tried to make folk music respectable for academics, Sandburg tried to make folk songs, and, more generally, an American folk wisdom, popular for all kinds of people; and it was his folk song collection, and, to a certain extent, his example, that would inspire many of the folksingers, composers, and songwriters of the Popular Front (Cantwell 1996). Sandburg had campaigned actively for the socialist

Eugene Debs before the First World War, and he never accepted the communist ideology that so many of his fellow writers adopted during the
1930s.[4] His politics were based less on doctrine than on a partisan empathy
for the people. Through folk song, as well as through the free-flowing verse
that he wrote throughout his life, the experiences, the creative potential, the
knowledge of the common people could be remembered and revitalized. As
he put it in 1916 in "I Am the People, the Mob," one of his early "Chicago
Poems":

> When I, the People, learn to remember, when I, the People, use the
> lessons of yesterday and no longer forget who robbed me last year,
> who played me for a fool – then there will be no speaker in all the
> world say the name: "The People," with any fleck of a sneer in his
> voice or any far-off smile of derision.
> The mob – the crowd – the mass – will arrive then.

Both Lomax and Sandburg can be contrasted to what might be termed
the "colonial" exploration of folk songs by Francis Child and Cecil Sharp,
who looked in the Appalachian Mountains for the remains of the colonial
British culture in the form of folk songs (Karpeles 1968). Where Lomax
and Sandburg identified folk songs, and eventually a folk music tradition,
with the values of the American frontier and the free spirit of American
cowboys, farmers, and workers, Sharp's and Child's ballads pointed to the
connections between European and American "folk" cultures. As such,
there was a tension, or at least a difference in emphasis, between a popular
and populist-inspired style of folk music collecting and a more cultured or
academic style of collecting, which came to be reflected in the academic
field of folklore as it developed into a scholarly pursuit (Bluestein 1972).
Both kinds of explorers, however, sought to establish a different kind of
popular music than the commercial, urban industrial framework of song
production which came to be known as Tin Pan Alley.

Folk song, for Sharp, as well as for Lomax and Sandburg, was something
authentic and, for the most part, anonymous and collective. This was the
difference between folk music and commercial music. Even when it was not
explicitly political – and few folk songs were – folk songs emerged and were
transmitted into the culture in a kind of structural opposition to the manufactured popular music of the music industry. In the 1920s, when black
folk music was being whitened into swing jazz and filling the night clubs
with popular commercial entertainers, folk music provided an alternative.
In the 1930s, that alternative musical "tradition" would be mobilized by the
radical labor and antifascist movements to strike deep chords in the
popular consciousness.

The songs of the popular front

The popular front of the late 1930s provided the movement context for the consolidation of a distinct folk music tradition. We have previously characterized the social movements of the 1930s in terms of a "pragmatic populism" and have pointed to the ways in which activists and intellectuals in the various left-wing organizations of the times attempted to redefine and reconstruct a distinctively American way of life. The uniquely American philosophy of pragmatism, which had emerged at the turn of the century in the writings of William James and John Dewey, became a part of the popular culture, as intellectuals sought ways to reconnect themselves to the "common people" (Jamison and Eyerman 1994). In what Stanley Aronowitz (1993) has characterized as the "cultural politics" of the popular front, there was a general spirit of nationalism, patriotism, and populism that arguably had a much more significant impact on American popular culture than on American politics. The "most enduring intervention" of the popular front era, according to Aronowitz, was "to have opened the way for a new American national popular culture, particularly those genres that drew from oral traditions, black and rural narratives, and music" (1993: 166).

Especially for many Communist Party sympathizers, "the people" became "a more effective revolutionary symbol . . . than the workers" and a strong interest in folk music and other popular art forms developed, along with an interest in collecting and preserving American folk material (Lieberman 1995: 34).[5] The slogan of the popular front was that "Communism is twentieth-century Americanism," as Earl Browder, the Communist Party leader, put it in 1935. And one of the lasting contributions of this multifarious cognitive praxis, inspired but by no means confined to those who were associated with the Communist Party, was the making of a folk song tradition.

In a wide-ranging review of the "culture of the thirties," the historian Warren Susman has pointed to the importance of the "idea of commitment" in defining the cultural activities of the decade:

It was characteristic in the 1930s for the idea of commitment to merge with some idea of culture and to produce, at least for a time, participation in some group, community, or movement. The 1930s was the decade of participation and belonging. The 1920s saw a growth in spectator sports; the 1930s mark a new era in sports participation. The 1920s found the intellectuals in revolt against the village; the 1930s witnessed the intellectuals in flight to the village. Such generalizations are obviously extreme, yet they do suggest a basic truth about the decade: the need to feel one's self a part of some larger body, some larger sense of purpose.

(Susman 1984: 172)

This quest for community was not confined to the Communist Party, nor even to a specifically leftist movement. On a general level, the idea of participation and the search for community was part of the spirit of the times. And it was expressed by intellectuals and groups that were far from falling under the influence of the Communist Party, even though in the red-baiting 1950s, the communist role in the popular front would be stressed, both by friends and foes. While the communists were popular in the popular front, for a few years reaching membership figures and a broader cultural influence that they would never come close to reaching again, it is important not to reduce the era merely to a "red decade" or a time of communist ideological hegemony. Many of the most lasting results of the period – and in particular the songs of Leadbelly and Woody Guthrie, the novels of Dos Passos and Steinbeck, the photographs of Dorothea Lange and the films of Frank Capra and Charlie Chaplin (e.g., *Modern Times*) – are not reducible to communist ideology. There was a broader "cultural front," which Michael Denning has recently characterized as a hegemonic "historical bloc" that extended from labor strikes to proletarian literature to political Broadway musicals (Denning 1996). As Susman puts it, "the genius of the Communist movement of the 1930s was its ability to use the obvious social and psychological needs of the period. It recruited effectively individuals who had no other place to go and who sought to belong and to do, those who had a commitment to ideals shared by those in the Party if not complete knowledge or understanding of its ideology" (1984: 173).

As a social movement, the popular front expressed its collective identity not merely through political tracts and strikes and demonstrations, but also, and perhaps more significantly, through art, music, and ritual. In Susman's words, "the Party offered more than political participation: there were its camps, its discussion groups, its magazines, even its dances and social affairs" (Susman 1984: 173). And, in addition to the political party building, there was the broader labor movement, which also took on new cultural activities at its schools, training courses, and even at its strikes and demonstrations. Florence Reese wrote "Which Side Are You On?" during the long coal miners' strike in Harlan County, Kentucky, and at the Highlander School, near Knoxville, Tennessee, singing and songwriting (as well as dance and theater) were actively integrated into the training of community and labor organizers (Horton 1990). It was at Highlander in the 1930s that several black gospel songs were transformed into labor songs (e.g., "We Will Overcome" and "We Shall Not Be Moved"). Interestingly enough, it would be at Highlander in the late 1950s that some of those very same songs would be transformed once again into songs of the civil rights movement (Reagon 1975).

Lee Hays, who would be one of the Weavers in the 1950s, spent most of the popular front period at Commonwealth College in Arkansas, where, like Zilphia Horton at Highlander, he used music and theater in labor struggles and the training of labor organizers (Willens 1988). Among other things, Hays liked to write what he termed "zipper" songs, simple songs with repeating verses "so constructed that you have to zip in only a word or two to make an entirely new verse. 'Roll the Union On' is the best example, with its structure allowing you to roll the union over anything you want to roll over" (ibid.: 57). Many of the songs were revised versions of the hymns of the religious camp meetings that Hays had attended in his youth in rural Arkansas. But not everybody liked the way he put the old songs to new uses in the radical labor movement. In 1940, in an early case of red-baiting, Commonwealth College was closed down, and Lee Hays took his songs up north, where he met up with Woody Guthrie, Pete Seeger, and Leadbelly.

It is perhaps not surprising that one of the legacies of the popular front was the innovation of a new, participatory form of music-making, the hootenanny, and the emergence of an open-ended song group, the Almanac Singers, which, at one time or another in the late 1930s and early 1940s, included most of the active folksingers in and around New York City (Lieberman 1995). In addition to the songs themselves – the Dust Bowl ballads of Woody Guthrie, the labor songs of Florence Reese, Lee Hays, and Earl Robinson, and the country blues of Leadbelly – the hootenanny represented a specific kind of cognitive praxis, which might be labeled collective song-making. At a hootenanny, songs were shared in a process of collective performance. And even though some of the songs and some of the singers were better than others, the idea was that folk music was not to be professionalized and made into the possession of a new elite of folksingers and collectors; it was also to be shared, as a ritualized part of collective identity formation.

Many of the songs were quite simple and were written to be hummed, chanted, or sung along at demonstrations or on a picket line, while others reinvented the topical song tradition of Joe Hill, mixing commentary with satire and often an uplifting message. But there had been in the intervening years a noticeable musical development that would help make the impact of the folk songs of the popular front so much more significant than the songs of Joe Hill had been, or would be in the future. Rather than merely writing a new text to a popular tune, the collective song-makers of the 1930s often drew on a rich and varied musical repertoire, which included both cowboy songs and the blues, as well as popular songs with a jazz inspiration. And they had the topical song tradition itself to build upon. What emerged was thus a creative remixing of musical traditions, as when Woody Guthrie joined forces, as he often did, with the blues duo of Sonny

Terry and Brownie McGhee, or the classical composer George Gershwin mixed jazz, folk, and blues rhythms into his folk opera, *Porgy and Bess.*

In the popular front, topical songs got rhythm, while the blues got sung in contexts very different from those from which they had come (Denning 1996: 323). The result was a much more musically interesting kind of folk song. To the older qualities of sharing a message were added the harmonies, driving beat, and spiritualism of the black music tradition. Huddie Ledbetter, better known as Leadbelly, was one of the most significant mixers of traditions and cultural innovators in the popular front era. Discovered in a southern prison by the folk song collector, John Lomax, Leadbelly was a living library of folk and blues songs, having written a good many songs himself and having heard and remembered hundreds more. When Lomax, partly for his own "academic" purposes, brought Leadbelly to Boston and New York, his vast collection of work and prison songs were brought into contact with a primarily white left-wing public as well as with a coterie of singers and song-makers.

As Leadbelly freed himself from the problematic relation with Lomax – a story that is filled with racial and class tension – he became a central figure in the folk music community in New York (Wolfe and Lornell 1992). Through his interaction with Woody Guthrie, Lee Hays, Pete Seeger, and perhaps especially Moe Asch of Folkways Records, Leadbelly helped give the black experience, and, in particular, the country blues tradition, a wider, more universal reach and impact. In the many songs attributed to him – e.g., "Goodnight Irene," "Midnight Special," "Rock Island Line" – the blues experience, which had grown out of the rural poverty and misery of southern blacks, became singable for whites in the northern cities. The meaning was much the same – the longing, the sharing of oppression, the envisioning of a better life – but, when sung together with whites in a popular, lively style, the songs were made more relevant for a much broader range of publics. In the early 1950s, Pete Seeger, Lee Hays, Ronnie Gilbert, and Fred Hellerman formed the Weavers, which was an immensely successful group until the red-baiting activities of Joseph McCarthy drove them underground. Their renditions of Leadbelly's songs sold in the millions, and were spread around the world as black folk music came to represent mainstream American popular song, as it has continued to do ever since. The combining of musical traditions that were opened up by the popular front thus outlived the social movement that had spawned them. Indeed, it can be argued that it was the Weavers, as a group, and Pete Seeger, as an individual (when he left the Weavers over a dispute: the others had agreed to sing for a cigarette commercial!), who did most to carry the folk song tradition into the postwar era, and into the cultural mainstream (Dunaway 1990, Willens 1988).

Woody Guthrie's "Talking Dust Bowl" and the other so-called talking blues songs of the popular front era represented, on a different level than Leadbelly's songs, a significant contribution to popular culture (Seeger 1993). Talking blues was not so much a song as a poetic performance, a rhythmic telling of a story. Like many other folk songs that became popular songs, talking blues did not require great singing talent in order to be performed; what it required, instead, was a talent for telling a story colorfully and humorously, and, in that respect, the folk songs of the 1930s helped to popularize poetry and public poetry readings even before the beats came along in the 1950s. Talking blues and other "novelty" songs also helped to expand the meaning of popular song itself. Not only did they open up new areas of subject matter, but they also made it possible for popular songs to be sung in new and different ways. Here again, the Weavers, and perhaps especially Lee Hays, who sometimes talked more than he sang at Weavers' concerts, served to carry the tradition of storytelling songs into the 1960s (Willens 1988). Appropriately, it would be Woody Guthrie's son Arlo who would modernize the talking blues tradition in the 1960s with his remarkable "Alice's Restaurant." In many ways, the talking blues can be said to live on today as rap music. Indeed, Pete Seeger refers to the "Talking Union" that he and his fellow Almanac Singers wrote in 1941 as the first rap song (Seeger 1993: 22–23).

The making of an alternative popular culture, or folk music tradition, was a collective enterprise, and involved a number of different types of artists and intellectuals. There were the singer-songwriters such as Woody Guthrie, Pete Seeger, and Huddie Ledbetter, and there were the organizers, such as Alan Lomax and Moe Asch, all of whom subscribed to the radical politics of the popular front. The systematization of folk song that had begun with John Lomax and Carl Sandburg in the 1910s and 1920s was politicized in the 1930s as part of the popular front's cognitive praxis. This politicization can be thought of in two main ways. On the one hand, there was a selection of the more "politically correct" songs for new folk song collections, which included a rediscovery of the Wobblies' and the populists' songs. On the other hand, and more importantly, there was a flowering of original folk music, i.e., the writing of new songs in the folk idiom which addressed contemporary concerns and social problems.

The Movement personified: Guthrie, Seeger, Lomax

More than any other single individual, it was Woody Guthrie who embodied the populist ideals of the popular front. As Robbie Lieberman has recently written, "Woody Guthrie was the major influence on those who began to link folk music with left-wing politics – an identity which young cultural workers absorbed as a given. Guthrie symbolized the potential for organically combining the music of the people with political concerns" (Lieberman 1995: 43). In the words of Moe Asch, who recorded Woody Guthrie for his Folkways label, Woody "had a driving force and a knowledge of what he stood for. He felt that he represented a group of poor people that needed to be spoken for, and he wanted to give them exposure" (quoted in Bluestein 1994: 119).

Guthrie's "This Land is Your Land," perhaps the most well-known folk song of all, projects a spirit of popular patriotism, with poetic images of the varied American landscape, subtly giving the country back to the people, making it clear that the land is to be shared – it was "made for you and me." As with most of Guthrie's successful songs, it is literally soaked in tradition, in a folk music idiom, but also unmistakably personal and contemporary. His more explicitly political songs like "Deportees" and "1913 Massacre" strike chords of shame and shared responsibility, taking real events and turning them into poetic ballads. There is preaching, but it is done in such a folksy, down-home way that it seldom disturbs: "see what your greed for money has done," he says at the end of "1913 Massacre." A Guthrie song usually does a bit more than tell a story; a little philosophy is woven into the folk tapestry. Guthrie was able to recollect the populist legacy in his very person, but at the same time he succeeded in bringing that legacy into direct contact with the contemporary music industry. After several years as a radio singer in California, mixing cowboy songs with stories of "hard travelin'," he brought to New York and the popular front movement in which he operated a unique combination of competences. For not only had he grown up in Oklahoma and been habituated into the dire living conditions of the poor farmer, but he had also accumulated knowledge of a wide range of folk and country musics. Unlike Joe Hill who mostly just added political words to popular tunes, Woody Guthrie managed to innovate new musical forms, like the talking blues. It was his involvement in a social movement, however, which gave his musical talent a structure and a focus. It was the regimen, discipline, and order imposed by the movement that, for a few years anyway, provided a kind of direction for his creative impulses.

It was a broader set of social conditions that stimulated Guthrie's individual genius – as well as that of Pete Seeger, Burl Ives, Aunt Molly Jackson, and all the others who contributed to the "folk revival" of the late 1930s and early 1940s (Eyerman and Baretta 1996). Not least important was the fact that the singers were no longer on their own; by the 1930s, there were those who earned their living collecting and recording songs. Several programs instituted through the New Deal job-creating activity dispatched photographers, writers, musicians, and folklore fieldworkers, such as John and Alan Lomax, to document the culture of the "common people." These programs included the Federal Arts Project of the Works Progress Association (WPA), and the collection projects sponsored by the Library of Congress (Tallack 1991). The artistic movements which grew out of this attempt to represent the general effects of the economic depression have been called the "documentary motive" of the 1930s, and there were few who acted on that motive more energetically than John Lomax and Charles Seeger.

The role of Charles Seeger was perhaps of special significance in raising the musical status of folk songs. As one of his assistants later wrote in relation to Seeger's New Deal work:

A number of people in various parts of the United States had of course been col- lecting folk music long before Seeger came on the scene. But with only two or three exceptions these were people whose orientation was literary, not musical at all; and the direction of their efforts was strictly centripetal. Seeger was the first American of standing among the best-trained musicians to interest himself in American musical traditions, so his interest gave folk music a position it had not had earlier in this country.   (quoted in Pescatello 1992: 47)

Another key individual who contributed to making the folk song tradi- tion into a part of the popular front movement and eventually an alterna- tive popular culture was Alan Lomax, John's son. As a teenager, Alan Lomax had accompanied his father on some of his explorations and helped him publish, in 1934, the most ambitious collection hitherto presented, *American Ballads and Folk Songs.* By the late 1930s, Alan had become politicized; he had been affected by the radical politics of the times, and his ideas about folk music had also taken a turn to the Left. In 1937 Lomax became the director of the Archive of American Folk Song at the Library of Congress, and played an important role in organizing concerts and recordings, and generally managing the affairs – and sometimes the reper- toire – of emerging new folksingers. He also helped them launch their careers by arranging for them to appear on the two radio shows he hosted. He was especially helpful to Leadbelly, after the black singer had fallen out with Lomax Senior, and he also encouraged Josh White, Burl Ives, Aunt Molly Jackson, and perhaps the two most influential performer-activists of the next decades, Woody Guthrie and Pete Seeger.

Pete Seeger, as the son of Charles Seeger, who became one of the most important academic interpreters of folk song while working with the Lomaxes in Washington, was exposed at an early age to folk music. Charles and his second wife, the composer Ruth Crawford, transcribed the musical accompaniments for the songs in many a folk song collection; Ruth had started transcribing songs already in the 1920s for Carl Sandburg's collection and was one of the first classically trained composers to take folk song transcription seriously (Tick 1995). The Seeger children – Pete, Mike, and Peggy – would all be inspired by Charles' and Ruth's interest in folk music, turning their father's and stepmother/mother's academic and theoretical interest into a more active, practitioner interest (Norm Cohen 1991). They were also inspired by their black housekeeper, Elizabeth (Libba) Cotten, who wrote the influential folk song, "Freight Train." They would all have long careers as folksingers and songwriters, which, of course, continue to this day.

Pete Seeger, born in 1919, was the only one who was old enough to be able to participate in the popular front movement. In 1938, he dropped out of Harvard and went to Washington, where he worked with Alan Lomax at the Library of Congress. There he played incessantly on the five-string folk banjo that he had first seen at a country music festival in the South with his father, while learning the songs that the Lomaxes and others had collected (Alan's sister Bess, who would soon be one of the Almanac Singers, remembers Pete that first year playing "almost continuously. One night Alan had to throw him out; Pete just never shut up, and it was driving everybody mad. Oh, he was *terrible*" [quoted in Dunaway 1990: 61]).

Eventually, he became better, and Alan helped him get on the stage and meet other folksingers in New York; and, in the words of Seeger's biographer:

Like the arms of a nebula compacting as it turns, a folk–political song movement began to take shape . . . No political commissar decreed folk songs in vogue; the change came through trial and error . . . It was as spontaneous as musicians sitting down together to sing, among them a trouble-tough Louisiana black; a New England boy, bouncy as a kid in sneakers; and soon, a wandering Okie. By themselves, these three could not have moved American musical history. But their tastes coincided with the New Deal's radical patriotism and folklore activities.

(Dunaway 1990: 62–63)

In their best songs, Guthrie, Seeger, and Leadbelly – and the larger contingent of singers and songwriters within which they worked – put the materials of folk music to new uses: they innovated within the tradition. It was a conscious effort to infuse meaning into the popular culture, and to give voice to the trials and tribulations of the common people during the hard times of the depression years. Woody Guthrie, Lee Hays, Leadbelly, and Molly Jackson combined their varied rural experiences of struggle and hardship with the idealism of young radical easterners like Pete Seeger, Fred Hellerman, and Ronnie Gilbert. What emerged was a new kind of music that the younger generation would carry further into the postwar era: to use song to change the world for the better, to "sing a song of social significance" (Denisoff 1972).

From the thirties to the nineties

While Woody Guthrie retrospectively came to epitomize the folk song movement of the popular front era – not least because of the way he served as a role model for the young Bob Dylan – the alternative popular culture that was largely formed at that time was, as we have tried to show, much broader. It mixed musical traditions, and it also mixed radical politics with realist, or documentary, aesthetics and populist, or patriotic, values. Its message was an American idealism that drew on the ideas of egalitarianism and frontier independence while trying to relate them to the concerns of the twentieth century. As a part of a social movement, it had a major political impact, particularly in mobilizing opposition to fascism and Nazism during the Second World War. But, as with the cognitive praxis of many social movements, its main influence has been on popular culture, in affecting structures of feeling and underlying social sensibilities.

In the 1950s, the message of community and solidarity that had been articulated during the popular front was challenged by the anti-communist crusade, and it was difficult for the folk song tradition to have much of an impact on American music until the death of Joseph McCarthy and the waning of the worst excesses of his red-baiting activities. The enormous success of the Weavers in the early 1950s did open up a small space in the popular culture for folk music that came to be further developed by Burl Ives and Harry Belafonte. But most importantly folk music went underground, to a handful of progressive college campuses, where Pete Seeger would be invited to perform even when he was blacklisted by the mass media and the commercial music industry, and to summer camps, where the children of the Old Left would be socialized into a left-wing tradition of values, solidarity, and folk music. And that tradition would be an important cultural resource for the new social movements that would emerge in the late 1950s and early 1960s. In the words of Todd Gitlin, one of the leaders of the early New Left:

From the Forties through the early Sixties, the music of the Weavers, Woody Guthrie, and others was an embattled minority's way of conjuring up an ideal folk . . . The folk taste could also be a way of expressing distance from and disdain for mainstream popular culture, yet without the avant-garde aura of jazz . . . The

Popular Front was dead, but the idea of it could be sung . . . The political generation of the Fifties was missing, but folk was the living prayer of a defunct movement, the consolation and penumbra of its children, gingerly holding the place of
a left in American culture.   (Gitlin 1987: 74–75)

With the coming of the civil rights movement in the late 1950s, a new
social movement context emerged for the reworking of the folk song tradition. As in the 1930s, when Leadbelly and Woody Guthrie combined their
talents with many other black and white folksingers and songwriters, the
early 1960s witnessed a remarkable outpouring of new songs and new collective events, like the Newport Folk Festival and the blues and folk
revivals. As we shall see, the reinvention of the folk song tradition that
began in the late 1950s fell victim to commercial forces that proved too
strong for most of the newer talents to resist, however. But the impact on
popular music – and popular culture more broadly – of the songs of Bob
Dylan, Joan Baez, Phil Ochs, Judy Collins, and many others remains
significant. Indeed, it can be argued that radicalism in the United States
continues to find its most appropriate and effective form of communication
in folk song. In 1995, Bruce Springsteen's musical evocation of "The Ghost
of Tom Joad" used folk song once again to draw attention to the plight of
the homeless and of the new emigrants to the United States from Mexico
and Vietnam. While the political climate has moved far to the Right, the
cultural climate remains open to voices of critical conscience.

4

The movements of black music: from the New Negro to civil rights

I, too, sing America.

I am the darker brother.
They send me to eat in the kitchen
When company comes,
But I laugh,
And eat well,
And grow strong.

Tomorrow,
I'll sit at the table
When company comes.
Nobody'll dare
Say to me,
"Eat in the kitchen,"
Then.

Besides,
They'll see how beautiful I am
And be ashamed –

I, too, am America.

Langston Hughes

From the beginning of the century, when W. E. B. DuBois analyzed the "souls of black folk" in his extremely influential book of 1903, African-American social movements have been closely identified with particular forms of musical expression. There had been other books which collected and represented the songs of African-Americans, such as the abolitionist era's *Slave Songs of the United States* (1867) and James Monroe Trotter's *Music and Some Highly Musical People* (1878), but DuBois's book put these songs in a social and historical context, and tried to give them clear political meaning. DuBois saw in what he termed the "sorrow songs" a central signifier of black culture, and he saw the spirituals as a central aspect of his own identity as a black man in the United States. As he wrote, "They that walked in darkness sang songs in the olden days – Sorrow Songs – for they were weary at heart . . . Ever since I was a child these songs have stirred me strangely. They came out of the South unknown to me, one by one, and yet at once I knew them as of me and mine" (DuBois [1903] 1994: 155–56).

For DuBois, the slave songs were not merely music, they were an expression of a life rooted in a rural past, and more generally they reflected an experience all African-Americans could recognize. The sorrow songs were, at one and the same time, a musical form and an expression of deep cultural truth. Hearing them is hearing history; they are part of a collective memory that when recalled connects the present hearer with his past. In the songs of the slaves, DuBois identified – and identified with – a common heritage, linking dispersed individuals to one another as well as transmitting the past into the present. This act of identifying, of naming, is central to the making of tradition. It is at once a process of identification and distinction, of bringing together and of sorting out. For DuBois sorrow songs were the authentic expression of African-American experience, while the then-popular "coon songs" ("a mass of music in which the novice may easily lose himself and never find the real Negro melodies"), also composed and sung by blacks, were not (DuBois [1903] 1994: 540). In this respect, DuBois was striking an elitist chord, and arguing that the only chance for black folks to advance was to prove their worth and not degrade themselves in order to win the respect of whites.

There was an underlying political purpose in this act of tradition building. The mapping out of the African-American heritage was an essential part of a cultural nationalism which, as we shall see, has formed an important resource in African-American social movements throughout the twentieth century. Two years after the publication of *The Souls of Black Folk*, DuBois joined together with other African-American intellectuals to form the Niagara Movement and shortly after that, in 1909, he was one of the founders of the NAACP, the National Association for the Advancement of Colored People. In this more explicitly political activity, music served as little more than background. After the First World War, however, the proper and "authentic" contents of the black musical tradition would become a source of open controversy, as a new generation of urban blacks – New Negroes – challenged the hegemony of those like DuBois (whom they called the "old" Negroes) to define what was authentically black music and what was not. For many of the New Negroes, it was the popular, secular, living black culture – represented in large measure by the rural southern world of the blues and its contemporary urban counter-parts in jazz – that was as important as the more cultivated or historical expressions that DuBois admired.

The country blues emerged at about the same time as DuBois was artic-ulating the characteristic double consciousness of "black folks." As the nineteenth century came to an end, blacks in the South were subjected to massive violence and oppression, and a segregated social order was being put into place, with "separate but equal" laws and rules and institutions for blacks and whites. No longer were the sorrow songs of the slaves sufficient to express this contradictory condition of free and not-free; a new form of collective music came forth, which can be seen to have translated the ambiguous social situation into words and stories. The blues helped rural blacks make sense of their emerging double consciousness, which was of a different order than the relatively benign dual identity that DuBois articu-lated for middle-class blacks in the North. Where the one tended toward a glorification of libidinal passion, carving out a haven of pleasure in a repressive social environment, the other strove to develop a highbrow black music grounded in the integration of African-American spirit and European musical form.

In their lively rhythms and their often tragically ironic texts, the blues managed to express something significant about the contemporary black experience. As developed by musicians and composers like W. C. Handy and singers like Bessie Smith, the blues became a popular form of entertainment, as the music traveled from the Mississippi Delta up the river to St. Louis and Kansas City and then moved eastward to Chicago and New York. It would be the mixing of blues and jazz – and their translation into literary and aesthetic discourses by writers and critics in the so-called Harlem Renaissance of the 1920s – that would prepare the way for the broader diffusion of African-American experience into American culture. By stressing the importance of rhythm and the particular characteristics of the black consciousness that were expressed in the music, "translator" intel-lectuals such as James Weldon Johnson, Alain Locke, Langston Hughes, and Zora Neale Hurston helped define the black musical tradition. At about the same time, some influential jazz musicians, especially Duke Ellington, explicitly sought to create a music that reflected the actual his-torical experience of blacks in the United States. In the 1920s and 1930s, Paul Robeson and Marian Anderson brought spirituals to the concert stage and their recordings spread black sacred music into American culture. The black composer William Grant Still wrote an impressive and influential African-American symphony and white composers like Aaron Copland and George Gershwin brought jazz rhythms into their operas and ballets.

In these activities, the underlying tensions of black music – and black culture more generally – were temporarily resolved; indeed, the so-called Renaissance, which spread from New York to Chicago in the course of the 1930s, can be seen as a kind of social movement, in which a common black aesthetic could be articulated in the diversity and range of musical expression amidst the hard times of the depression (Floyd 1995). Already in the 1940s, however, the tensions had reemerged, as the gospel blues of Thomas Dorsey and the bebop jazz of Charlie Parker challenged the integrationist tendencies of the big bands with more popular, blues-inspired forms of black music. And when the gospel blues was transformed by Mahalia Jackson into a music that could be sung both in church and on the streets, it helped inspire the "freedom songs" that would characterize the civil rights movement of the 1950s and early 1960s.

In the late 1960s, when black activists transformed their movement into a struggle for "black power" and a cultural concern with black consciousness and African-American identity took precedence over the more explicitly political battles for integration, a new kind of "soul" music emerged from the voices of black singers and composers. It brought into the popular culture a similar kind of longing and despair that had marked the spirituals and the blues; but in many of its versions, such as those of James Brown and Otis Redding, it also offered a new assertiveness, and an originality of expression that fundamentally transformed popular music. The rock music of the late 1960s, like the hip-hop, disco, and eventually rap musics of the 1980s and 1990s, is inconceivable without the energy, drive, and underlying meaning that comes from the black music tradition.

In this chapter we want to indicate how a good deal of the power of that tradition – its making and its remaking, its affirmation of itself as tradition and its periodic recombinations and reformulations – derives from its association to social movements. There has not always been a direct connection between music and politics; but as with the folk music tradition that we have traced in the previous chapter, social movements have, in a variety of ways, helped to define and redefine the contours of black music. On the one hand, the periods of social movement have served to open up spaces for musical experimentation – a new kind of black public sphere. They have provided contexts for critical reflection and analysis that have inspired, and, for some, even directly guided, musicians and composers in their innovative activity. On the other hand, social movements have given a kind of political focus or direction to musical expression, charging music with a special intensity and responsibility.

Musical developments are often seen as following a logic of their own, driven by the internal dynamics of aesthetic expression, or the external demands of commercial success. Music, for most musicologists, sociologists, and musicians, is a special sphere, largely sealed off from broader social and political processes. Musical innovations are seen to be the result of commercial opportunities for individual genius, of expanding markets and new audience "demand." Here, as elsewhere, entrepreneurs, those who recognize the new demands and act to meet them, are given the pride of place. It is not by chance, however, that new forms of musical expression seem to develop most strikingly in periods of social and political engagement. In the 1920s – and then again in the 1960s – social and political movements have provided a particularly strong set of "opportunity structures" for black musicians. Developments that had already begun in the commercial realm – the making of the blues and gospel, in the early period, and the emergence of soul and rock-and-roll in the later – have been given a much bigger audience and a much stronger cultural significance in periods of social movement.

Social movements provide a cohesiveness, a kind of social glue, that reconfigures the relations between culture and politics. But that cohesiveness is itself a historical process and, we would claim, a cognitive process of remembering. As cognitive praxis, music helps to constitute a collective actor by actualizing and articulating preexisting forms of social solidarity. In the case of the New Negro movement and the civil rights movement, that cognitive praxis has represented a mobilization of primarily oral traditions, expressing the African-American's truth-bearing claims for recognition, for visibility, for acceptance as free and equal to white Americans. But in taking on a political dimension within social movements, oral traditions – the forms of musical and cultural expression – are reconstituted. By becoming sources of empowerment, education, and "consciousness-raising," musical expression can thus serve as a form of exemplary social action.

As with the folk music tradition, it has been in the wake of the movements, after they have faded away as active political forces, that the music has diffused into the broader culture and changed popular mores and tastes; even more than has been the case in the folk music tradition, black music has served to keep alive the continuing discourse of black consciousness, that peculiarly double, or dual identity, that has been such an important part of twentieth-century American and Atlantic cultural experience (Gilroy 1994).

The secular and the sacred: blues and gospel

In the defeated South, in the remains of a collapsed economic and political system, emancipation made possible a more mobile and flexible black workforce (even in the face of a re-institutionalized racism), creating a background upon which the musical traditions from slavery and Africa could be reinterpreted. In addition to the small black middle class, part of which would find its collective voice with DuBois in the sorrow songs and the spirituals, unskilled laborers would find theirs in the blues (Alan Lomax 1993). For this group the blues served as much as a means of communication and source of identity as a way to make work bearable and leisure time entertaining.

Like the white country music of the same era, the blues emerged as the musical expression of a largely illiterate rural population. It grew out of the work songs, field hollers, religious songs, and dances of the rural poor and spoke to and of their experiences. Its African roots, of course, serve to distinguish it from its white counterparts, even though there would be a good deal of mixing between white and black (and Mexican) rural musics. But the blues came, in large measure, to reflect the experience of black workers, primarily male, who were scattered across the southern and eastern sections of the United States. The blues provided also an informal "network," a kind of community, into which migrant workers could immediately enter as they moved around the country (Cruz 1986). If for the first group the blues reflected and spoke to a real community, for the second, it helped create what Benedict Anderson has called an imagined community (1991).[1] It was not by chance that the clubs where the blues were featured or performed, citified jooks, lay in the marginal areas of cities and towns. It was these sections in which the newly arrived and the less well-off gathered, and which the more established and the better-educated avoided and disdained.

Some of the first written transcriptions of the blues were made by W. C. Handy at the turn of the century. Handy's sheet music text of "Memphis Blues" (1912) is often cited as the first example of popular, composed blues. As LeRoi Jones (Amiri Baraka) notes, Handy's transcriptions of folk material "invented" the blues "for a great many Americans and also showed that there was some money to be made from it" (LeRoi Jones 1963: 148). Handy, a black man, had heard blues tunes in Mississippi and Alabama, where he grew up. As he said, "Each one of my blues is based on some old Negro song of the South . . . Something that sticks in my mind, that I hum to myself when I'm not thinking about it. Some old song that is part of the memories of my childhood and of my race. I can tell you the exact song I used as a basis for any one of my blues" (quoted in Morgan and Barlow 1992: 117). The college-trained Handy collected his music, Steve Tracy (1988: 92) writes, with the approach of a folklorist and commercial entrepreneur, seeing the "folk song as a survival from the past and the commercial approach to folk songs as material to be mined and transmuted into something more respectable and grand."[2]

Handy's compositions were done in the style of Tin Pan Alley and helped open the blues to further commercial exploitation. His creations were central to the blues craze which rocked New York and other urban areas in the 1920s, even though "when W. C. Handy arrived in New York from Memphis in 1918, the blues had been there for years among southern immigrants, and female professional entertainers from southern minstrel and vaudeville shows were already important in entertainment circles" (Floyd 1995: 108). Before radio, Handy's written texts allowed the blues to circulate far beyond these small urban publics. Thus, at about the same time that DuBois' politically motivated interpretations were helping to articulate the slave songs as part of a "highbrow" black music tradition, Handy and others, such as Artie Matthews and Hart A. Wand, were developing other more secular and contemporary black musics in popular, commercial contexts.

Turning to the practitioners, not surprisingly many of the songs that can be categorized as blues deal with the problems encountered by the social strata whose experience they reflected: work and unemployment, traveling, drinking, social relationships, marriage and divorce, etc. (see Oliver 1960). One can also find, however, songs which comment on the emerging class stratification among African-Americans, such as this one collected by John Lomax in 1917:

> Niggers gettin' mo' like white fo'ks,
> Mo' like white fo'ks eve'y day.
> Niggers learnin' Greek an' Latin,
> Niggers wearin' silk an' satin,
> Niggers gettin' mo' like white fo'ks eve'y day.
>
> (quoted in Levine 1977: 245)

The blues provided a sense of identification, and of belonging to a group, and the texts reflected a range of diverse yet common experiences. This process of identification was different than that DuBois sought to express in relation to the sorrow songs, in that it was more immediate, less reflective, and less a matter of choice. This music also served as a form of negative distinction for the upwardly striving and integrationist middle class; the blues became something which many of them did not want to identify with. This, again, was an aspect which the blues shared with contemporary white country music. The term "nigger" used in the song quoted above carries this double connotation, this positive and negative distinction. This use of the term was a transposition of the dominant, white culture's racism, and was exactly what the upwardly striving middle-class African-American wanted to distinguish himself from.

The religious, the middle-class, and the educated African-Americans tended to view the blues as "nigger music," carrying the negative distinction. Willie "The Lion" Smith, one of the greatest of blues piano players, recalled a time when "the average Negro family did not allow the blues, or raggedy music to be played in their homes" (quoted in Lewis 1994: 59). David Levering Lewis questions such recollections, however, arguing that the same people who forbade such music in their homes in the daytime attended the parties and clubs where it was played at night.[3] Distinctions were meant primarily to keep up appearances, and the duplicity this involved was connected to class-related strategies of integration and accommodation. In addition to the ones already mentioned, such strategies had a geographical dimension as well. Cary Wintz writes, "by the 1920s few black intellectuals still believed that the future of the race lay in the South. As they turned their attention northward and focused their hope on the emerging black communities in the northern cities ... they also were turning their backs on their southern heritage" (1988: 6). The blues was part of that southern heritage, which was, in their eyes, rural and thus uneducated in origin, primitive in terms of emotional expression, and unskilled in terms of musical technique. The more blunt stated this straight out; the more subtle, like DuBois, found aesthetic criteria for dismissing the blues.

A similar development and struggle can be identified in religious music.[4] The first transcriptions of black religious music came in the late eighteenth century in the hymns which reflected the interaction between white and black religion (Floyd 1995: 58–59). Later, black religious music gained respectability among a broader segment of the white population when the Fisk University Jubilee Singers were formed in 1871. A market was uncovered for concert performances of spirituals to go along with the already-existing market for what have been called "pseudo-spirituals" and "Carry-me-backs," commercially popular nostalgic songs like "Carry Me Back to Old Virginny" from 1878. DuBois was himself moved by spirituals performed in concert format and they formed the basis for his own analysis of the sorrow songs. By the turn of the century, when DuBois was writing, the spirituals had become a central ingredient of the emergent black consciousness. For DuBois, the sorrow songs were not merely a source of identity – a common heritage for black people in the United States – but also among the main contributions that black folk had made to the country's development:

Little of beauty has America given the world save the rude grandeur God himself stamped on her bosom; the human spirit in this new world has expressed itself in vigor and ingenuity rather than in beauty. And so by fateful chance the Negro folk-song – the rhythmic cry of the slave – stands today not simply as the sole American music, but as the most beautiful expression of human experience born this side the seas. It has been neglected, it has been, and is, half despised, and above all it has been persistently mistaken and misunderstood; but notwithstanding, it still remains as the singular spiritual heritage of the nation and the greatest gift of the Negro people.   (DuBois [1903] 1994: 155–56)

James Weldon Johnson, who was a songwriter, politician, and writer – and one of the main proponents of the New Negro during the 1920s – was also fascinated by what he termed the "miracle" of the spirituals. In introducing a collection of spirituals in 1925, he stressed the dialectical combination of African "primitivism" and Christianity that had formed the basis for the spirituals:

What led to this advance by the American Negro beyond his primitive music? Why did he not revive and continue the beating out of complex rhythms on tom-toms and drums while he uttered barbaric and martial cries to their accompaniment? It was because at the precise and psychic moment there was blown through or fused into the vestiges of his African music the spirit of Christianity as he knew Christianity . . . Far from his native land and customs, despised by those among whom he lived, experiencing the pang of the separation of loved ones on the auction block, knowing the hard taskmaster, feeling the lash, the Negro seized Christianity . . . The result was a body of songs voicing all the cardinal virtues of Christianity – patience, forbearance, love, faith, and hope – through a necessarily modified form of primitive African music.   (Johnson [1925] 1944: 125)

The spirituals took on a new importance when they were presented in a controlled and disciplined performance before an essentially passive audience. Taken out of their original collective context and performed in this manner at concerts rather than in church, spirituals became, as Levine (1977) notes, more and more like European art music. When Paul Robeson performed them in London and on the Broadway stage, the shift in meaning and context of black music became a matter of open controversy among black intellectuals and creative artists in the 1920s.

There were a number of aspects to the controversy. One concerned the solo performance of what was essentially a collective music, another the role of black music in western civilization and, underlying it all, the more or less hidden question of class. According to Alain Locke, what was unique in the spirituals and essentially all other forms of black music was the way rhythm, harmony, and emotion fused as a form of collective expression. Separate out and emphasize any of these, and you are left with a distortion. The solo performance of the spiritual, in its focus on the individual performer and the emotional content, removed the songs, according to this view, from their authentic and anonymous collective basis (Locke [1925] 1968: 199–210).

In the early twentieth century, a shift in the style of black religious music has been noted in the compositions of African-Americans such as William Henry Sherwood and Charles Albert Tindley (the composer of "I Will Overcome"). To mark this shift, the period between 1896 and 1920 has been labeled "the first period of gospel singing" (Floyd 1995: 63). Gospel was a type of song and performance which stands in stark contrast to the concert hall or art music performance of the spiritual. Here the emphasis was on jubilation and active participation through collective singing, foot-stomping, and hand-clapping, with direct links to evangelical religion. The development of gospel out of the spiritual can be interpreted as a class-based reaction on the part of lower-class blacks to reclaim black religious music from more middle-class purifiers like DuBois (and Robeson). In the 1920s, gospel music achieved phenomenal success in part through the songs of a former blues singer named Thomas A. Dorsey. Dorsey is often called the father of gospel, as his transformation of an essentially oral musical tradition into sheet music opened the door to its spread and to commercial exploitation. Gospel became the religious music of the storefront churches in the sections of cities and towns where the lower-class blacks lived. In fact, for many of those who worshipped in the older, more established churches gospel was seen as bringing the devil's music – blues – into the church (Harris 1992).

The New Negro movement

After the First World War there was a great upsurge of creative activity among African-Americans. Centered in the industrial cities of the North, what could be called a black public sphere emerged as urban areas expanded to accommodate the waves of migrants arriving from the southern regions of the country and the soldiers coming home from war. Within the neighborhoods which were created or transformed, small clubs and meeting halls, restaurants, movie houses, theaters, and dance halls sprang up in the black sections of Chicago, Detroit, Cleveland, Philadelphia, and especially New York. Forms of popular entertainment were created as the newly arrived refitted their traditional cultures to fit the urban environment and lifestyle.

At the same time a growing interest in black history, literature, and art could be found among educated African-Americans. These processes, the emergence of a vibrant public sphere with cultural practices mixing the high and the low, the serious and the popular, were connected through a number of magazines, journals, and newspapers which served to link together a wide-ranging and often socially diverse racial community. While these media certainly tried to be commercially successful, the market mechanism was attenuated by a sense of racial consciousness connected with ideals of betterment and enlightenment. In addition to the commercial mass media ventures, there were some that were associated with organizations that sought to improve the condition of colored people, such as the NAACP's *Crisis* and the Urban League's *Opportunity Magazine.*

The editors of these journals, W. E. B. DuBois and Charles S. Johnson, were sociologists as well as political activists and, along with two other prominent intellectuals, the academic Alain Locke and James Weldon Johnson, executive secretary for the NAACP but also newspaperman and composer of popular music, they formed the core of an intellectual avant-garde. These men – and several other artists, musicians, writers, and activists – brought about what has come to be known as the Harlem Renaissance. Some of the younger generation associated with the Harlem Renaissance were more directly involved with popular music, by revealing how oral and literary traditions could be combined in cultural representation. Langston Hughes, for example, brought the blues into his poetry and Zora Neale Hurston found a musical quality basic to the folk tales she collected and recorded.

In spite of growing regional and class-related differences in musical taste, at the beginning of the 1920s, many African-Americans still favored a strategy of racial integration, if not cultural assimilation. The relative opening up of economic opportunity, higher wages, and the increased physical mobility raised hopes of accommodation with the dominant white society. These expectations were dampened by the reception accorded returning war veterans (black as well as white) and by the race riots which spread through northern urban areas in 1918–19. In spite of this, hopes of eventual acceptance into the dominant society remained as the 1920s began, and a vibrant black culture was seen by some influential ideological leaders to be one of the main ways to achieve that acceptance. As DuBois himself put it, "I do not doubt that the ultimate art coming from black folk is going to be just as beautiful, and beautiful in largely the same ways, as the art that comes from white folk . . . but the point today is that until the art of black folk compels recognition they will not be rated as human" (DuBois [1926] 1986: 1002).

Ben Sidran finds in the race riots evidence of rising black confidence amidst the often-violent confrontation with white society. Such riots, he writes, "brought out the fact that the black culture was slowly losing its fear of direct social action," and further, "the riots did *involve*, personally, large numbers of blacks, for the first time, in the process of urban decision-making" (Sidran [1971] 1981: 58, 59). And, partly as a result, the largest mass movement ever to involve African-Americans emerged in the early

1920s. Presenting an alternative to integration, Marcus Garvey's back-to-Africa movement attracted millions of the newly urbanized working-class blacks, becoming in the process "the first black social movement of any stature to express 'black pride' in no uncertain terms" (ibid.: 57).

Marcus Garvey, a charismatic Jamaican immigrant who landed in New York in 1916 by way of England, spearheaded the largest political movement of the age. His organization, the United Negro Improvement Association (UNIA), offered a counter to the integrationist and legalistic NAACP. The movement sponsored street demonstrations in the form of marches and pageants built around pan-African and cultural nationalist themes, as well as program of self-help. The UNIA's first annual convention, held in Madison Square Garden, New York, in 1920, was attended by thousands, and was accompanied by street marches and a grand parade which featured Garvey riding in a horse-drawn carriage, dressed in mock military uniform with a plumed hat. Such ritual was central to the Garveyist movement, whose officers dressed in similar fashion to Garvey, wearing feathered plumed hats and white gloves, bearing swords and medals. Movement recruits were trained at Booker T. Washington University in Harlem, whose name clearly revealed the links to Washington's earlier strategy and programs of self-help. Instead of the practical knowledge offered by Washington at the Tuskegee Institute that he had founded, however, Garveyism was heavy on symbolism and ritual which aimed at spreading racial pride and self-esteem in a black, urban setting. All this helped make Garveyism "the largest and most successful mass movement of blacks in the history of the United States" (Cone 1991: 14). The actual attempts to prepare for a return to Africa were mired in controversy and incompetence, and the miscalculations eventually led to Garvey's imprisonment for fraud.

The relations between Garveyism, which was essentially a working-class movement, and black music have not been accorded much historical attention. In a recent work, Ted Vincent has sought to correct what he sees as a bias found in many accounts of the 1920s, which have emphasized the importance of the middle-class movement of intellectuals, the Harlem Renaissance. Vincent has found a rich mixture of music and politics in and around the Garveyist movement. W. C. Handy and many other blues musicians took active part in the movement, and even black concert singers performed at movement events. Garvey and his movement inspired many jazz musicians, and actually formed the subject matter of many jazz hits of the time. For Vincent, Garveyism was a central factor in inspiring what he calls the jazz revolution of the 1920s, when jazz, for the first time, became a formidable force in American, and even international, popular culture.

Garveyism, like other social movements, provided contexts for experimentation, performance, and training in cultural activity. Instead of praising individual black artists who managed to project the African-American experience into the wider culture, as Alain Locke tended to do, Garveyism expressed itself through a collective music, and the songs that its members sang sought to relate the black musical tradition directly to the cause of black nationalism. As Vincent puts it:

> the relationship of the Garvey movement to the jazz revolution has not been explored in Garveyite terms – Black nationalist terms. As nationalists, Garveyites committed themselves to improving the lives of the entire captive Black nation in America. Garvey asked outside music stars to volunteer their services rather than spend association funds needed for his soup kitchens, neighborhood industries, and the like. As for money spent on music, it was more in the interest of the UNIA to invest in musical instruments for a community band than to pay a big fee for a one night engagement of, say, the Duke Ellington Orchestra. For the most part, the UNIA chose to spend its "national" allotment for music in the community.
>
> (Vincent 1995: 128)

Garveyism was only one of several political movements among blacks in the interwar years. In addition to organizations such as the NAACP and the Urban League, socialists and communists were also actively organizing amongst the emerging urban ghettos of the North. In the field of literature and the arts, the Harlem Renaissance represented a kind of cultural mobilization that was carried out alongside the more explicit political organizations. Taken together, these somewhat disparate activities nonetheless formed a context for experimentation and cultural reevaluation which can be likened to the space opened by a social movement.

To many participants and observers in the mid-1920s it seemed as if a new age were dawning. A "New Negro" – sophisticated, urbane, and above all imbued with a sense of racial pride – was said to be emerging to replace the stereotyped ignorant country bumpkin, the nigger, and the subservient Uncle Tom, which white America loved to hate, and which many African-Americans themselves appeared to accept as the inevitable outcome of the politics of racial discrimination.

While this sense of change was experienced more or less across the country, for reasons having as much to do with its being a center of cultural production as with the large number of blacks living there, New York City became the locus of this cultural revitalization. That section of upper Manhattan known as Harlem, a former rural paradise which offered country-style living to New York's most wealthy families as late as the 1910s, was quickly evolving into a "black metropolis," a cultural center and an urban ghetto at one and the same time.

The New Negro movement articulated what Raymond Williams called the "structure of feeling" of an emergent African-American culture, part of the process of race formation (Gilroy 1992). For Williams a structure of feeling

is a way of defining forms and conventions in art and literature as inalienable elements of a social material process: not by derivation from other social forms and pre-forms, but as social formation of a specific kind which may in turn be seen as the articulation (often the only fully available articulation) of structures of feeling which as living processes are much more widely experienced. (Williams 1977: 133)

Through literature and art, the participants in the Harlem Renaissance pursued a kind of exemplary action, putting into cultural form what many others were feeling. Alain Locke's anthology *The New Negro* published in 1925 is usually cited as the programmatic statement of the Harlem Renaissance, which brought together in one volume the various, even opposing strains of cultural expression. In his introductory essay, Locke presented the poems and literary pieces which make up the volume as representing a shared vision and collective project of racial reevaluation. Locke regarded the Harlem Renaissance not as a small literary movement, but rather as an intellectual avant-garde, the leading edge of a positive reformulation of what had previously been a negative demarcation. Harlem, Locke wrote, "is the home of the Negro's 'Zionism'" (Locke [1925] 1968: 14). The reference to Zionism reveals the cultural nationalism that was inherent in Locke's idea of the New Negro, and was consciously aimed at countering Garvey's pan-African movement, which was a strong presence in Harlem at the time. With roots in the urban, northern, and educated middle class, Locke's version of cultural nationalism put more emphasis on culture and less on nation – and on the founding of a national state, be it in Africa or some part of the United States – than Garvey's more working-class-oriented program.[5]

As christener of the new movement and a major actor in defining the New Negro, Alain Locke was more open than most of the educated African-American elite to popular forms of cultural expression, including music. Locke was sympathetic to the new generation's interest in all forms of black cultural expression, not only the spirituals, which in the 1920s were being further modified for general consumption by Paul Robeson, but also jazz and the blues, although the latter was a bit harder to accommodate. In a chapter of *The New Negro* entitled "The Negro Spirituals," Locke picked up the argument where DuBois left off two decades earlier, "It may not be readily conceded now that the song of the Negro is America's folk-song; but if the Spirituals are what we think them to be, a classic folk expression, then this is their ultimate destiny" (Locke [1925] 1968: 199). Yet, after acknowledging DuBois's contribution, he went on to criticize the basic categories upon which it was based:

Interesting and intriguing as was Dr. DuBois's analysis of their [the spirituals'] emotional themes, modern interpretation must break with that mode of analysis, and relate these songs to the folk activities that they motivated . . . From this point of view we have essentially four classes, the almost ritualistic prayer songs or pure Spirituals, the freer and more unrestrained evangelical "shouts" or camp-meeting songs . . . and the work and labor songs of strictly secular character.

(Locke [1925] 1968: 205)

Locke and the Harlem Renaissance he helped name can be seen as a forerunner of the cultural nationalism – and a challenge to the political nationalism represented by Garvey – that would reappear in the 1960s in the Black Power movement. The concept of race, like the New Negro who bore it, was here endowed with positive attribution, empowering rather than subordinating, as was the case when whites dictated the terms of distinction. As self-attribution, denoting a change from a race in-itself to a race for-itself, racial pride would replace self-hate. The Negro was New because he could now define himself, taking control over his own self-perception as a step toward controlling his own destiny. However, the folk traditions which formed the basis for this process of empowerment required interpretation and articulation by a black intelligentsia, the so-called talented tenth: "What stirs inarticulately in the masses is already upon the lips of the talented few, and the future listens, however the present may shut its ears" (Locke quoted in Tracy 1988: 26).

Not all of the participants in the "Renaissance" were as elitist as Locke, however. In their attempts to represent the New Negro, at least some activists in the Harlem Renaissance combined African and American folk traditions in innovative ways in the context of an emerging urban black public sphere. The spoken dialect and musical expressions of the rural, southern African-American were resources in this mobilization of tradition, a process, however, which was shaped (in-formed) by the conventions of the dominant European and American cultural frameworks of the time.

The New Negro movement was, in our terms, a part of a social movement, and even though many of its participants seldom articulated political goals in the narrow sense (that was left to Garveyism and the NAACP), they were nonetheless impelled by political motivations. They were political not only in their motives but also in their practice, in the artistic works they produced: the poems, the novels, the paintings, and the music were all objectifications of a new, empowering race consciousness.

In addition to providing spaces for the rediscovery of traditional practices and everyday frameworks of understanding, social movements express their identities through cultural innovations, thus serving as spaces for cultural experimentation. Music, as we have seen, has been a prime source of identity for African-Americans and was a core element in the notion of a distinct black perspective and way of life which was constituted in the New Negro movement of the 1920s. Traditional folk musical expressions, like the blues and spirituals, and newer genres, like jazz and gospel, were important in both the evaluative and innovative aspects of the movement's cognitive praxis as "movement intellectuals" drew upon and utilized the activities occurring around them in the bars, cafés, churches, movie houses, and dance-halls of the black public sphere.

In Locke's anthology, J. A. Rogers argued that, like the songs of the slaves, blues and jazz had common roots in the need for escape from domination and oppression, and this was intrinsic to the African-American experience. The music was rooted in and helped identify a distinct black culture:

Jazz isn't music merely, it is a spirit that can express itself in almost anything. The true spirit of jazz is a joyous revolt from convention, custom, authority, boredom, even sorrow – from everything that would confine the soul of man and hinder its riding free on the air. The Negroes who invented it called their songs the "Blues," and they weren't capable of satire or deception. Jazz was their explosive attempt to cast off the blues and be happy, carefree happy, even in the midst of sordidness and sorrow. And that is why it has been such a balm for modern ennui, and has become a safety valve for modern machine-ridden and convention-bound society. It is the revolt of the emotions against repression.   (Rogers in Locke [1925] 1968: 216–17)

Rogers was interested in explaining both the rootedness of the blues and the more universal appeal of jazz, which at the time was already beginning to be extremely popular among audiences around the world. This very rootedness in everyday experience also helps us understand why, in their less disciplined and sophisticated forms, jazz and especially the blues were anathema to the older generation of African-Americans. Rogers believed a great future awaited jazz in the "sublimated" form offered up by the current jazz orchestras, from Fletcher Henderson to Paul Whiteman, where "there are none of the vulgarities and crudities of the lowly origin or the only too prevalent cheap imitations" (Rogers in Locke [1925] 1968: 221). He quotes Serge Koussevitzky, conductor of the Boston Symphony Orchestra, to the effect that "jazz is an important contribution to modern musical literature. It has an epochal significance – it is not superficial, it is fundamental. Jazz comes from the soil, where all music has its beginning." He makes his position explicit in the closing lines of his essay: "jazz is rejuvenation, a recharging of the batteries of civilization with primitive new vigor. It has come to stay, and they are wise, who instead of protesting against it, try to lift and divert it into nobler channels" (Rogers, ibid.: 224).

It is significant that Rogers mentions blues only in relation to jazz, and legitimates the latter by citing the views of a white, European conductor. This was a standard strategy regarding folk traditions, to see them as residing in and reflecting an imagined past, and as useful resources for a more sophisticated future. As a folk and rural musical form, the blues was neither living nor valuable in itself. If not the embarrassment it was to the sensitive, upwardly mobile middle class, it was still something relegated to a bygone age, an historical document, not a tradition worth keeping alive. The younger members of the New Negro movement, Langston Hughes and Zora Neale Hurston, for example, had other ideas.

Hughes and Hurston offer an interesting contrast to the "old guard" of the New Negro movement. Both were raised in smaller towns and cities in the American periphery, Hughes in Kansas and Ohio and Hurston in Alabama and Florida; their paths to Harlem formed a sort of cultural coming of age. What separated them from their elders and helped unite them with a new generation was their feelings for and interpretation of their rural heritage. Both Hughes and Hurston sought to preserve – while at the same time transforming – the oral culture of African-Americans by transcribing it as literature for both a black and a white audience. Just as the transcribers of blues music had done, the poetry and plays of Langston Hughes and the novels and folklore collections of Zora Neale Hurston made the oral tradition accessible in written form, while at the same time attempting to preserve its distinctive voice and experiential authenticity. While Locke and DuBois could be moved by this oral tradition and recognize the authenticity of the experience it recalled, they saw little reason to preserve it, much less legitimate it as art or literature.

Langston Hughes spent much of his life on the road, but it was a road that always ended in Harlem. Like DuBois, Hughes counted whites amongst his ancestors, but he had less difficulty than the confrontational DuBois in navigating the United States' racial divide. Already in high school Hughes gained recognition from white schoolmates for his poetry and general writing skill. His first poetic models were drawn from a young American modernism, typified by Walt Whitman and Carl Sandburg. This was the more populist wing of modernism, which countered and counteracted its elitist brothers, like T. S. Eliot and Ezra Pound (Rampersad 1986: 29). Langston Hughes called Sandburg his "guiding star," in aesthetic concerns. In politics, however, that shining light came from W. E. B. DuBois, whose magazine *Crisis* published Hughes' poems and for whom he became a sort of "house poet." But these appearances in the NAACP's journal were closely followed by reprints in white literary magazines, something which helped cast Hughes into the role of interpreter and mediator between the black and white literary worlds. As James Baldwin would do two decades later, Langston Hughes helped open white eyes to the black world, something accomplished with the assistance of white agents like Carl Van Vechten.

Alain Locke included Hughes' poems in the special "New Negro" edition of the magazine *Survey Graphic* and in the book which followed. Hughes exemplified the new generation in one of those poems, entitled "Youth":

> We have to-morrow
> Bright before us
> Like a flame
>
> Yesterday, a night-gone thing
> A sun-down name
>
> And dawn to-day
> Broad arch above the road we came,
> We march!

The New Negro movement and wider public sphere in Harlem circumscribed an admiring black audience in behalf of which Hughes' creative energies could flourish. In the early 1920s this arena expanded to include patrons and go-betweens (like Van Vechten), and other interested parties from the white publishing world centered in midtown Manhattan. Hughes first met Zora Neale Hurston at an awards dinner arranged by *Opportunity Magazine*, another movement journal, in which judges, including Eugene O'Neill and Robert Benchley, and guests representing leading publishing houses, applauded Hughes and Hurston as first- and second-prize winners respectively. Although they met for the first time at this 1925 Harlem gathering, their paths followed similar routes and could have crossed earlier. Hurston was part of a circle of students around Alain Locke at Howard University in Washington, D.C., before moving to New York in 1925 where she studied anthropology with Franz Boas at Columbia University, where Hughes had also studied. Her first published poems appeared in Marcus Garvey's newspaper *Negro World*, part of the same movement sphere that nourished Hughes. But Hurston's professional training encouraged field work, which she carried out in New York's black ghettos for Boas and in the South with Alan Lomax, recording and transcribing the black cultural experience. While Hurston and Hughes worked within different professional spheres, their understanding of their role as movement intellectuals was similar. Both understood that role as giving voice to the multi-sided African-American experience, including its less uplifting sides, which the older generation looked down upon. The audience they addressed was both white and black, and the means they used mixed the high and the low, just as did the black cultural traditions that they did so much to articulate and diffuse. As the actor Ossie Davis put it, in a foreword to a posthumous edition of one of Hughes' numerous popular histories of black entertainers:

Langston Hughes was not only poet laureate, but also recording secretary to the tribe. Nothing about us, past or present, was too small or trivial for him to notice, hand down, or pass on as poem, story, or history book – certainly not our arts, our singing and dancing, which might be merely entertainment to White America, but to us were matters of life or death.

(Davis quoted in Hughes and Meltzer [1967] 1990: 1)

The new generation that Hughes and Hurston represented was working out its own aesthetic, something which would form a central part of the cognitive praxis of its collective identity formation. In literature and art, this would mean a search for authenticity and truth, a turn to realism and away from the uplifting romanticism of the older generation. It meant the realistic portrayal of Harlem street life in Claude Mckay's *Home to Harlem*, a best seller in 1928, which for DuBois was an expression of the "debauched" rather than the "talented" tenth, the use of dialect and street slang in the blues-inspired poetry of Hughes, the folk tales and stories collected and transformed by Hurston, and the primitivism and the naive realism in the paintings of Palmer Hayden and William H. Johnson.

The new generation was also more sympathetic than their elders to the mass-mediated reproduction of culture. Radio and recording had begun to play an important role in spreading a wide variety of musics across the airwaves, thus promoting a creative reworking and combination of musical forms and genres, across racial as well as regional and class lines. Like its latter-day counterparts, this new generation in the 1920s was more accustomed to listening to music in a mediated form and could readily accept experimentation and musical innovation. Hughes, for instance, had no difficulty fusing jazz and poetry, or writing poems in rural dialect, thus mixing the highbrow and the lowbrow, in both music and poetry. Nor did he have difficulty taunting those who did:

Let the blare of Negro Jazz bands and the bellowing voice of Bessie Smith singing Blues penetrate the closed ears of the colored near-intellectuals until they listen and perhaps understand . . . We younger Negro artists who create now intend to express our dark-skinned selves without fear or shame.   (quoted in Floyd 1993: 9)

There were, however, forms of music and types of musicians who made it easier to bridge the gap between the generations. In addition to the jazzy blues of Bessie Smith, there was a new jazz which combined larger orchestration with a softer tone. This was a kind of music that appealed to a larger and more diverse white audience, especially when performed in the sanitized environment of the supper clubs with their brightly lit dance floors. While this was not exactly the kind of integration that DuBois, for example, had had in mind, it could at least have been seen as a step in that direction. Central to this highly ambiguous process of mediating between races, generations, and musical traditions were musicians like Duke Ellington.

Raised in Washington, D.C., with a relatively large black middle-class population, Ellington personified the manners and appearance which appealed to the Old Negro. Ellington, as his nickname expressed, was an aristocrat in style and bearing, yet he was also young and hip enough to appeal to the new generation. As such, he could provide a role model for many other aspiring musicians, as well as a source of pride for blacks in general. It is important to remember that Ellington's ideas about music were formed in the context of the Harlem Renaissance project of racial empowerment, and throughout his life he sought to uphold the values of the New Negro movement. He sought explicitly to link concert music with popular forms of expression, in order to resolve the tensions between the artistic and political, the highbrow and the lowbrow, the two opposing traditions of black music. He shared the Renaissance interest in black history and was instrumental in transposing this literary interest into musical form. His compositions "Creole Rhapsody" (1931) and "Symphony in Black" (1934) put the African-American heritage to music.

Ellington's sophisticated jazz renditions made of him a cultural icon and a financial success, but he ultimately failed to become accepted as a legitimate concert composer by the arbiters of musical taste. In this respect, Ellington reflected the fate of the Harlem Renaissance as a whole. The dual project of racial empowerment and integration through art was inherently tension-filled if not self-defeating. White acceptance on equal terms was simply not (yet) possible for blacks, no matter how talented, sophisticated, or creative they might be. Jazz and blues, even when they were cleaned up and made more attractive to white sensibilities, were simply not able to claim the same kind of cultural capital allocated to European-derived concert musics. When black musicians and composers like Ellington and William Grant Still sought to communicate the black experience in a concert music idiom, they found little audience for their efforts, among either whites or blacks. What was possible was a commercial success, with more popular forms of music, which produced its own ambiguities and difficulties (Southern 1983).

White interest in black music interacted with commercial interest and with technological developments in recording and radio, all of which reproduced the American star system with its focus on individual performance and reward. It also created two publics for the stars, a black and a white, which sometimes mixed, but which were for the most part separate in the segregated cities and towns. This created the strange situation where Duke Ellington, as Ben Sidran notes, "kept two separate 'books' of arrangements, one for white audiences, one for blacks, and often went so far as to exchange parts in the middle of a piece" (Sidran [1971] 1981: 74).

As far as music and the establishment of a black music tradition is concerned, the role of the New Negro movement was to help reformulate the criteria which define artistic expression. It helped reveal that a creative and powerful interaction was possible between literate and oral forms of expression, while still maintaining music – popular and serious, sacred and secular – as the basic subsoil of black culture and black identity. For a time, the disparate forms of black music could be brought into one "discursive framework" and the highbrow could be combined with the lowbrow, the political with the artistic. The impulses given to black music and black culture were thereby enormous. As a result, black music made important inroads into the mainstream American culture, and yet the terms of the assimilation process were set by the hegemonic white culture. In this respect, the New Negro movement of the 1920s illustrates the relation between social movements and cultural transformation more generally. Social movements are always circumscribed by the broader culture in which they emerge. Cultural influence is achieved by a narrowing of ambition and a reduction of the emancipatory, transcendental movement project into something more limited, more instrumental. The price of commercial success, in this case, was a new separation of black music into its various component parts.

Between movements: bebop and gospel

Ben Sidran ([1971] 1981) labels the period between 1930 and the outbreak of the Second World War the period of underground communication and speaks of the development of a black underground as a sort of reaction to the rising popularity of black music and the increasing interaction between black and white musicians. He writes "after their initial exposure to Western forms and white society in the twenties, [black musicians] gradually became self-conscious of developing a separate and 'ethnically singular' idiom" (ibid.: 79). The creation of a racially distinct underground is the other side of racial integration, at least in terms of music. Black music, like black culture generally and even the ghetto itself, became at one and the same time something imposed and something sought after, a sort of haven in a heartless world. In black music as in the ghetto itself one could be one's self amongst one's own (for blacks, of course, but also for white "wannabes," called slummers at the time). After a few years of being in vogue among whites, at least some black musicians returned to the black community for sustenance and support; the ghetto provided the critical public for judging the authenticity of one's music and lifestyle. This underground was thus cultural and not directly political, although in the racial politics of the United States the two are not so easy to separate.

Despite the efforts of Locke and others, black culture in the 1930s remained rooted in an oral tradition, within which music retained a special place. (The current rediscovery of the Harlem Renaissance has much to do with the more central role the written word has in contemporary black culture due to the successes of the civil rights movement in higher education and the subsequent establishment of black studies programs.) The urban black public sphere, even in the depression which hit blacks much harder than whites, retained its vitality in places like Chicago, Kansas City, St. Louis, and New Orleans, and the growing sophistication of the audiences of the clubs and jook joints was crucial for the development of a black underground.

It was these small ghetto clubs which produced Charlie Parker and bebop as well as rhythm-and-blues. The development of these sub-genres of black music reveal a more differentiated, but also more socially fragmented, black public sphere. As Ben Sidran has written, "the strength of both the bebop and the rhythm-and-blues idioms that developed out of the black music of the thirties was that they excluded from participation many Americans (most of them white, although many were of the black middle class) who, as a matter of *taste* and of cultural *stance*, were unable to identify with the new assertion of 'blackness'" (Sidran [1971] 1981: 79).

This two-sided development of exclusion–inclusion materialized in subdivisions within black communities and even between larger cities. While more sophisticated forms of jazz and swing developed in New York, the midwestern cities – Kansas City, Chicago, and St. Louis – became centers for the urbanization of the blues and the development of rhythm-and-blues. In New York the links between the literate and the oral traditions were much stronger, while Kansas City and St. Louis remained more rooted in oral, southern traditions. Chicago produced Richard Wright, a product of the migration patterns from Mississippi northward, but Wright really came into his own as the leading black writer of the period after moving to New York. Muddy Waters would follow the same path from Mississippi to

Chicago in the 1940s, and remain there to become a key figure in the creation of the new, electrified urban blues.

Perhaps the most important single element of the black music tradition that would be mobilized in the civil rights movement was the gospel blues, especially the songs of Thomas A. Dorsey as sung by Mahalia Jackson, who raised the "new northern gospel singer to unprecedented status" (Harris 1992: 261). Jackson and Dorsey had started working together already in the late 1920s and their collaboration continued through the postwar era. According to Michael Harris:

Jackson had two distinct ways of working a crowd that attracted Dorsey to her. The first involved her personable manner . . . The second involved her powerful performance techniques . . . Jackson's appeal . . . rested on her adherence to the deeply emotive manner of singing that one finds referred to among enslaved African-Americans as being heard in their secret meetings . . . In Jackson Dorsey thus found two of the caller's major attributes: her sense of oneness with her respondents and her ability to capture the communal spirit of a performance so as to play it out virtually at will. Jackson's possession of these traits clearly emerged from her grounding in the urban brush arbor[6] experience. In the sense that she could lead out in the bush harbor, she could be said to embody the priestly function of bush arbor leadership. Dorsey, on the other hand, wanted a singer more like the hush arbor caller who could evoke shared emotion while she maintained an aura as leader.

(Harris 1992: 258–59)

While Jackson performed primarily for black audiences and continually toured and sang in black churches throughout her long career, she also managed to bring gospel music into the broader American culture through her numerous television appearances and recordings. As Billie Holiday and Ella Fitzgerald were bringing the blues up to date and into mainstream musical culture, Mahalia Jackson brought the spirituals up to date with her good-time religious music. And it would be, in no small measure, the updated, modernized, and more swing-like gospel music of Dorsey and Jackson that would inspire the emergent soul music of Ray Charles, as well as the freedom songs of the civil rights movement. From a base in the segregated black church – a kind of submerged social network where forms of social solidarity could be preserved and reproduced – both gospel music and the civil rights movement would lead to profound processes of cultural transformation.

The mobilization of music in the civil rights movement

As we have previously recounted, the cognitive praxis of the early civil rights movement reflected the rural, religious traditions of the South

(Eyerman and Jamison 1991: 120–45). The mode of dress and speech and, most importantly for our purposes here, the music that was so central to that movement's identity formation – and with which it has come to be identified – were drawn from the deep waters of African-American tradition. While the rest of the South was strongly conservative, the music of the black community contained a transcendental or emancipatory potential that could be mobilized in the struggle for integration.

Southern modes of behavior, white as well as black, spoke strongly for tradition in the anti-modern meaning of the term. John Egerton describes the situation in the 1930s:

this was a feudal land, an Americanized version of a European society in the Middle Ages. It was rural, agricultural, isolated. It had its ruling nobles, its lords of the plantation manor – and its peasants, its vassals. Its values were rooted in the land, in stability and permanence, in hierarchy and status, in caste and class and race. The highest virtues were honor and duty, loyalty and obedience. Every member of the society – man and woman, white and black – knew his or her place, and it was an unusual (not to say foolhardy) person who showed a flagrant disregard for the assigned boundaries and conventions.   (Egerton 1994: 19)

This was far different from the urban black public sphere which gave rise to bebop and the gospel blues, where a dynamic modernism was in full swing, in spite of the racial politics of the dominant society. Even, perhaps especially, in the "feudal" South, African-American music could take on connotations of hope and liberation, and mobilize a deep core of disguised meaning which had potential political significance. Tradition was kept alive in the entirely segregated black churches, where the influences of white culture and modern music were relatively limited.

Music was essential to the African-American religious experience and, as many have noted, the church, which ministered this experience, was the central institution of southern African-American life. Music was also central to the more secular sides of southern black life. The development of race records and radio in the early postwar era was a response to the general rise in standards of living, some of which trickled down to African-Americans, at least in the form of rising expectations. Except for New Orleans, jazz was not the music of the southern black; rather it was blues in a new, more mass-mediated and modern form dubbed rhythm-and-blues. Rhythm-and-blues added electrification and, like jazz, piano, saxophone, heavy bass, and drum beat to the blues guitar, which remained the central instrumental link to tradition. The other link was, of course, the singer and the song.

The first stirrings of the civil rights movement came with the bus boycotts in Baton Rouge, Louisiana, and Montgomery, Alabama, in 1954. Music was there from the beginning, since the church was the main meeting place, perhaps the only place outside the jook and the family living room where relatively large numbers of blacks could freely congregate. In the more well-known Montgomery boycott which lasted for more than a year, the church and its ministers, most notably Martin Luther King, Jr., and Ralph Abernathy, were the leading figures. With the church in such a central role, it should not be surprising that religious music was present from the outset. The first music of the movement were the traditional spirituals and gospel songs used, as was the custom, in their normal way at church functions. This familiar music identified the members of the congregation and welcomed outsiders as part of the same community, even in light of the new, secular circumstances. As in the church service, the song leader played an important role in this process of recreating group identity and solidarity. The song leader used voice to bring the group together, to call attention to common purpose, and to establish the opening of the meeting in the same way that a chairperson would do in another setting. Throughout the civil rights movement, finding a song leader was as important to local organizing as filling any other leadership function.

As the movement developed so too did the music and its functions. The music continued to serve as a means of identification, but added other communicative functions as the boycott took its toll and patience waned. Music served as a source and sign of strength, solidarity, and commitment. It helped build bridges between class and status groups, between blacks and white supporters, and between rural and urban, northern and southern blacks. It also bridged the gap between leaders and followers, helping to reinforce the notion that all belonged to the same "beloved" community. During the boycotts, traditional spirituals like "Walk Together Children" were given new meaning as people were forced to use their feet rather than ride the buses to work:

> Walk together children, don't get weary,
> Walk together children, don't get weary,
> There's a great camp meeting in the promised land.

Along the way, the basic sources upon which this movement music drew were expanded, in part as a function of the growth and growing differentiation of the movement itself. As the movement expanded beyond the local community to include wider sections and segments of the population, first black and then white, the music opened up to new influences and to new functions. When sit-ins in the larger southern cities drew in the more middle-class black college students, other musical traditions, like rhythm-

and-blues and Do Wop, were called upon. One song that became popular in the movement was called "Get Your Rights, Jack," modeled after the popular song by Ray Charles, "Hit the Road, Jack." It went:

> Get your rights, Jack,
> And don't be a "Tom" no more,
> No more, no more, no more.
> Get your rights, Jack,
> And don't be a Tom no more.

The song included local references to movement organizations and to opponents among local authorities. Such songs were both playful and serious, reflecting both the increasing influence of youth in the movement and the tradition of signifying in black humor and music. For Samuel Floyd (1995), signifying is one of the basic elements characterizing black music and black culture more generally, and it might be useful to apply the concept to the music of the civil rights movement. Signifying refers to a form of commentary which employs double meanings, jokes, and hidden references. It first developed as a running commentary on what Langston Hughes termed "the ways of white folks" – the title he gave to a short story collection, published in the 1930s. Like the jester in the medieval court, signifying permitted the subordinate to make serious comment about the behavior of superiors without threatening his own life. As a form of serious jest, signifying was a powerful survival strategy for the severely oppressed slave, allowing the maintenance of individual dignity, as well as cultural identity.

Through signifying talk, the we–them relation could be given a positive connotation. While it may not itself be rebellious or political, this form of cognitive praxis could readily serve as the basis for rebellious action, as it did in the songs of the civil rights movement, such as the Ray Charles adaptation mentioned above, and in "Dog Dog" by James Bevel and Bernard LaFayette, members of the Nashville Quartet and early leaders of the SNCC. Bevel described the circumstances surrounding the idea for the song in this way: "I lived next door to a man and he had a lot of children, and so did my dad, but we weren't allowed to play together because they were white. But we had two dogs. He had a dog and we had a dog. Our dogs would always play together. So we wrote this song for our group, the Nashville Quartet" (Seeger and Reiser 1989: 44).

Songs were not the only area of signifying culture brought to the movement by the college students. The following poem was printed in the first issue of the SNCC newspaper (1960) and reflects some of the wide-ranging sources from which the movement drew its inspiration:

> I, too, hear America singing
> But from where I stand
> I can only hear Little Richard
> And Fats Domino.
> But sometimes,
> I hear Ray Charles
> Drowning in his own tears
> or Bird
> Relaxing at Camarillo
> or Horace Silver doodling,
> Then I don't mind standing a little longer.
>
> (Julian Bond quoted in King 1987: 235)

This playful signifying recalls not only Walt Whitman, but also Langston Hughes' "I, too, sing America." This does not mean that the older, more religious traditions were discarded or even that they declined in use or meaning. Though educated and middle-class, the southern students who made up SNCC, the organization which formed out of the lunch-counter sit-in actions, were, at least at first, very religious in their symbolism and their praxis. In addition, singing religious songs served as a communications bridge between the students and other, less-educated and non-middle-class, blacks, whether in the movement or not. On the other side, singing rhythm-and-blues-inspired songs provided similar communications links to other outsiders, such as that to other prisoners in jailhouses, where activists often found themselves. This added to the other, more traditional functions of singing while in prison, such as holding up morale, courage, and commitment, which both secular and sacred songs lent themselves to:

> I know, I know we'll meet again,
> I know we'll meet again,
> And then you and I will never say good-bye
> When we meet again.

> Well, you come from Atlanta, Georgia, oh yes,
> And I'm from Memphis, Tennessee,
> We both met in the Mississippi jail
> Because we want to be free.
> . . .
> We've been together in this jailhouse, oh yes,
> And now we too must go.
> But we will be alone after you've gone,
> My friend, I'm gonna miss you so.
>
> ("Nashville 1960," by James Bevel and Bernard LaFayette quoted in King 1987: 33)

The signifying and adaptation of religious music was not without its friction. Guy Carawan, musical director at the Highlander Center, then called Folk School, recalls the resistance he encountered at song workshops for local civil rights activists when he suggested changing traditional songs for use in current political struggles:

> In 1959, when I came down here [to Tennessee], I knew about the old labor-movement tradition of changing an old song into something new, with words for the moment . . . but the songs that everyone in the South knew, the spirituals and hymns, weren't really being used in that way . . . I suggested adapting some of the spirituals and hymns. Some people were offended at first – these were very personal songs about salvation . . . [soon] people realized that these were their songs and they could change them to express what they were feeling.   (Seeger and Reiser 1989: 39)

As support for the movement widened, not least because of the coverage given by the mass media, other types of songs and singers became influential. The attempt to integrate the University of Mississippi at Oxford in 1962 gave rise to the Bob Dylan song "Oxford Town" and a year later Dylan wrote the classic, true-to-life folk ballad, "The Lonesome Death of Hattie Carroll" about the murder of an African-American maid by her rich, white employer. These songs, along with others by Phil Ochs, Tom Paxton, and Len Chandler, marked the convergence of the civil rights movement and the folk music revival stirring among white American youth. In 1963, the SNCC Freedom Singers, a group from Albany State College in Georgia which emerged out of the desegregation struggle in that town, performed at the Newport Folk Festival. Bernice Johnson Reagon, who later founded Sweet Honey in the Rock, was one of the Freedom Singers. She had been expelled from Albany State for her participation in the sit-ins, indicating that at least some of the black colleges remained tied to the conservative past, even while their students were breaking out of the southern "habitus."

In 1964, in conjunction with the Freedom Summer voter registration drives in Mississippi, the folklorist and folk song collector Robert Cohen organized the Mississippi Caravan of Music, bringing white folksingers to the South. In *Don't Look Back*, the film about the early career of Bob Dylan, one can see a clip of Dylan dressed in bib-overalls singing his "Oxford Town" to a group of young blacks. Phil Ochs contributed a song called "I'm Goin' Down to Mississippi" which began,

> I'm goin' down to Mississippi
> I'm goin' down a southern road
> And if you never ever see me again
> Remember I had to go.

For the white folksinger from New York, it was indeed a long road down to Mississippi. However, the gap between these cultures was made easier to bridge with music. The ballad tradition also had roots in the rural South, and the topical song which reached back to the Wobblies and the popular front helped cross the multidimensional cultural divide. The folksingers helped bring the long-standing American tradition of protest song into the civil rights movement. Long-time activist-singers like Pete Seeger and institutions like the Highlander School were both important in this process.[7]

The songs of the civil rights movement became sources of collective identity formation not so much by being musically innovative or even commercially successful as by lending themselves to shared performance. Their melodies were simple but emotive, geared to being sung collectively. They invited participation, simple repetitive choruses, and rhyming couplets, with an emotional and political content:

> We shall overcome, we shall overcome,
> We shall overcome some day.
> Oh, deep in my heart I do believe,
> That we shall overcome some day.

The songs were not ideological in any dogmatic way; they dealt with universal themes of brotherhood, integration, and racial discrimination without presenting any specific political line or strategic action. They reflected the political openness of the civil rights movement, and many of the young songwriters sang their songs at the March on Washington in 1963, giving in musical form the same kind of utopian, hopeful message that Martin Luther King, Jr., propounded in his "I Have a Dream" speech. Older black singers, such as Mahalia Jackson and Marian Anderson, who had been important in maintaining and transforming the black music tradition out of which the songs of the civil rights movement emerged, also performed at that demonstration. The songs envisioned a tolerant society, racially integrated, where different cultures were respected and indeed honored. In retrospect, we can see the songs of that time as having planted some of the seeds for the contemporary, but highly controversial, multicultural practices in American culture.

The cognitive praxis of the civil rights movement combined the sacred and the secular components of the black music tradition to create a historically significant collective actor. As cognitive praxis, the songs and their performance at events like the March on Washington represented a kind of exemplary action that expressed the ideals of the movement. In songs, the movement was made real and objective, and it is in their recollection that the movement can be recalled and reexperienced, and its songs continue, to this day, to be transferred to other places and movements in many different parts of the world.

From civil rights to rap

According to Stokely Carmichael, the man who made Black Power into a worldwide slogan when he shouted the words at a rally in Greenwood, Mississippi, in 1966, the phrase was meant to emphasize the need for African-Americans to break loose of the white "dictatorship of definition, interpretation, and consciousness" (Van Deburg 1992: 27). Like the poets and writers of the Harlem Renaissance, Carmichael was reminding his audience of the centrality of culture in social change. The call for Black Power emerged in the mid-1960s as the civil rights movement appeared to bog down amidst its partial successes and the failure of its integrationist strategies to achieve real change and understanding among white Americans (Carson 1981).

If the movement culture of the early civil rights movement reflected the rural, religious traditions of the South, the later stages in the late 1960s and onward harked back to the urban culture that the New Negro movement had expressed and represented. Fading from the scene were the bib-overalls, and the notion of the "good Negro," as well as the suits and ties of the preaching leaders, and the religious metaphors and rhetoric that were expressed in songs and speeches. Even the non-violent philosophy with its moralism and its sense of salvation through suffering fell on hard times when the war in Vietnam was escalating and, for many young blacks, racial discrimination seemed to be escalating as well.

A harder, tougher style and symbolism emerged in the culture of the Black Power movement – from the raised fists of the Black Panthers to the aggressive music of James Brown. This was in large part, of course, a matter of generational change. Martin Luther King, Jr., the most urbane of the civil rights movement leaders, was born in 1929; Stokely Carmichael was born in 1941. But it was much more than age that separated them. King, as James Cone points out, was rooted in black religious tradition. "No tradition or thinker influenced King's perspective as much as the faith which blacks created in their fight for dignity and justice . . . One discovers King's faith primarily in his *preached word* . . . delivered at . . . black churches and in his *practiced word* during many of his nonviolent, direct-action demonstrations" (Cone 1991: 122–23). Carmichael, and later H. Rap Brown and the Black Panthers, came from the urban ghettos and spoke an urban, secular language.

Like King, the early civil rights movement articulated, as we have seen, its religious roots in its cognitive praxis. But that cognitive praxis also mobilized secular traditions, musical and political. In the late 1960s, the integrative praxis began to split apart; the street dialect, and what movement activists and leaders referred to as the language of "the people," came to be seen by many as the defining characteristics of "blackness" and of "soul," while others sought to institutionalize black studies as a new academic discipline. By so doing, the popular and the academic tended to part company. As roots of authenticity and collective identity, street talk and urban street life became the ground upon which the Black Power movement moved. The language provided the fundamental structures of feeling through which black experience and thus black culture was said to form. It provided also the backdrop against which black experience could be measured and judged. It was, in Bourdieu's terms, the African-American habitus, the unreflective practices and categorical frames which both grew out of and circumscribed African-American culture. To get too far from this habitus was to become white, to lose contact with your roots, where it all came from. If one was successful in the white world, it was important to have paid one's dues, on the street, with the people, and to have walked that walk and talked that talk, to show that one was still a member, black on the inside, where and when it counted. This was to view blackness and African-American traditions in a very different way both from the white culture and from those "Negroes" who proposed integration or social mobility as the answer to the United States' racial conflicts. From that perspective, folk or street culture was something to overcome, a "culture of poverty" to get away from, through education, learning proper English, changing manners and mannerisms from clothing to hair color and texture. Subsequent tensions in the civil rights movement have often seemed, at least to sympathetic outsiders, to derive from this split between separation and integration, and between attempts to emphasize the separateness of black identity or the universality of the black experience.

For Black Power activists the movement's cognitive praxis involved adjusting the received evaluative frames through which the world was understood, where all that was white appeared at the top and all that was black at the bottom. Through its exemplary action, from music to more violent forms of resistance, the Black Power movement sought to upgrade black experience. Black people should want to be themselves, not emulate the whites, to be proud of their dialect, their hair, their bodies, and "doing their own thing." Music was central to this process and this strategy. Soul music and, in our day, rap music have emerged to express these more variegated manifestations of black consciousness. And the debates about rap, as about jazz earlier in the century, reflect the special double character, the essential tension in black music (Paul Anderson 1995).

Rap music emerged in the late 1970s as an electrified folk poetry of the streets, as a way for young blacks to speak their minds and, as its influence has spread and many of its artists have become commercially successful, the older tensions between highbrow and lowbrow reappear. Rap has been vilified by many music critics at the same time as black intellectuals have defended its importance and sought to give it cultural legitimacy – much as Langston Hughes once did for the blues (Baker 1993). Rap has it all – affirmations of African-American pride and dignity, technical innovation, and accompanying dances and rituals, as well as a range of texts and sub-texts – all of which make for new markets, and also seeds for new movements. The form is particularly exciting in its open-endedness and its improvisational possibilities. Rapping is not merely singing; it is a kind of thinking out loud in a melodic and rhythmic fashion. One of the more interesting groups, from our perspective, is Arrested Development, which expresses the tensions of black identity in so many of its songs.

Arrested Development asks their young listeners, "Do you know about the Panthers, the MOVE organization, Kwame Nkrumah, the Zulu nation, or just Nike and Pumas?" Black identity, these rappers are saying, is not merely playing basketball well, or looking good in the right sneakers; there is also a history, a tradition to relate to. Arrested Development is one of the many rap groups that, in a relatively non-political time, tries to carry the messages of African-American social movements on to a new generation via MTV and compact discs. Like the civil rights songs, they express the struggle of African-Americans for respect and equality in musical form. However, in contrast to the civil rights songs which drew on the spirituals and gospel and the styles of church and folk music of the period, rap music makes use of the rhymes and rhythms of the urban black culture as it has developed throughout the 1980s and 1990s. Even more significant is the difference in movement context. In the 1960s, music was a part of a massive social movement that, in many ways, linked whites and blacks together to overcome racism and injustice. In the 1990s, rap groups help keep the message of the movements alive in the collective memory and thus help inspire new waves of opposition and dissent, when organized movements have unfortunately gone out of fashion.

5

Politics and music in the 1960s

> We're trying to crystallize the thoughts of young people who have stopped accepting things the way they are. Young people are disillusioned; we want to reinforce their disillusionment so they'll get more involved and do something – not out of a general sense of rebellion, but out of a real concern for what's happening – or not happening.
>
> Phil Ochs, interviewed in *Vogue*, September 1, 1964 (quoted in Gottesam 1977: 70)

In this chapter, we will explore the interrelations between politics and popular music in the 1960s in the United States. We will refer to popular songwriters and musicians, as well as to some of the songs that have continued to stand for the spirit of the sixties in the popular consciousness. But even more than the songs, we want to emphasize the importance of the contexts in which these songs were written and performed. In the 1960s, songs contributed to the making of a new political consciousness, and were often performed at political demonstrations and collective festivals. Singers and songs were central to the cognitive praxis of the 1960s social movements, but it is important to realize that the relations between movements and music shifted dramatically in the course of the 1960s. It was primarily in the period of transition from the civil rights movement to a broader political opposition to the war in Vietnam, that is, in the years from 1961 to 1965, that popular music could serve as the site, perhaps the most important site, of a remarkable process of experimentation and innovation, which would lead to major transformations in American and "global" culture, as well.

By the end of the 1960s, with commercialization, fragmentation, and depoliticization, the "movement phase" of that development had largely come to an end. For one thing, the era of the rock concert had taken over, with its individual band or artist ego-tripping across the stage. The context of performance had generally been altered from a spiritual community, or at least collective group, setting to a far more commercial and individualistic form. At the same time, the intense collaboration of the songwriting community broke apart in the course of the 1960s; instead of "trading songs" as they did in the early sixties, singing their newly written works together in a spirit of camaraderie, the successful singers – Bob Dylan, Joan Baez, Carly Simon, for example – became commercial artists, subject to the production techniques and role differentiation of the corporate music industry. The singer, who earlier had often been a songwriter, performer, producer, and activist all rolled into one, became an "artist" projecting a personal vision rather than a collectively political one. The songs, with few exceptions, were turned into products manufactured for private consumption on a mass market rather than the vehicles for collective identity formation and shared consciousness-raising that they had been earlier. As the audience broadened, it became more diffuse and less political; and subtly the substance of the songs also shifted. As the contexts of production, performance, and consumption all changed, the gap between politics and popular culture which had been bridged in so many ways in the mid-1960s widened once again.

It is somewhat limited to refer to these developments primarily in terms of a "folk revival." For what was going on was much more than a new wave of popularity for folk music, although that was, of course, also happening; in terms of cultural transformation, it was rather the recombination of folk music with other musical genres (rock-and-roll, jazz, country, even classical) and the shaping of a totally new kind of oppositional "youth" culture that seem most significant and long-lasting. For our purposes, the period is important not for the musical innovation per se, nor for the political movements in and of themselves. What is central is their interaction, and, in retrospect, that curious sense of overdetermination, often neglected by both the political and the cultural historians, that the one "movement" is inconceivable without the other. It is their contemporaneity, their mutual dependence, however difficult it might be to explain, that is so important to emphasize. The transformation of popular culture was dependent on the politics, while the very meaning or content of the politics was substantially shaped by the popular cultural forms of representation in which it was expressed. The project of liberation that the movements of the sixties stood for – what Herbert Marcuse at the time termed the Great Refusal (Marcuse 1964) – has been difficult for subsequent analysts to grasp; some have emphasized the politics while others have focused on the music. For us, the 1960s are interesting primarily as a key stage in the recurrent attempts by activist and artist alike to confront the dialectical tension between cultural and political practice, between "changing society" and its public policies and ideological programs, and "changing people" and their values, mores, and tastes. This dialectic of liberation was what the sixties were all about, and the difficulty, not to say impossibility, of resolving the tension was what was ultimately learned.

During the early to mid-1960s the collective identity of what was then called the Movement was articulated not merely through organizations or even mass demonstrations, although there were plenty of both, but perhaps even more significantly through popular music. As Richard Flacks has put it, "In the early sixties music and protest were more deeply intertwined than at any other time since the days of the Wobblies" (Flacks 1988: 182). Movement ideas, images, and feelings were disseminated in and through popular music and, at the same time, the movements of the times influenced developments, in both form and content, in popular music. In particular, the "fusion" of what Flacks calls "the avant-garde and the pop" took place in the aftermath of the movements of the early 1960s. It was not just the folksingers of the civil rights movement who projected new themes and ideas into popular culture. According to Flacks, the diffusion of a more serious, and socially critical, kind of music was a much wider-ranging affair:

By the mid-sixties, it was evident that the most popular singing group of all time, the Beatles, were interested in the same sort of thing. By the later years of the decade, the predominant themes and forms of youth-oriented music derived directly from the traditions of "romantic" art (rather than the traditions of popular music genres). Songs were filled with symbolism, surrealism, and literary allusion. They expressed apocalyptic visions, strong hostility to industrial society and encroaching technology, explicit paranoia about official authority, deep antagonism to conventional morality, and affinity with a variety of non-Western spiritual and religious traditions. (Flacks 1988: 183)

Other interpreters of the sixties have noted the role played by the political folk music of the early 1960s in the development of rock music. Indeed, rock music represented a further mobilization of tradition, namely of the black secular blues music tradition (stimulated, to a large extent, through the mediating intervention of some of the main bands of the so-called British "invasion": the Rolling Stones, the Animals, the Yardbirds, etc.). The mobilization of blues and its transformation into rock complemented, but also built upon, the mobilization of the black spiritual music tradition that characterized the civil rights movement and the mobilization of the topical folk song tradition that was so central to the "folk revival." The commercial strength as well as the cultural resonance of rock music derived from this multiple legacy. It is no accident that it was especially those who could draw on all of the traditions in their very person, people like Jimi Hendrix and Janis Joplin, who would be most successful in bringing rock music into the popular culture (but who would also destroy themselves in the process). Hendrix and Joplin brought all three traditions into their music and into their lives. Other key innovators, like Frank Zappa, Miles Davis, Van Morrison, and Gram Parsons, would bring still other kinds of musical traditions – classical, jazz, Irish, country – into the rock mixture, along with the oppositional politics that was shared by the "counter-culture" as a whole. By the late 1960s, however, the commercial opportunities for rock music, together with the increasing fragmentation and radicalization of political mobilization, took many of these artists, often by surprise, into an Establishment world that in many ways their music and lifestyle critically negated. Popular culture was permanently changed, while the politics soon reverted back to "business as usual." Our argument, however, is that much of the subsequent development of rock music drew on the social movements of the early 1960s for its intrinsic meaning.

By providing resources for collective identity formation, innovative developments in popular culture can, we suggest, be traced directly back to the influence and the impact of social movements. In particular, the increasing multiculturalism – and reactions to it – that is to be found in American education, historical consciousness, and popular values and behavior can be traced back to the 1960s, when a politically charged music helped project a new vision of American society. Similarly, the more general search for new personal identities and for connecting the present with the past – that is, for mobilizing traditions – that is so widespread in the world today can be traced back to the early 1960s. The social movements of the 1960s offered and practiced a new vision of participatory democracy, and that vision formed a central part of the cognitive praxis of the "folk revival." The play-it-yourself participatory approach to music that has subsequently fueled so many youth movements around the world reinvents something that took place in the early years of the 1960s. In this chapter, we will seek to identify some of the factors, both contextual and textual, external and internal, that led to the creative recombination of culture and politics that took place in the United States in the 1960s.

Contextual factors

What were some of the key social processes affecting the mediation between popular culture and social movements in this period? Why was popular music able to become so pregnant with ideas and innovations? One obvious sociological factor is the size, as well as the economic and creative power, of the prime audience for both sides of the mediating process – youth. With the possible exception of the civil rights movement in its early stages, the prime constituting public of both the Movement and the creators, users, and consumers of popular culture were people under thirty (Frith 1978). Throughout the 1960s this age-group was expanding and gaining increasing self-awareness. This self-awareness encompassed both cultural and political modes of thought and behavior, something which did not go unnoticed by either marketing promoters or social theorists. It led sociologists to characterize these movements as youth movements (Flacks 1971) and to speak in terms of a war between generations (Feuer 1969). More generally, young people and their problems became a growing area of sociological and social-psychological study.

In an issue of *Daedalus* from the early 1960s, entitled *The Challenge of Youth*, Kenneth Keniston, one of the most important American scholars to reflect on the meaning of youth, wrote:

The gap between childhood and adulthood will not explain why in our society at present the youth culture is becoming more and more important, why it involves a greater and greater part of young men's and women's lives, or why it seems so tempting, compared with adulthood, that some young people increasingly refuse to make the transition at all. Rock'n'roll, for example, is probably the first music that has appealed almost exclusively to the youth culture; catering to the teenage market has become one of the nation's major industries. And, as [David] Riesman has noted [in *The Lonely Crowd*], the very word "teenager" has few of the connotations of transition and growing up of words like "youth" and "adolescent," which "teenager" is gradually replacing. (Keniston 1965: 210)

The emergent potential of a youth market was recognized by the mass media and other consumer products industries; not only did they re-tailor their marketing strategies, they also developed new product lines and forms of production that were amenable to the preferences and lifestyle orientations of "youth."[1] The concept of generation became commercialized. But, by creating a youth market, the corporate establishment unwittingly also contributed to the creation of a generational self-awareness, which linked rebellious working-class urban rockers with disaffected suburban middle-class youth, who had all the material comforts imaginable but were still searching for something different. Seen from this perspective, distinct forms of making music and of doing politics were essential elements in this process of generational self-awareness, both at the original time of occurrence and today, as part of a recollective nostalgia. Being young became a factor that could transcend and partly overcome both the traditional barriers of race and region, as well as economic stratification and ethnic division.

Simon Frith has discussed how during the 1960s the idea of youth and the notion of the teenager were glossed over by those with clear interests, whether they were commercial, moral, scientific, or ideological. The idea of youth and of a youth culture, Frith argues, arose in the context of post-Second World War affluence and contained particular assumptions about the decline in importance of social class (and race and gender, we would add) for shaping such things as musical taste. As an all-inclusive concept, youth was meant to define both an age-group and a stage in the life of modern western individuals. For the commercially interested, youth represented potentiality, a growing population between the ages of sixteen and twenty-five that was becoming a significant market for consumer goods. Here the room for individual choice was expanding at the same rate as the economy. For the functionally oriented sociologist, youth was that period of transition between childhood and adulthood, a relatively purposeless stage of the life-cycle when identity was more related to leisure and subject to peer-group pressure than to the constraints of work and family. For both types of interested observer, youth contained in itself both the possibility and the risk that circumscribe the parameters of the western idea of freedom. Possibility stemmed from the range of choices available to the unburdened and relatively affluent young person, in terms of lifestyles connected to leisure activities and consumer goods. Risk followed from the same premises: being unburdened by the constraints of work and the control of the family meant being outside the normal controls imposed by society. This carried with it the risk that impulse and peer pressure, rather than reason, would rule choice of lifestyle.

This in fact is precisely what the critics of mass society and mass culture were saying about the "consumer" society which emerged in the 1950s: the dangers of conformity and status anxiety that came from living in self-enclosed suburban enclaves, where lifestyle was a function of income and image, rather than imposed by social class. For mass culture theorists like C. Wright Mills, what functionalists and more conservative commentators were saying about teenagers might very well be applied to their parents as well. Since youth was elevated to a universal condition, class, race, gender, and region were considered of secondary importance to age- and peer-group identity. In this sense, the concept of youth replaced the earlier notion of the teenager, which was more clearly class-related, with working-class being associated with masculinity, gangs, and rock-and-roll, and middle-class with femininity, bobby sox, and Tin Pan Alley love songs. Frith is good at exposing the built-in bias this implies and in suggesting the need for a more nuanced appreciation of class differences (Frith 1978).

Recent studies have revealed the significance of Frith's warnings about an all-too-inclusive analysis of youth and generation. American studies, for example, have indicated the continuing significance of race in affecting musical taste and consumption. It has become common, for example, to argue that rock-and-roll emerged out of a white appropriation of black musical traditions and that the "folk revival" emerged in the mid-1950s when rock-and-roll went into decline in the wake of the tragic deaths and confinement of some of its leading stars. For black "youths," not only did the folk revival go unnoticed, rock-and-roll never died – in fact, it never even emerged. For African-Americans the rhythms that characterized rock-and-roll had been around at least since the 1940s; the military service of Elvis Presley, the imprisonment of the cross-over Chuck Berry, and the deaths of Richie Valens, the Big Bopper, and Buddy Holly were of little significance to the fans of Sam Cooke and Jackie Wilson. The so-called lull in rock-and-roll, Daniel Wolfe, S. R. Crain, Clifton White, and G. David Tenenbaum write, "was based on a definition that limited rock & roll to rebellious dance music sung by young white men. If that had died, then Sam [Cooke] and his friends Jackie Wilson, Ray Charles, James Brown, Dee Clark, Darlene Love, and the Shirelles danced on its grave" (Wolfe, Crain, White, and Tenenbaum 1995: 198–99).

When class and race are added to a more nuanced notion of youth music, then rock-and-roll or rhythm-and-blues can be seen as musical forms developed by lower-class whites in the South and which began to have a much wider appeal in the mid-1950s. Its audience, however, was primarily "youth," that is, young people under thirty years of age. And, as many accounts show, performers were treated accordingly, that is, badly. Don Everly reports, "To be a rock & roll star in the fifties was to be low-class. You were treated terribly, especially in the States. The people that ran the business hated it and made fun of it. You'd go to interviews and, especially being from the South, they would look and check if you had got your socks on" (in Wolfe et al. 1995: 176).

This class and racial aspect affected the performance conditions as well as the treatment of the performers. Youth may have been a universal condition, but in reality it was very particular, segregated. In the southern United States white and black performers were not allowed to appear on stage at the same time, audiences were also kept segregated, and it became a matter of conflict and concern how a performer faced the audience: should a black performer face the white or the black audience?

However one looked at it, the proportion of the population under thirty was expanding in both numbers and importance. And the social movements of the 1960s were both a cause and an effect of this. The movements were fueled by young people and the movements were forces in transforming an age-group into a self-conscious generation. There were commercial forces and interests at work here as well, but for a time they were followers, rather than leaders. Within the youth movement the many racial, regional, gender, and class divisions were, at least at the level of feeling and intention, transcended. This was part of the utopian dimension and exemplary action of the movement. And music was essential to its expression. It was in the music that the utopian images of a multicultural society gained coherence and form. And it is in the music that this multiculturalism lives on. During the 1960s youth not only gained self-consciousness, it became the model and set the standards for the rest of society in many spheres of culture, from the most superficial like clothing and hair-styles, to the most deeply rooted like the basic social interactions of men and women and blacks and whites. That much of this would quickly be turned to commercial advantage – from outside as products and lifestyles were bought and sold, tried on and discarded, and from within as forms of cultural capital to be exploited on the commercial marketplace – does not detract from the transformative power of the movement. Rather, it enhances it.

Another important contextual condition is what could be called the "mediability," the disposition to accepting a mass-mediated reality, of this new generation. As the second postwar generation, these youths were raised not only in an atmosphere of relative economic comfort and political security, they were also well acquainted with mass media and fast becoming used to consuming its artefacts, like phonograph records. While American intellectuals in the 1940s and 1950s wrestled with the problems of "mass culture" and "mass society" which were seen by many as evidence of decadence and decline, by the 1960s these were taken-for-granted realities, especially by the young. Brought up on situation comedies and *Mad* magazine, as well as on comic book renditions of classical literature, the new generation perceived culture in far different terms than their elders, although there were, of course, attempts by the arbiters of high culture to bridge the emergent gap between the generations. Leonard Bernstein, the conductor of the New York Philharmonic Orchestra, wrote the musical *West Side Story* in 1958 with the expressed purpose of creating an artistic representation of youth and its problems, which could have a broad appeal for different tastes, classes, and age-groups. In the 1960s, several popular musicians utilized classical instruments in their performances, and some of their compatriots wrote rock operas and rock musicals. It was not uncommon for the new generation to mix "high" and "low" culture; for many young people, they were not seen as separate realms of experience and expression, as they had been for their elders. Thus, the politically conscious youth of the 1960s saw no contradiction in reading social theory in readily available paperback form or in seeing their own forms of political and artistic expression as genuine culture, which would have horrified the cultural effetes of earlier generations. In any case, the size and force of the new generation encouraged a creative interchange between usually more conservative culture industries and change-oriented social movements.

As the habitus of youth expanded to include regular trips to the record store, the commercial potential of "rebellious" music like rock-and-roll was readily accepted by the corporate giants. In the 1960s the recording industry was itself in a state of development and change. Tapes were in the process of becoming the central mode of recording, with the multitrack tape coming into increasing use in production, making possible a new sort of sound, as well as permitting overdubbing and the recording of different segments of a recorded piece at different times and even places. The cassette band was fast coming into popular usage, which would make recordings cheaper as well as more easy to use and store (Steve Jones 1992).

These changes in the material process of producing and distributing popular music must be understood in relation to the social changes that were taking place in American society, and especially those that were brought to a head by the escalating war in Vietnam. By 1965, opposition to the American intervention in southeast Asia had become the single most important issue defining the social movement sector in the United States, which until then had mostly focused on issues of racial equality and civil rights. The anti-Vietnam war movement was more divisive than the civil rights movement had been; and it thus altered, as we shall see, the forms of interaction between politics and culture that had been so intimate during the early 1960s.

All of the movements of the 1960s contained within them, of course, a critique of militarism, and of the role of the military in American life. The movements of the 1960s were, at one level, a massive protest against the military-industrial complex, and the dominant position of the military in American political, economic, and cultural life. The predominance of military values and military priorities meant that other important social goals – racial equality, elimination of poverty, social welfare – could not be adequately addressed; but it also meant that aggressive and violent behavior had become defining characteristics of American culture. For all its simple-mindedness, the hippie slogan "Make Love Not War" articulated at least part of the meaning of the movements of the 1960s.

On another level, the military provided part of the contextual background for the mixing of the races – the multiculturalism – that would prove to be such an important part of the 1960s legacy. After having been exposed to the relative equality of the military, even in the segregated army of the Second World War, returning black soldiers were important sources of influence for the next generation that would make the civil rights movement in the late 1950s. In addition to crystallizing the contradiction between the ideology of creating democracy abroad and segregation at home, the experience of life in a large bureaucratic organization where (in theory anyway) authority and treatment were a function of rank, not skin color, was an important learning experience for blacks as well as whites (Sullivan 1991). The American military had been officially integrated by Harry Truman in time for the outbreak of the Korean war in 1950. The military followed a policy of locating northerners in the South and southerners in the North, as well as practicing at least formal racial equality. This mixing of the races, the classes, and the various regions was a central, though largely unnoticed, element in preparing the way not only for the civil rights movement but for all the movements that characterized the early 1960s.

It was thus not only radio, often recognized as a key source of musical integration, that helped bridge cultural and social barriers; at least as important, perhaps even more so, were institutions like the military, and even war itself. Later, scenes like the one in *Platoon* (Pratt 1990), which vividly portrayed the experience of Americans in Vietnam, where black and white, northern and southern male soldiers dance together to the strains of a rhythm-and-blues tune, would become as common as the white ethnic mixing which characterized films about the Second World War.

What great cultural transformation this helped prepare the way for, and what these social movements actually achieved, were the integration of black culture, if not blacks themselves, into American society and the elevation of youth as exemplar for the culture generally. If (white) rock-and-roll was a transformed and translated (black) rhythm-and-blues, then the new (white) urban folk music was (at least in part) a transformed and translated (black) country blues. Its "authenticity" derived much from black southern roots. At the same time, the youth culture that cohered in and through the social movements of the 1960s became the standard-bearer for the society at large. It was to youth that one turned for guidance, assurance, and legitimation. They knew and defined "where it's at," especially in music.

In the 1930s and 1940s recorded blues had provided the basis for a common experience and identity for a widely dispersed, itinerant, and largely illiterate black proletariat. In the 1950s, rock-and-roll, that newly contrived mixture of black and white, urban and country, sounds had, with the aid of records and radio, helped congeal a new generation's self-identity.

In the 1960s, a pregnant mixture of acoustic folk and electrified rock music and eventually a creative recombination of a wide range of other musical genres – blues, gospel, jazz, even classical – spread a spirit of cultural pluralism through the airwaves by electronic means. This popular musical innovation process was, we claim, a major force in the collective will formation of a new generation, and a source of fundamental cultural transformation in American society.

Music in movement

Several accounts of activists, from Todd Gitlin, a president of Students for a Democratic Society (SDS), the main proponent of a New Left in the early 1960s, to Bernice Johnson Reagon of Sweet Honey in the Rock, a song-group which grew out of the civil rights movement, confirm the importance of popular culture in helping solidify collective identity and individual belongingness in the social movements of the times (Reagon 1993). As Gitlin remembers one moment in the early 1960s, the "years of hope" that preceded the "days of rage" at the end of the decade:

Dylan sang for us: we didn't have to know he had hung out in Minneapolis' dropout nonstudent radical scene in order to intuit that he had been doing some hard traveling through a familiar landscape. We followed his career as if he were singing our song; we got in the habit of asking where he was taking us next. It was a delight but not altogether a surprise, then, when Dylan dropped in on SDS's December 1963 National Council meeting. We were beginning to feel that we – all fifty of us in the room – were the vibrating center of the new cyclonic Left . . . A recess came, and Dylan told a group of us he'd be interested in working in one of our incipient ERAP [Economic Research and Action Project] projects . . . Dylan wasn't just putting us on; or if his political commitment was a put-on phase designed to catapult him to stardom, as he said in a later and cynical incarnation, he was probably putting himself on as well.   (Gitlin 1987: 197–98)

For Gitlin, as for so many other student activists in the 1960s, the music was central to the politics. His story of the sixties is, to a large extent, a story of how the music grew more violent and aggressive – as did the politics.

While there is no doubt that songs and popular culture generally played a significant role in solidifying activists in the social movements of the sixties – as they had done for "old" social movements, as well – the effects of those movements on developments in popular culture have been less acknowledged. Peter Guralnick, one of the foremost critics of popular music in the United States, has written the following about the development of soul music as a new musical genre:

Certainly [soul music] can be seen as paralleling the Civil Rights Movement stylistically as well as chronologically, emerging with stealth at first, slowly gathering strength, then learning to assert itself without apology or fear, until forced to retrench in the face of a series of traumatic events and jarring disappointments.

(Guralnick 1986: 18)

Guralnick goes on to illustrate his thesis by analyzing the changing nature of soul music against the background of the biographies of some of its greatest innovators – in the context of the historical events of the 1950s and 1960s. Another music critic employing a similar methodology to make broad claims about popular music is Greil Marcus. In *Mystery Train*, Marcus offers a series of biographical sketches (including subjects like The Band, Randy Newman, and Elvis Presley) in an "attempt to broaden the context in which music is heard; to deal with rock-and-roll not as youth culture, or counterculture, but simply as American culture" (Marcus 1990: 4). The portraits he paints are of musicians who attempted through their art to redefine the ways in which people think about themselves and about American society.

Influence can be direct and obvious, as in the example of the music (and preaching) of Solomon Burke, who used the recorded speeches of Martin Luther King, Jr., to introduce a number of his own songs and records; or it can be less obvious, as in James Brown's musical revolution which helped bring about a whole new appreciation of black history and culture in conjunction with the Black Power stage of the movement.

Social movements develop in specific historical periods, as well as in national political cultures. These contexts form a distinct environment which affects the formation of a social movement, and which is in turn affected by that movement's formation. Popular culture, in its specific national and international forms, is a distinctive part of the environment affecting the formation of new social movements. Not only are movement activists raised in a milieu permeated by popular culture; as activists they also draw upon and use many of its forms and contents – its symbols and its "stars" – to further movement ends. Movements, through their activists and their activities, are both consumers and producers, takers and shapers, of popular culture. They do this, however, in ways defined by national contexts. The Free Speech Movement at the University of California at Berkeley in 1964 offers an example:

Here They Come! Get ready! . . . The cops start with the people nearest the elevator, and methodically work their way through the tightly packed crowd. I'm about two-thirds of the way down the hall, leading singing. It's amazing – I can remember every word to every song I've ever heard. Usually I have trouble, and bog down after a verse or two. Not this morning. Civil rights songs, FSM [Free Speech Movement] Christmas carols, Leadbelly songs, chain-gang chants, spirituals, folk songs – anything I can think of that has a call-and-response; it doesn't much matter, what's more important is that we keep on clapping and singing.   (Goines 1993: 1)

This quotation is from a first-person account of one of the very first manifestations of the student movement in the United States. The mixing of music and movement was already clearly established, the sources were popular, and traditional tunes were transformed and put to new uses. The songs provided a sense of identification as well as rallying strength to resist authority.

The American student movement which began in direct connection to the civil rights movement was contemporaneous with a revival of interest in folk music. This paralleled the development of soul or roots music and the civil rights movement, as mentioned above. The music and the movement grew together and at the same time as many of those instrumental in the folk music revival – Bob Dylan, Peter, Paul, and Mary, Pete Seeger, Phil Ochs, Tom Paxton, Joan Baez, Judy Collins, and many more – found a ready audience on the front lines of mass demonstrations. The songs, and the singers, formed part of the process of collective identity formation of the movement, just as the "freedom songs" had in the civil rights movement – so much so that it is difficult to think of one without the other.

The folk revival as a social movement

The Movement provided the folksinger with more than an audience; it provided content and a sense of mission over and above the commercial. In fact, it helped justify an anti-commercial attitude and foster a sense of authenticity, as well as lifestyle, that motivated an interest in folk music as such. What was opposed, by both the politicos and the folkies, was the massification of American society, the domination of commercial and military values over American life. Even Robert Cantwell, who is at pains to emphasize the non-political nature of the folk revival, sees a certain convergence of movement and music in a shared attitude of opposition:

The folk revival . . . was a short-lived response – flowing out of various elite, progressive, radical, avant-garde, bohemian, and popular cultures and movements into the commercial marketplace, with little coherent ideology of its own but derived from many ideological traditions – to the conditions of life in America after World War II . . . In a sense the folk revival represents a reconciliation of originally antagonistic socio-political developments, temporarily making common cause against what must have been understood, on some level, as the same adversary, mass or commercial culture.   (Cantwell 1996: 355, 356)

If it were not for the political movements there would not have been a folk music revival in the United States in the early 1960s. In any case, it would not have been as popular or as widespread as it was. And the folk revival would not have been able, as Cantwell puts it, to carry "a culture of personal rebellion across normally impermeable social and cultural barriers under the influence and authority of folk music, at once democratic and esoteric, already obscurely imbued with a spirit of protest" (1996: 346). The movement helped make folk music popular and popular music more open to the influence of folk traditions and musical forms. But the flow of influence can also be traced the other way. In this period, popular music was one of the main mediating forces, forms of translation, between the movement's more obvious expressions – demonstrations, organizations, books and journals – and the wider population. Through the media of popular culture, the ideas, values, and attitudes expressed in the movement reached a broader segment of people, and (perhaps) to more long-lasting effect. The political protest was colored by what Cantwell terms the "romantic claim of folk culture – oral, immediate, traditional, idiomatic, communal, a culture of characters, privileges, obligations, and beliefs – against a centrist, specialist, impersonal technocratic culture, a culture of types, functions, jobs, and goals" (1996: 349).

By seeing the "folk revival" in terms of the cognitive praxis of a social movement, it becomes possible to specify the nature of that claim somewhat more clearly than Cantwell, and others, have done. For this was not merely the reaffirmation, the revival, of a tradition and of traditional folk musics, although that was certainly involved. Indeed, the propagation of traditional, "oldtime" rural instruments and lifestyles was central to the movement: we might say that a new kind of folk music instrumental competence represented the technical dimension of the movement's cognitive praxis, the appreciation of a traditional, often non-commercial musicianship, such as playing bluegrass mandolin or mountain dulcimer. This aspect of the movement's cognitive praxis had been available for quite some time; Bill Monroe's version of bluegrass music, for example, was developed and became commercially successful already in the 1930s. What was needed, however, was a new kind of audience, a new public space, for appreciating, and eventually appropriating, the technical skills involved in invented traditions like bluegrass or, for that matter, topical folksinging.

That audience was generated by the broader political and social movement, in which the criticism of a mass, technological culture was of central importance. The artisanal skill of the traditional musician and of the topical songwriter and an interest in the "authentic" acoustic instruments that they mastered became socially significant when put into the context of a social movement opposed to mass, artificial, technologically mediated culture. Bill Monroe, Doc Watson, Clarence Ashley, Jean Ritchie, and Jack Elliott – and, for that matter, Woody Guthrie – represented something real, something oppositional, for the young people in the suburbs who discovered them within the context of a social movement. As Peter Guralnick has written, "It was all about a world that continued to believe in democracy, about political commitment and long-term struggle . . . They [the songs of Woody Guthrie and Leadbelly] represent a commitment to a progressive social tradition, a belief not just in the common man and woman but in the necessity of struggle – for each of us, for our own sakes. They represent the one kind of affirmation that is real, a declaration of belief in what we share rather than in what separates us" (Guralnick 1988).

Cantwell contends that it was no accident that many of those who were drawn to traditional music most strongly were of Jewish heritage; their "outsider" status in the United States allowed them to appreciate musicians who were marginalized by the mainstream culture. He notes that Jews in the United States have been consistently drawn to left-wing projects, and "wildly idealistic" ideas (Cantwell 1996: 378). In any case, as it so happens, the competence of Bill Monroe and Doc Watson needed politically minded, often Jewish, music lovers to "discover" and spread their talents into the popular, mass culture. But even more than the Jewish component, the promulgation of folk music had a strong non-Jewish family component to it – there are Seegers almost everywhere you look. It is almost as if folk music needed a particular family legacy to make it seem even more authentic and homey. Of course it was not just the Seeger family that made and then remade a folk music tradition in the United States. In the earlier period, Alan Lomax and Moe Asch joined forces with Charles Seeger and Ruth Crawford Seeger, as we have seen; and in the 1960s, Ralph Rinzler, Guy Carawan, and a host of others joined with the younger Seegers in "reviving" folk music once again. But the family continuity is striking in any case. As their parents had earlier done – but less as performers and teachers than as explorers – Pete, Peggy, and Mike Seeger would do in the 1960s; for political reasons, they would promote traditional music, and a broader folk culture as a counterpoint to the synthetic technological culture of mass American society. The Seeger siblings would each be attracted to somewhat different types of folk music, but they would all be united in their shared aim of fostering authenticity and taking on, in various ways, a more rustic, rural, "traditional" lifestyle than their parents.

In the Seegers, one finds a (modest) generational revolt against their modernist parents, but also a continuity. Pete's promotion of the banjo, Mike's taking on the mannerisms and clothes of a backwoodsman (and mastering traditional musicianship and dancing like few others), and Peggy writing women's folk songs and helping to promote the British folk revival after leaving the United States – they are different aspects of the same cognitive praxis, which builds on but also transforms the cognitive praxis of their parents' movement. For the children, the politics are less doctrinaire and the ties to the traditional cultural establishment are broken more strongly and personally. Instead of continuing to operate within the mainstream culture as promoters of a dying alternative, the children become "movement intellectuals," teaching and training new cadres of folk musicians in an emergent oppositional culture. Rather than simply struggling to have folk music accepted by the hegemonic culture (although they have done that, as well, throughout their lives), the children helped carve out a new social movement space, and create new institutions. While Charles and Ruth, along with John and Alan Lomax, sought to save folk music from extinction while working primarily in established institutions, the children have helped to build alternative organizational frameworks, and develop alternative skills and competences, within the context of a folk music movement. They became innovators and teachers in support of what Raymond Williams has termed an emergent cultural formation.

As Robert Cantwell and other historians of the "folk revival" so well describe, the movement was innovative not just in individual terms but in collective ways as well. In the 1950s, McCarthyism forced folk music "underground" to summer camps and a few liberal college campuses, but it could nonetheless survive and even spread to new enthusiasts so that, when McCarthy died and the peace and civil rights movement brought politics back into American society, folk music could be part of a new public sphere. Folk clubs and, eventually, major festivals, particularly at Newport, Rhode Island, provided a new social space for experiencing a sense of community and collective identity, a new organizational form for cultural expression. The festivals were not just mass concerts; they also provided opportunities for social learning, both of the new music and of the lifestyle and philosophy that came with it. There were workshops and informal exchanges between performers and their public; and, along with the magazines and instruction books, the festivals helped to spread the interest in folk music in a highly participatory mode.

Everyone could play or sing folk music; and this became one of its most significant and attractive features, central to what we would term the organizational dimension of the movement's cognitive praxis. In projecting new criteria of musical competence and in organizing those forms of competence in new ways, the folk revival was a kind of social movement, or cultural process. It could be distinguished from the more explicit political manifestations, and there were certainly many people who liked the music but not the politics (as Robert Cantwell himself apparently did). But what made the folk revival into a social movement that had lasting repercussions for the broader culture was more than music; it was the direct connection to political activities, the fact that folk music, for a few years, could serve as an important "medium" for communicating the multifaceted message of protest.

For, besides its form and its technical dimensions, the content of the new music was also distinctive: this was not merely, or even primarily, a revival of old, traditional songs. The quiet sounds of folk music perhaps encouraged a focus on text as a prime source of meaning, while the open-ended nature of the protest lent itself to a poetic, or at least more emotive, form of political communication. The "folk revival" brought ideas into popular songs; it was in the songs that the critique of mass culture – with its homogenizing tendencies, its environmentally destructive products, its dependence on war and weaponry – could be most effectively articulated. Along with the intimate connection with the collective identity of a rising generation, this intellectualizing encouraged the development of a new sort of folk music, a non-traditional, urban folk music, which easily admitted cultural and political criticism into its lyrical content. In addition, the songs provided the movement with a sense of its own history. As in the civil rights movement, many of the new folk songs recorded events significant to the development of the movement itself. Again, largely due to the potential commercial benefits to be accrued, mass media industries soon opened to producing and distributing this new music. The result was eventually to become a mass-produced form of social criticism.

Examples come readily to mind. Peter, Paul, and Mary's commercially successful versions of Pete Seeger's "If I Had a Hammer" and Bob Dylan's "Blowin' in the Wind" in 1962 and 1963, respectively, were perhaps the earliest protest songs to reach a mass audience. But, "paradoxically," as Charlie Gillett puts it, "despite their genuine political beliefs which they expressed by singing free at political rallies around the country, the sound of Peter, Paul, and Mary . . . was soft and easy on the ear, unlikely to stir activity in the passive pop audience" (1970: 297). Bob Dylan himself remained unknown to a wider public until 1965, when he went electric with his song "Like a Rolling Stone." In the early 1960s, in addition to Peter, Paul, and Mary, it was primarily Joan Baez, who, through her performances on college campuses and at folk festivals, as well as at civil rights demonstrations, attracted the most public attention.

Dylan's songs, and those of Phil Ochs, Tom Paxton, Pete Seeger, Buffy Saint-Marie, Ed McCurdy, Malvina Reynolds, and many others, became sources of collective identity formation, not so much by being top ten hits as by lending themselves to shared performance. They invited participation, by simple repetitive choruses and rhyming couplets, with an emotional and political content.

These were songs that almost anyone could sing, but while singing them one shared in a common experience of "consciousness-raising." But this was, of course, not a traditional ideological or even ethnic consciousness, although the rhythms and forms of the music were derived from a mixing of several traditional musics – blues, spirituals, folk, and country. Some of the most popular songs – "All My Trials," "This Land is Your Land," "We Shall Not Be Moved" – were older songs that were remembered by a new generation. But rather than being merely a reinvention of tradition, the consciousness that was being formed by singing these songs was of a generation in revolt against a society that was drifting, losing direction, and, most certainly, losing its revolutionary spirit. In protest against racism and war and injustice, the songs helped shape a new kind of politics which was as much a longing for community as it was a protest against the conformity and "one-dimensionality" of the modern United States. The political meaning could be slight and indirect, as in the longing to go home in the refrain of "Sloop John B" or the remembrance of Michael's struggle to row his boat ashore across the Jordan River. But it was often quite direct and quite pointed, as in Malvina Reynolds' social criticism, satirizing the society of "little boxes made of ticky-tacky" that gave Pete Seeger one of his few commercially successful records. It was an oppositional consciousness, which named the other and envisioned a utopian future. It turned out, however, to be a consciousness that was extremely difficult to transform into effective political results; its larger impact, we suggest, was instead to be on the mores and values of popular culture.

In his analysis of the myths of American popular songs, Timothy Scheuer refers to the songs of the 1960s as seeking to "redefine the role of the individual in the context of a new mythic vision," adding to the critical language of radical dissent a new kind of existential pathos. The exemplary songs were of "individuals who wandered on the borders of an absurd technocracy, which threatened them with a loss of freedom, equality, opportunity, and individuality. This image of the outsider," writes Scheuer, "proved to be the locus of the reexamination of the myth of America and the key concept in the continuing attempt to create a new myth through the next two decades" (1991: 167, 181). No longer could the radical seek redress in the one big union or in a popular front, or even in a political movement; the message that was projected in the topical songs of the 1960s reflected the growing sense of alienation in American society, and a resistance to what Mario Savio, the leader of the Free Speech Movement in Berkeley, referred to as the "machine." While Herbert Marcuse and Lewis Mumford criticized, in academic, theoretical terms, the reification of technology, the domination of the megamachine, Bob Dylan looked out with his "lady" from the rows of desolation where they were "making postcards of the hanging." For a few years, Dylan, Ochs, and the others provided a musical variant of critical social theory, mixing into the political discourse a new kind of insight, derived not so much from literature or philosophy as from a rural populist tradition, in which the lone individual – Dylan's "blue-eyed son" – could come back from his wanderings, tell of the horrors and the visions that he had seen, and proclaim a poetic truth: "it's a hard rain's a-gonna fall." The fear of nuclear war, and of environmental crisis, inspired many a songwriter, and when Barry McGuire singing "Eve of Destruction" reached the top of the pop music charts, "protest songs," for better or worse, had permanently entered the popular culture.

The dialectic of Dylan and Ochs

Bob Dylan, who was the great innovator and key figure in the folk revival, made his long journey from Hibbing, Minnesota, to New York's Greenwich Village by way of country blues. His strength would derive from his range of sources, and his ability to put into words a collective experience, not in the ever more personal and highly limited individual vision that would all but replace politics in his songs in the mid-1960s. At Gerde's Folk City in April 1961, in one of his first public appearances, Dylan played alongside John Lee Hooker, one of the all-time blues greats. But country blues was not, of course, the only kind of music Dylan absorbed and eventually synthesized. For a time he took on the identity of Woody Guthrie, and went through the song collections of Alan Lomax and Pete Seeger as if they were college textbooks. Liam Clancy, an Irish folksinger who met Dylan at the time, said: "Do you know what Dylan was when he came to the Village? . . . The only thing I can compare him with was blotting paper. He soaked everything up" (quoted in Heylin 1991: 42). Bob Dylan was not alone. Traditional folk music, country music, blues, rhythm-and-blues, and even rock-and-roll were being blended together in a great, creative melting pot, as cultural and political forms of expression ran together with a new generation in the early 1960s.

The folk-rock which was to emerge later was yet another step in the cumulative process of social and musical integration. A key factor was electrification and the addition of a drum beat. This was not a bloodless process. In one of the most famous incidents in the history of modern music, Bob Dylan was booed off the stage at the Newport Folk Festival in July 1965. A week before the festival, Dylan had released "Like a Rolling Stone," which, with electric backup, was already moving up the pop charts. He arrived at the Newport Festival, a yearly celebration of traditional folk and blues music, to great anticipation and tense expectation. Dylan played three numbers on stage, all with electric backup provided, among others, by members of the Paul Butterfield Blues Band, a white group that was also creating havoc with traditionalists at the Festival. During the set, musically conservative members of the Festival Board of Directors, Alan Lomax and Pete Seeger, tried, and failed, to have the volume turned down. It was more the noise than the electric guitars and the drums in themselves which they were opposed to. In the end, after leaving the stage in a shower of boos, Dylan returned with his acoustic guitar to play a few solo numbers to quiet the crowd and the Board. But the message was clear; a turning point had been reached and Dylan would soon produce two electric albums with next to the same backup as at Newport, "Highway 61 Revisited" and "Blonde on Blonde" (both on Columbia Records, which boasted of having "all the revolutionaries" under contract) which would establish him as the "King of Folk-Rock."

As its name implies, folk-rock was a mixing of genres, combining not only the pulsating beat and electrified sound of rock-and-roll, but also the significant text which characterized folk music. The new urban folk music had developed an interest, under the influence of a vibrant social movement sector, for what Dylan called "finger-pointing" songs. In 1963 and 1964, Dylan recorded finger-pointers like "Masters of War," "The Death of Emmett Till," "A Hard Rain's A-Gonna Fall," and the more generalized "Blowin' in the Wind," which, along with "We Shall Overcome," became an anthem of the civil rights movement, particularly among white supporters. "Blowin' in the Wind" was sung at demonstrations by traditionalists like Pete Seeger and popularizers like Peter, Paul, and Mary, as well as, of course, by millions of activists. The merging of folk and rock was thus a mixing of content-rich text and rock beat. Bob Dylan's "Like a Rolling Stone," a title revealing roots in the country blues, added a driving beat and a synthetic sounding organ to powerful lyrics expressing alienation and anger. The song pointed an accusing finger at an anonymous and amorphous Establishment and, addressing no one in particular, and thus everyone, asked, "How does it feel, to be on your own, with no direction home, a complete unknown . . ." It climbed high up the popular music charts and stayed there for weeks. It would become, for many, the theme song of the sixties, and, more than any other, it was the song that brought a kind of truth-bearing meaning into popular music. "Like a Rolling Stone" was a poetic cry of critique, a diatribe against pomp and power and pretense, and a renewed, for Dylan almost a final, call for justice and compassion, and for authenticity.

The song was rooted in the folk and blues traditions but up to date in its rhythmic, electric rockiness. The theme of alienation connected back to the situation of the hobo from Woody Guthrie's "I Ain't Got No Home" and "Hard Traveling," but Dylan broadened the experience to a contemporary world in which even the mighty could fall, a world in which all were ultimately in danger of losing their way home. It would be one of Dylan's last great songs as a "movement intellectual" and a unique cultural turning point. It changed the standards of popular culture, in a number of ways, by showing that hit songs need not be formulaically three minutes long, that rock texts could be free-flowing, complex, and poetic in the tradition of Whitman, Sandburg, and Hughes, and, finally, that pop songs could be a kind of exemplary, truth-bearing action: by singing them, dancing to them, comprehending them, something significant about one's self and one's world could be revealed. Dylan's unintended transformation of himself into a prophet brought not merely commercial success and fundamental changes in popular culture. It also signified a break with the movement from which he had emerged and for which he spoke. By asking others how it felt to be drifting, and achieving respectability and wealth in the process, Dylan removed himself from the movement and started to seek what his nameless victim had lost: personal contentment. In commenting on the song at the time, Phil Ochs said that, in rejecting politics, Dylan was making a "dangerous" move; he was reaching out to the broader culture, but Ochs feared he would be swallowed up by that very mass audience that he so desired to have (Ochs 1965). Dylan's next song, "Positively Fourth Street," would be the extremely bitter – and less commercially successful – result.

As Ray Pratt puts it, "Dylan's movement away from explicit protest themes coincided with the deepening radical critique then emerging in the country" (1990: 208). In 1965, the American involvement in Vietnam expanded considerably, and the opposition to the war mobilized major demonstrations that increasingly took on a more aggressive, radical edge. Dylan reacted by retreating into himself, but also by becoming a more self-conscious poet. Some of the songs on "Blonde on Blonde," his double album from 1966, are masterpieces of lyric poetry, while the message or meaning becomes increasingly difficult to decipher. "Visions of Joanna" could be about Joan Baez and the long-lost folk revival, but it could also be about a lost era, perhaps the new frontier of John F. Kennedy, with its youthful idealism and public compassion. The song criticizes hypocrisy, but also the role of public spokesman that Dylan had, perhaps unwittingly, taken on. It was as if songs weren't enough any more to express the horror of the war and of the failure of the dreams that Dylan had shared with so many of his contemporaries in the early 1960s. Instead, as he put it, bluntly and far from poetically, in another song on that album, "everybody must get stoned."

Dylan's "going electric" in his albums of 1965 and 1966, along with the highly successful rock versions of some of his earlier songs by the Byrds, opened the door to a wave of folk-rock, the most substantial of which would be written by a young New Yorker named Paul Simon, who with his schoolmate, Art Garfunkel, would record several number one hits in the late 1960s, from "The Sounds of Silence" to "Bridge Over Troubled Waters." Simon would turn out to be the tradition-bearer, almost single-handedly keeping meaningful pop music alive in the 1970s, and then rein-venting folk music (and his flagging career) in the guise of world music with his Graceland project and record in 1985. In the late 1960s, Simon and Garfunkel were the most consistently commercially successful folk singers, but there were a few others – Joan Baez, Janis Ian, Richie Havens, Arlo Guthrie – who brought into the emerging rock music something of the legacy of the early 1960s. Janis Ian pointed forward to the women's move-ment of the 1970s, and Richie Havens connected back to the freedom singers of the civil rights movement (and his rendition of "Freedom" at Woodstock in African attire also points forward to the innovative improvisational performances of contemporary rap artists and the tradi-tion-bearing hybrids of world music). While folk music had broken apart as a social movement, its cosmology, its message of protest, peace, com-munity, and authenticity did enter into the rock culture, but increasingly as a "minority" position. In the wake of Vietnam, escapism and decadence grew ever more popular, and social criticism increasingly took on more doctrinaire, dogmatic forms (Edward Morgan 1991).

By then, Dylan himself had rejected both the "finger-pointing" of the early 1960s folk revival as well as the more moderate and less explicit polit-ical lyrics of Paul Simon-style folk-rock and moved on to become an almost mythical figure, detaching himself from the political conflicts of the late 1960s and the antiwar movement into a private world of artistic reassess-ment and self-exploration. In 1969, Dylan recorded "Nashville Skyline," a collection of country tunes; and on his "Self-Portrait" album of 1970, Dylan combined a number of old popular songs – "Blue Moon," "Let It Be Me" – with some of his own, exchanging the powerful, aggressive song voice of the early 1960s for the laid-back twang of a country crooner. The album pictured him relaxing and recording on his country estate, as clean-cut as the hippies were dirty; like the boxer in the Paul Simon song that he also recorded on that album, Dylan had seemingly "squandered his resistance for a pocketful of mumbles." Of course, Dylan would return through the following decades in many different incarnations, some of them even overtly political, and he would often rekindle the spirit of the 1960s on his concert tours, but he would henceforth be the detached and reclusive artist rather than the activist, ever further from the "movement intellectual" that he, perhaps more than anyone else, had once been, for a few short years in the early 1960s. He had, of course, "been so much older then," as he wrote already in 1965 in "My Back Pages," but it was then, when he was older at least in spirit, that he wrote the songs that would have the most enduring significance.

The careers of Phil Ochs and Tom Paxton followed a different kind of trajectory, as both singers continued to mix their songwriting with political activism even after the excitement of the sixties had passed. And while they still managed to sell some records, they had largely lost their mass audience, which followed Dylan and Creedence Clearwater Revival back to the country, when it wasn't "flipping out" on drugs. Ochs' was an especially tragic story, ending in suicide in 1976 after a number of failed attempts to recreate the unique combination of culture and politics that he had done so much to articulate in the early 1960s. He traveled and performed in Africa, even recording a song in Swahili with a local band in Kenya before he was attacked and robbed in Tanzania; in the words of Robin Denselow, "he was discovering a whole new world of international music, way ahead of the rock field" (1989: 118). A benefit concert for Chile, which he organized after the military coup in 1973, prefigured the rock benefits of the 1980s, but musically it was apparently a fiasco, as a drunken and overweight Ochs tried to bring back the spirit of a different era, even getting his old friend Bob Dylan to put in an appearance (Eliot 1990).

Perhaps more than any other single individual, Phil Ochs epitomized the message of the sixties in both his personal and his musical life. Like Dylan, he started out by trying to reinvent the tradition of the political songwriter, which Joe Hill had played before the First World War and Woody Guthrie had played in the 1930s and 1940s (Ochs wrote songs about both Joe Hill and Woody Guthrie). When Pete Seeger introduced him at the Newport Festival in 1963, he said that Phil Ochs wrote topical songs rather than folk songs; and it became Ochs' particular identity to mix his songwriting with all of the political movements of the sixties, from civil rights through the student revolts of the mid-1960s ("Oh, I am just a student, sir, and I only want to learn, but it's hard to read through the rising smoke from the books that you like to burn. So I'd like to make a promise, and I'd like to make a vow: that when I've got something to say, sir, I'm gonna say it now") on through to the antiwar movement of the late 1960s. In the early days of the civil rights movement, he sang his "The Ballad of Medger Evers," "Too Many Martyrs," "Here's to the State of Mississippi," and "In the Heat of the Summer," both in the South and at the large demonstrations in the North. But it was the Vietnam war that became his special topic, from the satirical "Draft Dodger Rag" to the later and more significant "I Ain't Marchin' Anymore," "We're the Cops of the World," "Canons of Christianity," "White Boots Marching in a Yellow Land," and "The War is Over." In these and several other songs, written during the second half of the 1960s, Ochs provided an understanding of American imperialism that brought the experience of the war home and into at least a certain segment of the popular consciousness. His songs offered another kind of social theory, providing political analysis mixed with his characteristic ironic observations of the inherent absurdity of the war:

> Silent soldiers on a silver screen;
> Framed in fantasies and drugged in dreams;
> Unpaid actors of the mystery.
> The mad director knows that freedom will not make you free,
> And what's this got to do with me?
> I declare the war is over,
> It's over, it's over.   (Phil Ochs, "The War Is Over")

As with his more reflective and poetic songs, which questioned the values of American society, and perhaps especially the values of his fellow progressives – "Changes," "Flower Lady," "Outside a Small Circle of Friends," "Jim Dean of Indiana," "Pleasures of the Harbor" – the political messages that Ochs sought to infuse into popular culture largely failed to reach a mass audience. Ochs was one of the few who criticized the drug culture – the "smoke dreams of escaping soul . . . [that] dull the pain of living as they slowly die" – but he himself slowly died in the late 1960s as the political movements grew more radical and extremist, and many of the musicians with whom he had shared so much in the early 1960s put politics behind them. As he reflected on the violence that he had witnessed first-hand at the Democratic Party convention in Chicago in 1968, he recorded a moving, largely forgotten testament in the form of an album, "Rehearsals for Retirement." On the cover was a gravestone, showing that Phil Ochs had died in Chicago, and the record was filled with powerful songs bemoaning the demise of the political folk song era.

At an appearance in Vancouver in late 1968, recently released as a compact disc after being discovered in an archive, he said how hard it was to keep going. The country was captured by the "media syndrome, when they fill everyone's mind by use of fairly mindless, mind-distorting distortions of the facts . . . which led all of us into the Vietnam war." He still sang protest songs, which could be defined as "a song they don't play on the radio." By 1970, however, even Phil Ochs could see that the political and cultural movements had gone separate ways:

> Hello, hello, hello,
> Is there anybody home?
> I only called to say I'm sorry
> The drums are in the dawn
> And all the voices gone
> And it seems that there are no more songs.
>
> (Phil Ochs, "No More Songs")

Joan Baez, who earlier in the decade had had one of her few commercial successes by recording an Ochs song ("There But For Fortune"), performed at the famous Woodstock Festival in 1969, but by then the political movement had largely parted company with the so-called counterculture that had taken on such prominence. Along with Ochs and Baez, it was Pete Seeger and Tom Paxton – and, with "Alice's Restaurant," his immortal tale of draft-dodging and garbage collection, Woody Guthrie's son Arlo – who tried to keep alive some of the earlier ambitions, but the music industry was moving on: into psychedelic, drug-dominated hard rock music for some, sexually suggestive soul music for others, and soothing country rural music for still others. Rather than inspiring political change, popular music seemed to be trying to provide the satisfaction that Mick Jagger couldn't get in the early, more political days.

The appropriation of the blues: Janis and Jimi

For Edward Morgan, the rock music of the late 1960s represented a "retreating inward" from the explicit political mobilizations of the early 1960s. Rock, he has written, "reflected and expressed the subjective impulses that permeated the counterculture . . . The importance of Sixties rock music lies in its connection with other aspects of the counterculture, as part of the search for personal liberation and community" (Edward Morgan 1991: 188, 193). But that utopian search for community ran into the reality of the commercial marketplace, and, perhaps as a kind of negative synthesis, rock turned against the very spirit that had spawned it. In the 1970s, rock would become ever more theatrical, decadent, and violent, but it would also transform the mores and tastes of the popular culture as no other single element. Nothing better illustrates this than the careers of two of the stars of the period, Janis Joplin and Jimi Hendrix, who, as we mentioned earlier, are representative not so much because of their popularity, but because of the way they combined traditions stemming from the blues, the spirituals, and folk songs in the context created by the social movements of the 1960s.

Much has been made of the deaths of Joplin and Hendrix, a few weeks apart in the fall of 1970. Both deaths involved a fatal mixture of drugs and alcohol and were probably accidental. For many they symbolized the death of a generation, a lifestyle, the counterculture itself. The *New York Times* wrote at the time: "God, what a year this is turning out to be. The king and queen of the gloriously self-expressive music that came surging out of the late sixties are dead, the victims, directly or indirectly, of the very real physical excesses that were part of the world that surrounded them." Just as the previous example of Dylan and Ochs, their respective paths are at one and the same time unique and reflective of the broader social forces which help constitute the period and create a new generational consciousness.

What characterizes the music of the late 1960s and early 1970s is the willingness to cross established boundaries, be they racial, social, regional, sexual, or genre-specific. The Movement, now by all accounts in decline, had opened spaces for cultural experimentation. As key innovators, Jimi Hendrix and Janis Joplin came to their boundary-crossing "cognitive praxis" from very different directions. Hendrix, raised in a small black working-class section of Seattle in the northwest of the United States moved southward and eastward across the country to New York City and then to England, where his blend of blues and rock revolutionized the sounds a guitar could make and, with the help of new global media, re-educated musicians and audiences alike. Joplin, a middle-class white woman from Port Arthur, Texas, followed Jack Kerouac's advice and went on the road in the general direction of San Francisco, where she helped create a new kind of music combining down-home country blues with the psychedelic rock emerging with the counterculture. Creative as they were as individuals, both Janis Joplin and Jimi Hendrix were nourished by the social and cultural movements of their time. Their creativity – in our terms, a kind of innovative cognitive praxis – cannot be thought of apart from those movements. For Hendrix a nurturing community was provided by the urban blues and folk circles, part of the expanding bohemian middle class, with bases in Chicago and New York and, in his case, London. For Joplin it was the newly forming California-based counterculture, which provided the collective basis for her individual experimentation, both musical and social.

This was a period of unprecedented creativity in the recording industry.

Fueled by the success of the "concept" records by Dylan and the Beatles, a freer hand was given to singer-songwriters for experimentation in the production of music, even though marketing, publicity, and distribution remained pretty much as narrowly defined as before. There was, however, a growing number of independents ready to challenge the majors by seeking out new talent and producing the newly labeled "rock" music for more specialized and localized markets. For a short period in the mid-1960s before the major companies settled in and reestablished their control, one could almost speak of a creator's market. Into this walked the likes of Jimi Hendrix and Janis Joplin, both of whom were central to the reinvention of the blues in a multiracial and aesthetically open context. As representatives of social and cultural movements, Joplin and Hendrix were important carriers of black musical traditions into the mainstream American culture. Through their music they helped break down some of the barriers that had previously existed. American cultural history reveals a constant interest and interchange between black and white musical styles and audiences, and the enormous popularity of rock-and-roll from the mid-1950s onward was based on a blending of white and black musical and performance styles. While the sales of rock-and-roll records were increasing amongst middle-class white youth, the musicians were largely working-class. There still remained much territory to conquer.

The civil rights movement was an important force for exposing white audiences to black music. The dramatic televised events which brought the civil rights movement to public attention, from the demonstrations in Little Rock to the freedom rides and the mass jailings, included a vast array of music and song in their footage. The anthem of the movement, "We Shall Overcome," remains one of the most recognized songs of recent American history, without ever becoming a major commercial hit. Such songs were also performed on college campuses where they coincided with a revived interest in folk music, and at the mass gatherings and demonstrations which were, throughout the 1960s, a common feature of college life.

Singers like Bob Dylan, Janis Joplin, and Jimi Hendrix were thus part of broad historical processes through which black and white musical cultures interacted. However, the social context of the 1960s set the bounds and the agenda for that interaction in a particular way. In the late 1960s, Janis Joplin and Jimi Hendrix, as well as practically all of their contemporaries, built their music around an interpretation and appropriation of the blues and/or rhythm-and-blues music. Jimi Hendrix had learned the ropes of a musical career by playing backup for some of the best. Janis Joplin was perhaps closer to the norm: she picked up a "classic" blues intonation and performance by listening to phonograph records of old blues singers. Jimi

Hendrix had, of course, done his share of that too, and had even visited Chess Records in Chicago to listen to Muddy Waters and Willie Dixon directly. But both Hendrix and Joplin did more than accommodation, i.e., fitting their music to preconceived audience expectations. In their interpretations of blues songs, as well as their own compositions, which developed blues and rhythm-and-blues themes, they literally reinvented the blues tradition within the social and cultural contexts of the 1960s. Some of this refitting was consciously done and some not. Ellen Willis writes, for example, that Janis Joplin's interpretation of Big Mama Thornton's classic blues number "Ball and Chain" is noticeably different from the original because of Joplin's experience of being one of the lone women singers with any standing in the counterculture of the 1960s. Her interpretation, in other words, brings new meaning to the song because of the particular social context in which it is sung. Allan Moore suggests that Joplin's "musical device" on the same song, by which she stopped the music in order to express her feeling even more directly, in a non-singing voice, without musical accompaniment, "intruded on her listeners' sense of reality, leaving them to surmise that she meant it, every word of it. The device communicates the strength of her meaning far more incontrovertibly than words alone could ever have managed" (Moore 1993: 85).

All of this has nothing particular to do with adaptation or with "whitewashing," an attempt to please either the new audience or the record companies. To say that both Janis Joplin and Jimi Hendrix refitted black music to the new context is thus not necessarily to say that they were part of a great conspiracy to destroy or undermine "authentic" black music or culture. But there were aspects of that music and that culture – and many musicians as well – which got lost in the appropriation.

It should be repeated once more that one exemplary characteristic of their generation of musicians was to publicly acknowledge the sources they drew from. Many blues singers would have died unknown, at least as far as the wider public is concerned, if not for the public recognition of their work made by sixties rock and folk stars like the Rolling Stones and others of the British Invasion. This is in stark contrast to previous generations of appropriators. But such a process has its victimization and its victims and if the 1960s people were kinder than most generations, they were not altogether innocent either. Alan Lomax has suggested that there is a folk aspect to blues music which ties it to the community from which it emerged. To the extent that it formed part of the oral tradition of a folk culture, the blues expressed at least some of the experience of earlier generations of African-Americans. To that extent also, the blues can be said to share the fate of this folk group: as the community from which it emerges changes, so too does its forms of cultural expression. Janis Joplin and Jimi Hendrix, each in their own way, reinvented the blues tradition for a new audience, helping give voice as well as form to *its* common experience. Their blues articulated the collective identity of a youth "movement" in the midst of an amorphous generational revolt. To this end, they reinterpreted aspects of this traditional music for a new audience in much the same way as folk revivalists like Dylan and Ochs had done. In the process of reinvention both the music and the audience were transformed. The music was given new meaning and the audience was provided with a new source of identity.

Hendrix's songs gave expression to the anger and confusion, the "purple haze," that had implanted itself in so many young people's brains, while Janis Joplin's insatiable longing for true feeling, for true love, expressed the widespread alienation of the times. Hendrix is perhaps most remembered for his violent, impassioned rendition of the national anthem at Woodstock, when he made one electric guitar sound like an entire battlefield gone berserk. Janis Joplin's cries for love made it sound as if her life depended on being given "just a little piece of your heart, now, baby." Her live performances gave vent to the near-desperation that so many felt in the heat of the Vietnam war. Her own songwriting efforts included "Mercedes Benz," where she ridiculed consumerism, but also indicated how caught up she was in it. Obviously a song that meant something to her, she introduced it, on record, characteristically tongue-in-cheek fashion, as a "song of great social and political import." She sang it a cappella, without any musical accompaniment, a little prayer to her own god, asking him to buy her a Mercedes Benz, since her friends "all drive Porsches, I must make amends." In form, it was a classic blues song, but its content was pure counterculture, laughing at, but also wanting, ever so badly, the fruits of postwar prosperity. She even ended the song, on record, with a little smirk, so the listener was left in ambiguity: was Janis serious or just having a good stoned laugh?

With the help of this multidimensional rock music, an emergent genera-tion came to know itself and make itself heard. This new multicultural blues- and folk-influenced rock music played an important role in the iden-tity formation of a new community. As expressed through the musical per-formances of Bob Dylan, Phil Ochs, and especially Janis Joplin and Jimi Hendrix, popular music acquired new meaning, as well as a range of new interpretative functions. It came to express the experience of the generation that appropriated it, not that out of which it had originally come. This gen-eration-in-the-making, though primarily middle-class, white, and sub-urban, with a great deal of exposure to higher education and formed within a de-centered popular culture, was open to breaking down national, regional, cultural, and ethnic barriers. This was blues and folk played in a different manner and conveying a different experience, even where it shared some of the same sense of alienation, restlessness, and fascination with physical sensation, alcohol, drugs, and sexuality with the older blues music.

This was the blues of the affluent, not the poor, the blues of the franchised, not the disenfranchised; it was the blues of the majority, the dominant culture. It expressed the revolt of the masses, from within the good life itself. The blues were reinvented to express the longing of this generation because they were seen as sources of real feelings, as authentic reaction against a hostile and oppressive society and its culture. As jazz had done for the white beats in the 1950s, and American folk music for the radicals of the early 1960s, so electrified blues served the youth of the late 1960s as an authentic source through which to express their alienation from the mainstream American culture, their culture. Reinventing the blues, they reinvented the underground, the counterculture, the culture of revolt in the new historical context.

The battle between underground and mainstream culture was thus refought by a new generation partly through its music. Traditionally, this struggle involves dealing with the commercial and technological possibilities offered by mainstream culture, its avenues to fame and fortune, as part of the struggle to establish the specific norms and values, the way of life, which will define the generational identity. How much of the mainstream can one make use of and remain shielded from its clutches? This question has faced all countercultural movements from the first conscious attempts to live the bohemian life amongst bourgeois Parisians in the middle of the nineteenth century to our own time's punk and post-punk alternative music movements. In the 1950s, existentialists in Paris and beats reacted in different ways to what radical, New York intellectuals in the 1940s understood as an emerging mass society in the postwar United States. With a little help from German exiles like Theodor Adorno and Max Horkheimer, Dwight MacDonald had been among the first to glimpse the new mass culture which would come to define American society. Standing on the high ground of the fine arts, MacDonald and others argued that American culture was being industrialized and trivialized at the same time, through mass media which catered to the least common denominator principle of commercial rationality: never do or say anything to offend a potential customer.

The beats took another tack, seeing in the same mass media the potential to reach a larger audience with a radical message. As a way to immunize themselves against cooptation, the danger of success that participating in these media opened, they chose an aesthetic lifestyle and a nihilistic attitude. In this way one could use the media without being used by it. Real meaning was found in the inner self and not the ornaments of material success, even if you wore them. The folksinging radicals of the early 1960s followed a similar line of attack, developing a lifestyle which expressed their rejection of the mainstream, including a simple form of musical expression, while at the same time participating in the commercial media. Monterey Pop was an interesting event from just that point of view, the attempt to define the line between using the media and being used by it. That this more "authentic" lifestyle could be manufactured and sold as fad and fashion to others less endowed with talent or principle was seen as not really their problem. The counterculture of the late 1960s thus extended this venture into mass culture and style even further than the beats. And of course the power of the mass media to circumscribe the forms and content of success, with national and global networks, would grow with each passing year.

There were genuine attempts to create an alternative to the commercial culture around them: groups like the Diggers in San Francisco who opened a "free" store where goods but no money could be exchanged; rock groups like Country Joe and the Fish in San Francisco and the Fugs in New York who actively sought to put the same sort of idea into musical practice; the communes, alternative newspapers, concerts, bookshops, food stores, and restaurants that covered the social and cultural landscape throughout the 1970s – all helped constitute an alternative public sphere that was relatively autonomous from the mainstream. Especially in light of the social background of those who made up this alternative, these two cultures lived side by side. The white middle-class youth moved back and forth between city and suburb, east coast and west coast, alternative and college environments, like the musicians moved between electric and acoustic guitar. Al Grossman, manager of both Bob Dylan and Richie Havens, gave Janis Joplin and Big Brother two scenarios when he offered his management services after the group's success at Monterey: to be like Havens, the committed artist who sang commercially only to make enough money to work politically, or to be like Dylan, the rich and famous superstar. He could do it either way; it was up to them. We know which one Janis Joplin chose, and we know the consequences. Jimi Hendrix made a similar choice.

All this was made possible by the economic boom which was still in progress. There seemed to be room for everybody. The mainstream was growing wider and more flexible because of it. And, like Mom and Dad, it would be there when you needed it. What about the mainstream? Did it remain untouched by the counterculture? It is easy to be either cynical or romantic about this. The cynic can point to the bloodthirsty competition, the struggle for fame and fortune that went on among singers and groups, the million-dollar contracts that resulted from "free" concerts, the drugs and the alcohol, the excessive sex and so on that marked the lives of all but the most idealistic, naive, or strong-willed of musicians. The cynic can wink knowingly and sneer at any suggestion that counterculture was anything other than part of the hype. The romantic, on the other hand, can wax lyrical about the good times and the good intentions of those like Phil Ochs, whose suicide was but one of the great tragedies to befall the ideologically committed singer-songwriter, or the misguidedness of Janis Joplin and Jimi Hendrix in dealing with the fruits of their pact with the devil. He can point to Joan Baez or Richie Havens, who resisted temptation and survived the hype with dignity and values intact.

Each side has their point, but neither has the whole story. That the counterculture was never entirely alternative cannot be denied, especially given the actors and the possibilities involved. But neither were its musical representatives, its movement intellectuals, entirely corrupted through participation in the commercial public sphere. Even if much of the altered appearance of the music industry was just that, altered appearance, as beads, beards, and pot replaced the gray flannel and alcohol favored by an earlier generation of corporate executives, some more permanent, deep-running changes can be identified from the interaction between underground and mainstream cultures in the 1970s. Songs with more serious meaning than teen problems became much more acceptable. The long, free-flowing verse of Bob Dylan which was revolutionary in both form and content as far as the mass pop market was concerned became part of the normal fare of AM radio. For the cynic this would be just another example of what Herbert Marcuse called "repressive tolerance," cooptation through acceptance, a form of normalization or routinization of rebellion – killing at best with kindness, at worst with indifference.

But is the media really the message? Do people merely listen to the radio, as Marcuse's more cynical colleague Theodor Adorno claimed, not to music on the radio? We think not. The musical performances of Janis Joplin and Jimi Hendrix, even in their recorded and mass-mediated versions, expanded the notion of what was acceptable in the mainstream, fundamentally altering its form and content. Joplin's powerfully expressive music, her open-hearted emotionality and sexuality, her cry of pain from being a lone female rebel in a male-dominated counterculture, are there for all to hear. Her recorded and mass-distributed musical performances have inspired countless young women to follow in the path she opened up. She made it easier for the next generation of "normal" women to express their emotional independence, just as she made it possible for a new wave of feminist singers to find their own voice and their audience in an alternative

women's community and the mainstream as well. Since the 1960s it is best
to view the mainstream as a river, where different currents wash over into
each other, than, as in the 1950s, as an independent and all-powerful force,
against which alternatives must fight.

The same can be said regarding ethnic, regional, and class cultures. The
distinctive black musical culture of which the blues can be identified no
longer exists as it did even as late as the 1950s. Its passing can be mourned,
but cannot be easily denied. The "race" market, with its different genre,
regional, and class specifications, rhythm-and-blues, jazz, gospel, and soul,
has given way to a multivaried, multicultural musical mainstream. The wid-
ening and induced flexibility of mainstream culture which directly followed
the sixties made this possible. How else can one explain the predominance
of rap as the musical genre of urban youth, white and black, male and
female? Rap has roots in the blues, the topical talking folk song, jazz, and
so on. Its multiple roots and multicultural framework are obvious to the
serious listener. All one has to do is turn on the AM radio to hear it.

Conclusions

What we hope to have illustrated in this chapter is that the relations between
social movements and popular culture can be reciprocal and mutually rein-
forcing. Rather than representing two distinct modes of activity, social
movements and popular culture can interact with each other in synergetic
ways, and thus contribute to wide-ranging and long-term processes of cultural transformation. This is, we contend, precisely what occurred in the
United States of America in the 1960s, where the effects are still being felt
today.

In both form and content, some popular music in the 1960s could function as another kind of social theory, translating the political radicalism
that was expressed by relatively small coteries of critical intellectuals and
political activists into a much different and far more accessible idiom. Like
theory, the best popular songs of the time identified social problems, gave
names to vague feelings of alienation and oppression, and even offered
explanations, albeit in poetic terms. But in addition to theory, popular
music could also provide a sense of belongingness, a sharing in a collective
vision, by making use of more emotive language and rhythms – and innovative performance practices that linked the musical and the political.
Music could, for a brief period of time, provide a basis of common understanding and common experience for a generation in revolt. It worked only
briefly, when the conditions allowed it; when the contextual factors that
shaped it disappeared, the music was "incorporated" into more established

channels. The forces of commercialism and professionalism, already present at the outset, reasserted themselves, at more or less the same time that dogmatism and sectarianism came to dominate the political arena. The intricate balance between culture and politics dissolved into its component parts, leaving both fundamentally different than before, but diffusing the revolutionary potential into disparate and often destructive directions.

Primarily through music, processes of personal and political change were linked into a common project of liberation, and at least some musicians became "movement intellectuals," leaving their artistic identity behind in pursuit of some larger, more all-encompassing societal role. As a result, American culture was transformed. By virtue of its appeal to the natural openness of youth, as well as the accessibility of its forms, popular music invited participation; and, under the contextual conditions of the 1960s, music could serve to create a sense of collective expression that was then diffused into the larger society. In the 1970s and 1980s, it would be that unique combination of the political and the cultural that would most come to symbolize the spirit of the 1960s; and periodically, that spirit, more than the actual issues of the 1960s, would come to infuse and inspire new movements of political and cultural change – from the ethnic and sexual movements of the United States to the movements for democracy in China, eastern Europe, and South Africa (see Garofalo 1992).

6

From the sixties to the nineties: the case of Sweden

> When people ask me if I really think that songs can affect political developments in society I usually answer that I see culture as the substance of politics. I mean that culture (songs, for example) gives expression to what we think and feel, what we dream and long for, and what we are ready to fight for. And that is exactly what politics is about.
>
> Mikael Wiehe (1980: 11–12)

The politically charged music of the 1960s has been diffused during the past thirty years in a variety of ways. On the one hand, there has been a process of globalization by which American music has entered into, and in large measure served to define, a worldwide culture industry. From the end of the 1960s, rock music has come to exert an enormous influence over international popular culture, and, in economic and financial terms, has become one of the major commercial activities in the world. Rock music has stimulated developments in technology – from synthesizers to CDs, from electric guitars to the Internet – as well as in other leisure and consumer industries, and it has become a crucial ingredient in many other areas of culture, from film and theater to art and advertising.

As a result of these multifarious processes of diffusion, the music has, of course, been continuously depoliticized: the trajectory that was already visible in the sixties, from political folk music to harmless rock music, and from songwriting "movement intellectuals" to individualized rock artists, has become a kind of norm. By streamlining one's act and image, by writing innocuous but melodic songs, and by utilizing the technologies of production, performance, and marketing to their fullest, a steady stream of young musicians have become celebrities, encouraging thousands of others to follow suit. The music industry has offered a new set of career opportunities for young people throughout the world, although the central power and decision-making, as well as the most marketable artistic commodities, remain primarily American.

In many ways, what is being diffused in contemporary rock music is the legacy of the sixties, whether it be an aging Bob Dylan singing his old songs, or Kurt Cobain repackaging the sixties experience in new musical form. The particular sense of a generation in revolt against an anonymous Establishment – a generation in search of authenticity, peace, and even collective love – continues to fuel rock music, even when it has become one of the most important industries in the world. The revolutionary quest for liberation may have become big business, but it nonetheless remains the core meaning, or sign, of rock music. The paradox is that, by providing a transforming influence on popular culture, rock music has lost much of the socially critical force it once had. While some rock musicians choose to take sides, and contribute money and musical performances for political causes, far more musicians reject a political role. While benefit concerts and records have been produced to help starving people in Ethiopia, save small farmers in the United States, preserve Brazilian rain forests, and support the anti-apartheid movement in South Africa, they have represented only a proverbial drop in the bucket, providing a way to soothe the guilty conscience for a handful of rock millionaires (Garofalo 1992). The dominant messages and uses of rock music are commercial, exploitative, and aggressive; and in the balance of things, it seems that rock music causes more social problems than it helps alleviate. By becoming mainstream music, rock has also become, as it were, dependent on the commercial industry, the Establishment that many of its aging superstars once rebelled against.

On the other hand, there has been a range of "alternative" folk musics that have emerged, especially over the past fifteen years or so, building in somewhat different ways on the legacy of the sixties. One important factor is the increasing recognition on the part of the music industry of the commercial potential of non-western musics, particularly from Africa (Moore 1993). But it also has to do with a new wave of mobilization of tradition, inspired, to some extent, by the globalization of production in general, and the globalization of the music industry in particular. The commercialized and globalized culture has spawned a reaction, a searching after roots, authenticity, tradition. Folk music has, in many countries, thereby experienced a new "revival" of interest; and with it a revival of tension between traditionalists and innovators. But while traditional musics are growing in popularity, what marks the new wave of interest in folk music, and serves to distinguish it from the folk music of the 1960s, is a far more sophisticated musical experimentation and a much more explicit "global consciousness." Under the genre title of world or roots music, an exciting process of mixing and combining is taking place, often with direct political implications. As racism and ethnic nationalism take on increasing importance in many parts of the world, the new globally oriented folk music has come to represent for many a kind of counterforce, often indirect and non-political, but nonetheless conjuring up a spirit of international solidarity in the form of musical hybridization (Lie 1996).

While this new dialectic of globalization in the realm of folk music has begun to generate some discussion among music critics, musicologists, and musicians themselves, rather less attention has been given to the relations between world music and social movements. For all the talk about tradition and modernity from social and cultural theorists, it is noteworthy that there is little reflection and analysis of one of the more visible arenas of globalization. World music is a field of ambiguities and tensions where the marketplace meets traditions head on, and, even more crucially, where the meanings of the music itself are filled with connections to other social and political discourses and movements. Most of the folk musics that are being commercialized are, of course, bastard versions of the real thing, and they are usually chosen for a variety of non-political reasons; in sociological terms, the contexts for their selection have a local contingency but also follow more general patterns. In many cases, however, there is a broader non-musical, or social, motivation for their selection, be it anti-imperialist, religious, or more explicitly political. And, as the Swedish experience well illustrates, the new revival of interest has a direct connection to the "new social movements" of the 1970s – especially the movements related to environmental and anti-nuclear activism and movements related to women's liberation.

Our aim in this chapter is to try to relate these recent developments to the theoretical and historical material presented in earlier chapters, by focusing on the interaction of popular music and social movements in one particular national context, Sweden. Besides being the country where we live, it is also a country in which many of the tensions and dilemmas of post-1960s political music were first played out most clearly and visibly. The Swedish progressive or non-commercial music movement, a network of companies, organizations, musicians, and activists which flourished in the 1970s, was fairly unique in its strength and longevity, and in its long-term impact on popular culture, compared to similar phenomena elsewhere (Wallis and Malm 1984). And it was also far ahead of its time in opening spaces for musical experimentation, and in reviving popular interest in folk music and in traditional musics from other parts of the world. As one journalist put it in 1981, "In retrospect, folk music appears to be the most important of all that happened in the seventies" (quoted in Kjellström, Ling, Mattsson, Ramsten, and Ternhage 1985: 179).

The Swedish music movement, as we see it, was a movement of mediation between the 1960s and the 1990s; on the one hand, it was a movement that appropriated the American experience into a different national culture and idiom, and, on the other, it was a movement through which Swedish traditions were mobilized, leading to the new wave of Swedish folk music in the 1990s, through which Swedish music enters into the ambiguous realm of "world music."

The Swedish movement brings out the work of translation that was so widespread to the decade that followed the 1960s: a translation of the American experience into other national cultures, but also a translation of the political message of the 1960s into different movements and political struggles. The Swedish case shows how the rediscovery of traditional folk music, or "roots" music, started to emerge as part of this process of international exchange, or transfer.

The Swedish music movement is a fascinating example of the relations between music and social movements. It represents an important mediating influence on Swedish popular culture, and continues to have an impact on Swedish society, as a source of inspiration and bad dreams. It also provides a good way to explore more general issues of politicizing music; in Sweden, the tensions between traditionalists and innovators, between commercial and anti-commercial and between folk and popular musics were all played out in public within an organized movement space. The results of the movement are equally visible: a wide-ranging folk music and folk-rock "movement" has become an important component of Swedish popular culture, while the active propagation of participatory ideals in music-making has led to an explosion of young, talented pop musicians, many of whom are doing quite well in the global marketplace. What has happened in Sweden, we suggest, thus has a more general relevance for countries where these issues have been taken up in much less organized and coherent form.

What was the Swedish music movement?

There were many elements in the Swedish music movement, and, now, in retrospect, there are a variety of possible interpretations of what was happening (Fornäs 1993). At the simplest level, there was a translation of Anglo-American rock music into a Swedish idiom. Rather than singing in English, or singing direct translations of English or American pop hits, many young Swedish musicians around 1970 started to transfer the meaning of American rock music into a Swedish context. And while this national appropriation process was taking place in every European country, in Sweden there was a somewhat stronger political element to this translation work, and a great deal more organizational activity: there were many who defined the making of Swedish rock music in political, i.e., "anti-imperialist" and especially non-commercial terms. There was also a broader range of musical genres and traditions that were applied to the task of appropriation than was the case in other countries. Most significantly, and uniquely, the Swedish music movement gave rise to an integrative cognitive praxis, through which a vision of a "non-commercial" music, with a do-it-yourself, participatory flavor, was given a coherent organizational and ideological structure. The movement was an important cultural force in Sweden through most of the 1970s; in its own journal, concerts, records, meeting places, and record companies, it carved out a public space that was, in many respects, more significant than those of the other "new social movements." As Leif Nylén put it at the time:

Of all attempts to create alternatives to the industries of capitalist culture, the Music Movement is probably the most surprising and the most successful. A politicized, socially critical musical culture has grown up in a few short years outside the framework provided by established culture. What's more, it has grown without any real ideological or organisational support from the socialist left. In an increasingly polarised culture, the Music Movement is so far relatively alone in having the characteristics of a sort of alternative mass popular movement and at the same time giving concrete examples of how radicals can make real inroads in mass culture.

(Nylén 1977: 120)

In the pages of the journal, *Musikens makt* (The Power of Music), which came out between 1973 and 1980, there was a continuous debate and analysis about the meanings of the music movement, and this debate was reflected in some of the songs and especially the broader cultural manifestations of the main activists in the movement. These included the alternative festival in 1975, held in opposition to the Eurovision song contest in Sweden (after ABBA had won the contest the year before), and the so-called "tent" project of 1977, taking a collective musical theater about the history of the Swedish labor movement around the country in a circus tent (Fornäs 1985).

The music movement was contemporaneous with the rise of environmental and anti-nuclear movements, as well as movements for women's liberation, and the relations between the different movements are interesting to consider. The women's and environmental movements are part of a process of specialization of social movement energies that set in after the 1960s (Eyerman and Jamison 1991). The use of music in these movements throughout the world – at demonstrations, festivals, and large collective manifestations – was reminiscent of the early sixties experience, and especially of the music of the civil rights movement; but the difference is that the environmental and women's movements have been more limited, specialized movements, and thus the music is more exclusionary than the inclusionary music of the early 1960s. Women's music and environmental music was not meant to be for everyone; the themes were not universal, but rather particularistic, emphasizing one set of issues or social problems over others. As such, these movements prefigure the ethnic and sexual identity movements of our day.

When the new social movements of feminism and environmentalism fragmented in the 1980s, splitting apart, in Sweden as elsewhere, into radical and reformist wings, the music was similar, affecting mainstream popular culture – with new genres of women's music and new age music emerging – as well as, on the more radical side, inspiring the new wave of post-punk participatory music movements that are to be found in most every industrialized country. The point, however, is that the new social movements in most countries were separate from each other, "specializing" politics, and their cultural impact or influence followed suit – leading to new specialized musics. In Sweden, where the emphasis was, more than in most countries, on the common musical denominator rather than on the specialized political campaign or set of issues, the "new social movements" could have a somewhat different and perhaps more substantial impact on popular culture.

In Sweden, however, there was an extraordinary emphasis on music in the movement activity of the 1970s, and, as we shall see, this was to be a source of strength for the music movement as well as an important cause of its rapid demise in the 1980s. The music movement tried to include all progressive causes, and this would lead to dissension and confusion for some, and to a dogmatic "political correctness" for others. Without a unifying program or cosmology broader than "anti-commercialism," the music movement could not survive its own problematic, commercial successes. The ambitious tent project was an expression of the movement's cognitive praxis as well as the beginning of the disintegration of the movement. Similarly, the commercial success of some of the records that were produced by the movement's record companies – particularly those of the Malmö group, Hoola Bandoola Band, and the Gothenburg rock band, Nationalteatern – led to a contradiction in terms, and an eventual breaking down of the barrier between the alternative movement space and the mainstream popular music industry. One result was a larger share of the music industry for "alternative" companies and groups, and a wider set of opportunities for less commercial music than in many other countries (Wallis and Malm 1984: 161–62).

The Swedish context

Much like the situation in the United States in the late 1950s, when the initial excitement of rock-and-roll had begun to wane and popular music showed signs of commercial and artistic stagnation, thus creating an opportunity for a politically charged folk music to win market shares and influence people, Swedish popular music in the late 1960s was also in a kind of stagnation. Record companies failed to see the possibility of producing an indigenous Swedish rock music. As in the 1950s in the United States, where "teeny-bopper" music dominated the airwaves, popular music in Sweden was dominated by dance band music and "schlagers," and both artistically and commercially lagged behind many other European countries. As Leif Nylén, one of the stalwarts of the progressive music movement, would later put it,

While foreign record companies put great efforts into the artistic expansion of pop music and the liberation of the entertainment industry from traditional values and functions (e.g. Beatles' "Sergeant Pepper," Dylan's "Blonde on Blonde," Jimi Hendrix) and utilized the emerging romantic-anarchistic underground culture as a kind of social and aesthetic laboratory (Jefferson Airplane, Frank Zappa, Velvet Underground, Pink Floyd, Incredible Stringband) – in Sweden the pop industry was simply cast aside. This left a sort of vacuum. There was no Swedish pop music which could claim to represent and put into focus the collective identity of Swedish youth. (Nylén 1977: 124)

In the words of Johan Fornäs, "the dependence upon imported popular music from the commercial music industry was overwhelming, and, while the domestic popular music was still dominated by older 'schlager' traditions, the young rock scene did not yet have any strong political edge, nor did it contain any influential and self-conscious public networks" (Fornäs 1993: 39–40). Unlike the situation in many other European countries, even in neighboring Denmark and Norway, there was a lack of vision and awareness on the part of the national music industry, which "created a space for the rise of self-organized alternative structures, and this space was quickly filled by a sudden flow of youth subcultures and progressive movements that experimented with new forms of political and musical expression" (ibid.: 40).

Nylén emphasizes, as well, that "a new collective identity, with common values, symbols, and ways of interacting was developing among the large groups of students and young people taking part in the Vietnam movement and in the struggles at the universities . . . What grew out of this was Swedish underground music which had a political definition from the start: it was socialist, or at least anti-imperialist, independent, and suspicious of commercial values and attempts at exploitation" (Nylén 1977: 124).

The movement started as one ingredient in the making of a counterculture, Swedish style. It was at Gärdet, a large open field in Stockholm, that a number of hippies and musicians gathered together for a happening-like festival in 1970, and, from then on, a coherent and self-conscious movement gradually took form. A number of formal and informal concerts and festivals were held – many of them modeling themselves on Woodstock and its countless imitators and rivals – and soon a record company was established to start to produce and market some of the results. There had already been some pop music in Swedish, but most of it had been highly imitative of the real (British/American) thing; indeed, in the late 1960s, the most marketable musicians were those who tried to resemble the Beatles or Elvis Presley most closely. Much of Swedish pop was sung in English, or directly translated from English. What eventually emerged as a Swedish progressive music movement was thus, first and foremost, an effort to produce a more meaningful kind of popular music, and the sources for the movement would be many and varied.

Not surprisingly, perhaps, the main influence was the rock music of the American counterculture – the folk-rock of Bob Dylan and the Byrds, the psychedelic rock of Jimi Hendrix, the rock-blues of Janis Joplin, the experimental rock of Frank Zappa, and the British variants thereof. In Sweden, these kinds of music fed into an alternative culture that was, intriguingly, highly and vocally anti-American. Almost all the progressive groups opposed the American involvement in Vietnam; many of the early festivals included antiwar speakers and activities ranging from book tables to agit prop theater. The music accompanied, as it were, the antiwar movement, which, in Sweden, was dominated by support groups for the National Liberation Front, many with an explicitly socialist or communist ideology – often even avowedly Maoist (Salomon 1996).

With its long tradition of neutrality and independence, opposition to the war and support for the Vietnamese were widespread in Sweden, in many ways more widespread than in other European countries. When Olof Palme, who had taken part in demonstrations against the war (marching on one occasion alongside the ambassador from North Vietnam) became prime minister in 1971, there was a freezing of diplomatic relations with the United States. Even though, or perhaps because, Palme like so many other Swedes had close personal ties to the United States, having spent some high school and college years on the road, he became a vocal opponent of the

American war. Many Swedes felt personally involved, almost personally attacked by the bombings of Hanoi and Haiphong. After all, almost a quarter of the population had emigrated in the nineteenth and early twentieth centuries to the United States, and the ties between the two countries had remained strong (Eyerman and Jamison 1992). Swedish academic life, policy doctrines, and general moral stance were all colored by American progressivism, and almost everyone had a relative or friend across the ocean. There was a complicated mixture of outrage, disappointment, and personal betrayal in Swedish anti-Americanism, and this had an impact on the appropriation of American rock music. It was both familiar and foreign at the same time, which would make it fairly easy for some Swedish groups, from ABBA to Ace of Base, to become extremely successful in the global music industry. But it would also make possible an alternative American-style music, a political pop, that would win a greater foothold in Sweden than in just about any other European country.

Partly because of this historical connection, Swedish culture was, and still is, extremely dominated by the United States as a powerful commercial and ideological influence, but also as an ever present danger to be avoided and criticized. The youthful ambitions to break free, and to revolt against the domineering parent, but also to moralize about American transgressions, were combined in the Swedish music movement. In a sense, American rock music was turned against itself; by adding elements from Swedish music traditions, and by taking ideological cues from the antiwar movement, the curious love–hate relation with the United States took on new life. What seemed to have died in the United States was thus reborn in Sweden as a progressive music movement.

Nowhere else in Europe was the diffusion of American rock music given such a political coloration as in Sweden, and nowhere else was a self-consciously progressive music organized as effectively as in Sweden. As in the British Isles, and especially in Ireland, where indigenous folk musics were brought into the mainstream pop culture in the 1970s, in Sweden, the progressive music movement helped bring about a renewed interest in folk music that is now an important force in "global culture." But in Sweden, there was a political component to this appropriation process that was fairly unique. There was a mobilization of tradition, and traditional musical forms, within the context of an avowedly political movement. Even though the most commercially successful groups played a more mainstream popular rock music, the movement provided opportunities for musical experimentation and the rediscovery of traditional forms of Swedish folk music. While the political songs of the 1970s now seem anachronistic, Swedish folk music continues to grow. While the music movement largely failed in its efforts to contribute to political change, it played an important role, largely unintended, in the making of a new Swedish folk music.

The sources of the movement

In the 1960s, Jan Johansson, one of Sweden's most influential jazz musicians, recorded versions of Swedish folk tunes before he tragically died in an automobile crash. The jazzy, humorous renditions of traditional music became quite popular, and certainly led a good number of urban youth to the real thing – the traditional fiddle festivals that every summer were held in the Swedish countryside. Folk dancing and traditional fiddle music had a distinctly conservative, oldtime meaning to most of the makers of the Swedish model welfare state in the postwar era. But for the alienated young people, who had grown up in their little boxes in model suburbs, folk music and rural traditions in general represented something authentic, something that was in danger of being lost. Johansson helped give folk tunes a kind of musical legitimacy, and the music movement, with its critical attitude to commercial, American music, opened the way for a more direct, first-hand experience. It was at progressive music festivals that many young Swedes heard their first country fiddling; and, for many, that experience would only be the beginning.

Other kinds of folk music also came to be "reinvented" within the context of the progressive music movement. Like Johansson with the instrumental music, a bearded immigrant from the Netherlands, Cornelis Vreeswijk, had already, in the early 1960s, started to breathe new life into the Swedish ballad, or visa, tradition. In the eighteenth century, Carl Michael Bellman in Stockholm had written hundreds of songs about wine, women, and the emerging bourgeois order, and, accompanying himself on the guitar, he succeeded in inventing a musical genre that mixed poetry and music in a distinctively Swedish way. The main twentieth-century figure in the development of the genre was probably Evert Taube, who, in his youth, had traveled the world and written hundreds of songs about his travels and his amorous conquests. It was perhaps an indirect influence from the tradition that had affected the young Joel Hägglund before he emigrated to the United States and became Joe Hill; in Sweden, however, the songs that were sung were primarily romantic and nationalistic, songs of summer and flowers and love. The labor movement had its own songs, which were far from the sentimental pathos of the visa. Rather, they glorified the diligence of the worker and the importance of his organizations. In Sweden, many labor songs were directly taken over, and translated to Swedish from the larger European countries (e.g., the French "Internationale" and the Italian "Red Flag"). The distinctively Swedish working songs were those of the lumber camps in the north or the railway construction workers. The unions themselves contributed little in the way of musical innovation, and whatever there was sought to break explicitly with the traditions of the past.

Only a few singing poets had brought the life of work and hard times into the folk song tradition in the twentieth century, and the one who had done it most successfully, Dan Andersson, had been a loner, a drinker, and a rather unpolitical sort. Unlike the situation in the United States, where a topical folk song tradition was constructed as part of the political movements of the 1930s, traditional musics did not enter into the "middle way" of Swedish social democracy, which favored instead the marches and songs of struggle that were imported from Germany and Italy. Andersson's songs, which told the stories of outcasts and rural workers, came the closest to mobilizing the visa tradition for the cause of social democracy, but, until their rediscovery by the progressive music movement in the 1970s, their message was not considered sufficiently progressive for Swedish socialists to take to heart.

Vreeswijk brought his own troubled, and complicated, personality into the visa tradition; but he also brought something of the spirit of the sixties – of revolt and alienation – into what by then had primarily become a conservative and rather marginal musical genre. His music was inspired by American folksingers (Woody Guthrie, Leadbelly, Pete Seeger, Bob Dylan), and one of his early hits was a Swedish version of Ed McCurdy's "Last Night I Had the Strangest Dream." There were other newcomers to the folk song tradition in the 1960s, as well: Fred Åkerström, who combined socialist songs with Bellman; Alf Hambe, who brought an early environmental consciousness into his song poems; and a number of younger, urban singers, inspired as much by Bob Dylan as by Evert Taube. Many of them would be activists in the progressive music movement, and the organization of the troubadours would be a kind of musicians' labor movement and record producer, in alliance with the political rock groups. Jan Hammarlund, who continues to write and sing topical folk songs, was particularly influenced by the songs of Malvina Reynolds, whom he brought to Sweden, where she recorded a collection of songs for one of the progressive labels.

It was in the cities that the progressive music movement would have its strength, and its most popular groups. But while Stockholm, the commercial and cultural capital, would provide much of the support, both in terms of media propagation, record production, and distribution, and in terms of publicity and commercial opportunities, it was the second and third cities of Gothenburg and Malmö which would be the main bastions of musical creativity and innovation. Malmö – close to Copenhagen and the Continent, as well as to the university town of Lund – would offer intellectual pop songs from a number of different groups, while Gothenburg would offer a harder, working-class political rock, more extreme in its radicalism and harder in its rock rhythms. Stockholm contributed the eclectic Gunder Hägg (Blå tåget), a collection of artists and poets who banded together to write some of the sharpest lyrics that have ever entered into Swedish popular music. Leif Nylén and Torkel Rasmussen, both now cultural critics for a Stockholm newspaper, brought something of the beat consciousness, as well as components of the Swedish literary tradition, into the progressive music movement. With an infectious musical amateurism, Blå tåget mixed styles that ranged from the European avant-garde to Swedish and American folk music, and their songs were filled with biting commentaries on the issues of the day, and whimsical, philosophical reflections on the meaning of life. Reinventing the poetic legacy of Almqvist and Strindberg, Blå tåget sang of the decline of the welfare state, the tristesse of Swedish urban and suburban life, and, of course, the American war in Vietnam – all formulated in a radical socialist rhetoric that placed their songs in the center of the progressive music movement's cosmology. Their most famous refrain, accusing the capitalists and the social democratic government of sitting side by side in the same boat, would become an anarchist slogan when it was recorded ten years later by a punk band. And their songs would be listened to and analyzed with some of the same literary attention that Bob Dylan's early texts had attracted:

> Side by side, they help each other out
> The state and the capitalists, they sit in the same boat
> But it's not them who row the boat,
> Who row so that sweat starts dripping
> And the whip that cracks over the rowers' necks,
> It's not their necks it's whipping.

From the smaller towns, and from the countryside, folkier musics would emerge, bringing the sounds of traditional fiddles and other folk instruments into popular music, and linking, however tenuously, the concerns of the urban-based progressive music movement with the very different concerns of rural Sweden. In retrospect, one of the movement's main failures was its inability to resolve the urban–rural tension; the rock dogmatism of the urban Left literally overpowered and drove away the softer, folkier rural music. In commenting on the new folk music wave in 1979, Jan Ling, the country's leading folk musicologist, noted that a left-wing ideology had encapsulated the folk music "vogue" – in much the same way that folk music in the 1930s had been appropriated by right-wing, nationalist movements. He characterized the revival of folk music, under left-wing "music movement" auspices, as a real contribution to Swedish musical life, but also as a limited kind of appreciation:

> In their search for an alternative to the music of international commercialism and upper-class art music, some of these young people began to turn their interest toward folk music . . . The reaction against the establishment included a form of "antiprofessionalism" which led some to go so far as to refuse to tune their guitars, so as to sound as amateur and "folky" as possible. Such reactions to the art music of the concert platform and to the music of international entertainment led people to seek music with *proletarian* roots. This resulted not only in a fertile production of new music, which was of profound importance to Swedish music in general, but also to short-lived deformations in which musical creativity was restricted by the decrees of ideology.
>
> (Ling in Rönström and Ternhage 1994; quoted from Kjellström et al. 1985: 179)

The breadth and relative commercial success of Swedish folk music and folk-rock in the 1990s are, in part, a belated recognition of folk instruments and sounds by urban rock musicians. Several of the most influential folk musicians today were active in the music movement of the 1970s, and record on the non-commercial companies that were created at that time. Many of the political ambitions of the 1970s remain alive, as well, in Swedish folk music, particularly the international solidarity, and the identification with the poor. The orientation toward the past – to remember the rural peasantry's way of life – is often politically motivated, and the widespread use of folk music in theater and film seems to draw at least some inspiration from the experiences of the 1970s, and especially the tent project of 1977 (Fornäs 1985). Several participants in the tent project went on to work with theater groups in smaller towns, as well as "digging up" musical history and reviving long-lost folk instruments, like the bagpipe and the bouzouki.

In July 1996, the two most popular groups in the progressive music movement reunited to serve as warmup bands for – who else? – Bob Dylan when he performed in Malmö. Malmö's Hoola Bandoola Band had been the first commercially successful progressive group in the 1970s; and its two leaders, Mikael Wiehe and Björn Afzelius, had both gone on to have long-lived careers as singer-songwriters. Wiehe translated many of Dylan's early songs into Swedish, and he has written several classic progressive songs. His first big hit with Hoola Bandoola – "Vem kan man lita på?" (Who can you depend on?) – had been a kind of anthem for the progressive music movement, satirizing the sell-out of John Lennon ("who has gone into psychoanalysis") and Bob Dylan ("who is in the country counting his millions") as well as many other cultural heroes.

Wiehe wrote songs about the slaves who built the pyramids of ancient Egypt (which, in 1996, he dedicated to the European Union, "our contemporary pyramid"), about the CIA, about the sinking of the Titanic, about freedom of expression, and about fighting and struggling for justice. He later formed several bands, many with folk artists like Ale Möller, who would become a major contributor to the new folk music "revival" of the 1990s, and he, like Afzelius, has continued to speak out on public issues and take part in benefits and support concerts for a wide variety of progressive causes. One of his best songs with Hoola Bandoola, a eulogy over the Chilean folksinger, Victor Jara, well expressed the international solidarity, but also the broader political ideals, of the progressive music movement:

> There are many who do tricks
>   for those who hold onto power.
> And there are many who grovel for crumbs
>   at the tables of the rich.
> But you made your choice, to sing for the many.
> And you laughed at the promises
>   and threats of those who rule.
> Yes, Victor Jara you gave voice
>   to the prisoner's longing for freedom
> and for those who believed in a future
>   with only people in power.
> And you gave strength and courage
>   to the trampled-upon's dreaming.
> But for the rich and the few
>   you sang out your disgust.

Björn Afzelius' love song to freedom ("You are the prettiest [thing] I know, You are the prettiest in the world") became a pop staple in Sweden, a melodic pop tune with a message. Reuniting the Hoola Bandoola Band that had split up in 1976 was thus more nostalgic than meaningful; it was a way to return to their youth, but it was also meant to rekindle some of the politics of the 1970s, the anti-imperialism that had been so central to the anti-war and progressive music movements. Most of the members of Nationalteatern, the other "prog" group that reunited in 1996, had not been as successful as Wiehe and Afzelius. Thorstein (Totte) Näslund had become a blues singer, while Ulf Dageby had continued to write music for films and theater as well as for other pop singers. But the group's hard-nosed politics had gone out of fashion; in the 1970s, they had sung of the problems of the working class and they had fashioned an aggressive rock music that formed

the dominant tone of the progressive music movement in Gothenburg. Nationalteatern's songs, like so much of the Swedish antiwar movement, after the war had ended in 1975, were more of the Old than of the New Left. The tent project that many of the progressive music and theater groups produced in 1977, a huge collaborative effort that told, in rock music form, the history of the Swedish labor movement, underlines the strengths but also the weaknesses of the kind of progressive music that Nationalteatern sang. On the one hand, the songs were extremely powerful and suggestive, but, like the finger-pointing songs that Bob Dylan rejected in the mid-1960s, they were far too ideologically direct to appeal to a mass audience. And they were overly serious, forgetting the humor, the satire, and irony that are so essential for making political songs work. Even before the tent project, Leif Nylén could see that the amateurism and fantasy – and not least the eclectic musical experimentation – that had characterized the movement in its early years had been replaced by a more streamlined political rock, filled more with slogans than real political content:

We've reached a situation when the typical progressive record consists of competent but anonymous rock with elements of blues and reggae, containing one song about women's oppression, one about nuclear energy, one on commercial pop garbage, and one on the new suburban ghettos . . . Meanwhile developments within the movement are toward a greater division of labor and specialisation. A relatively few musicians have become professional and tour around the country to the music forums – whose activists see their role reduced to the distribution of progressive show packages. The combination of different functions which was so typical in the movement's early years – when musicians were also arrangers, administrators, political activists – that combination is splitting apart. It's not only that we have a musical elite but also the media structure, record companies, etc. are isolating themselves and losing touch with the movement's base.   (Nylén 1977: 127–28)

Nylén hoped that the tent project would revitalize the movement. As it turned out, the result was a further professionalization of a progressive music elite, many of whom, a few years later, would occupy leading positions in Swedish cultural life. Indeed, there would be a kind of revolt against "prog" music from punk bands, which flowered in Sweden in the early 1980s and tried to bring rock music back to its simpler, and more proletarian roots. As with so many movements before and since, the Swedish progressive music movement by becoming successful and an influential contributor to popular culture, lost its *raison d'être* and ceased to be a movement (Fornäs 1993). By 1980, the forums had become concert halls, the record companies had become commercial, and the internal cohesion of the movement, and, with it, the magazine that had served to define the movement, had disappeared. New movements would spring up, but none with the unique combination of musical experimentation and political involvement that had characterized the progressive music movement in the early 1970s.

The demise of the movement

The very success of Nationalteatern, Hoola Bandoola, and some of the other progressive and near-progressive rock bands helped to signal the demise of the progressive music movement. If aggressive rock in Swedish could sell, then it could sell even more if it was produced more professionally and marketed more effectively. But that, of course, would inevitably mean that the message would have to be watered down. If the movement was primarily a movement for participation, for making your own music, as most of its spokesmen described it, then a group that was professional and commercially successful was a kind of contradiction in terms. A group like Nationalteatern required discipline and professionalism; if Näslund, for instance, was to develop as a musician, the political packaging would soon become a burden rather than an inspiration. And if other groups were to have an impact on the popular culture, they would also have to get their act together and not just mouth political slogans. So while the progressive music movement opened up a space in the popular culture for integrating politics and music, that space proved to be temporary.

The organizational dimension – making and distributing records, arranging concerts, performing for free, linking quality to equality, prioritizing participation – simply could not survive commercial success. In the 1980s, progressive rock and innovative folk-rock came to have a major impact on the music industry, paving the way for the international success of groups like Roxette and Nordman, but the politics and the music came to be separated once again. Roxette and Ace of Base are products of the widespread pop music culture in Sweden, the garage music-making that is, in part, a result of the participatory principles of the progressive music movement, and, for that matter, of rock music in general. Nordman and Hedningarna, on the other hand, build on the mobilization of traditional sounds and instruments that formed part of the progressive music movement's search for alternative music. In both cases, however, commercial success has been won, at least in part, at the cost of a political cosmology. The meaning of the songs is once again meaningless, and the promise of an emergent culture, an alternative, non-commercial culture, has not been fulfilled. It lives on in the fringes of Swedish society, perhaps most visibly among the new immigrant communities for whom folk music remains an important source of collective identity in an increasingly hostile and difficult foreign environment.

As such, the cognitive praxis of the progressive music movement has become fragmented as the remnants and memory of the movement have become incorporated into the established political culture. Participation – the main element of the progressive music movement's organizational dimension – has lived on in the punk and neo-punk culture of the cities and their suburbs; garage bands are everywhere in Sweden, and they are often supported by public funds and institutions as a legacy to the struggles that were waged in the 1970s. The progressive music movement, in town after town, fought for meeting places for young people, forums for music-making, and opportunities for practicing, recording, and performing. Much of that struggle was won in the distinctively Swedish spirit of compromise; the movement activists gained public support at the expense of autonomy and control over their own locales. Now, Sweden's music forums – its festivals, rock concerts, and record companies – are commercial and non-political, but they are widespread, and that is due, in large part, to the progressive music movement. The movement carved out a space in the Swedish popular culture for the new musics that young people themselves wanted to make.

The cosmological dimension of the progressive music movement's cognitive praxis has meanwhile wandered along different paths. Much of it lost its vitality already in the late 1970s in the ideological disputes between different Marxist sects, and between adherents of the different "new social movements," in the quest for ideological purity that affected the New Left in Sweden as much as elsewhere. Some of the ideas of the Swedish progressive music movement continue to inform Swedish politics, particularly the ideas of feminism and environmentalism, which also found a good deal of their singing voice, for the first time, within the music movement. Many were the women's song groups and environmental troubadours who performed at the festivals of the music movement of the 1970s, and, if environmentalism and feminism never came to dominate the music movement's cognitive praxis, they were nevertheless an important part of the eclectic mixture.

The few environmental songs that were most successful were those that replicated the songs of earlier social movements. In Sweden, a particularly good example is the translation of "We Shall Not Be Moved" that was sung at many anti-nuclear demonstrations and became for several years a kind of theme song for the anti-nuclear movement. It was a song of collective identity that sang well in Swedish, exchanging the phrase "we shall not be moved" for a Swedish phrase that literally meant "we shall never give up." It was not a song about nuclear energy as much as it was a song about an anti-nuclear movement, and it thus managed to do what so few environmental songs have attempted to do, provide a sense of solidarity for activists. The song, however, was too old-fashioned for the arbiters of musical taste in the progressive record companies. Its author, Roland von Malmborg, says that, when the anti-nuclear movement intensified in 1979 with the people's referendum campaign, he tried to get his song included on two anti-nuclear records that the progressive music movement's record companies were preparing. Malmborg, who remains a movement artist, and has sung his songs at all of the congresses of the Swedish Green Party since its founding in 1981, was rejected in favor of a number of highly commercial artists, whose songs evoked little of the collective spirit and identity that his song conjured up.

In the ensuing years, environmentalist music has largely moved out to the country where it has taken on a number of manifestations: as "new age" music, as country music, as traditional music, while the music of the women's movement has inspired, in Sweden as elsewhere, a number of women singer-songwriters, who have brought their personal politics into the world of popular music. As feminism parted company with socialism, many of the women's singers have also left a movement space behind them, but the meaning of their songs often draws on the more explicit struggle for liberation that was originally expressed in women's song groups.

The technical dimension of the progressive music movement's cognitive praxis has changed fundamentally. In the 1970s, the interest in folk music and technical musical competence was certainly a part of what the progressive music movement stood for; but the world of folk music and even of folk song was never really integrated into the music movement. It was primarily a pop music movement, its main activists playing the typical rock instruments rather than experimenting with music itself. And this was one of its main limitations. In its American dominance, the progressive music movement did not open itself sufficiently to the indigenous musical traditions in Sweden or the rest of Scandinavia. The movement apparently became a barrier for many who grew interested in folk music in the 1970s, forcing the musicians to be "politically correct," censoring their experimentation, channeling the folk music interest into ideologically superimposed categories. In the 1990s, many Swedish musicians have come to take part in world music, and the folk festival in Falun is one of the major events on the European folk music calendar.

It was, however, not so much because of, but in spite of, the progressive music movement that folk music has had such a renaissance in Sweden.

Partly because of its ideological purism, its endless debates about what the "movement" was all about, the short-lived journal could not play a major role in stimulating folk music, in mobilizing tradition. The doctrinal lines were drawn too strictly in a "socialist" direction; and many musics were simply excluded from interest. Chilean folk musicians and Russian balalaikas were acceptable, but most rural folk dancing and Swedish fiddle music were more questionable, due to their connection to a feudal, even imperial past. It was not so much that folk music was forbidden for the progressive musician – indeed, several musicians active today in folk music played in progressive groups – it was rather that the movement did not encourage and give priority to learning and teaching the kind of artisanal skill that folk music embodies. The technical dimension of the progressive music movement's cognitive praxis was largely imitative rather than innovative, a transfer of British and American rock music techniques rather than an original mixing of various musical competences. The multiple legacies of the progressive music movement thus became separated. While they have influenced the Swedish popular culture, that influence is fragmented and differentiated, and probably less than it would have been if the movement had been somewhat less doctrinaire and more open. But then it probably would not have happened.

Conclusions

A major problem that all social movements face in their relations with music and other forms of cultural expression is being flexible. Artistic creation in general, and songwriting in particular, can be inspired by the concerns of social movements, but songs have, as it were, a logic of their own, a kind of poetic logic or rationality that cannot be mandated or imposed. To be successful, songs have to work in their own musical terms; the rhythm, melody, structure, and words must all make separate sense and function within particular kinds of acceptable forms. And there should be, as well, a personal, human touch to fuse the different ingredients into a coherent whole. If the song is driven too much by an external, social doctrine or idea, then it can easily fail as a song. In many ways, the demise of the Swedish progressive music movement corresponded to a death of the New Left itself; in the late 1970s, the dogmatic Marxist sects and revolutionary groups fell into arguing with themselves, and leftist terrorism emerged in several countries, helping to bring on a politically conservative backlash, as was the case in the United States as well. The progressive musicians became extremist, on the one hand often giving up music-making altogether in favor of anarchistic, often violent manifestations, or on the other joining in the conservative backlash, choosing a mainstream musical career over politics.

The remarkable thing is that, for a few years, the political environment could provide an opportunity for a movement to emerge around political pop music. Nowhere else in Europe was there an explicit progressive music movement, a movement that appropriated rock music into the popular culture in an avowedly political way. That there would be limitations and problems with such an effort goes without saying. That there could be such a movement in the first place is probably due to the special kind of relationship between Sweden and the United States, and the rather unique position as a social laboratory – a pilot plant for the world – that Sweden occupied through much of the 1960s and 1970s. For many of the same reasons that Swedish environmentalism could play such a significant international role in the early 1970s, the progressive music movement could emerge only in Sweden. Independence, neutrality, affluence, and international consciousness could combine for a brief period of time. In the 1990s, Sweden has lost most of those qualities; and the progressive music movement lives on as a remembrance of things past, but also as a source of so much of the sounds of the contemporary culture. The week-long festivals that now light up the rather drab city life, and the rich array of music that is to be found throughout the country, are unimaginable without the progressive music movement. It is a memory of better times, when Sweden, through its prosperity and its independence, could exert some moral influence on the world.

7

Structures of feeling and cognitive praxis

Structures of feeling and cultural transformation

We have discussed social movements in this book as articulators and transformers of culture. As forms of collective action emerging in social and historical contexts, social movements presuppose and make use of preexisting forms of social solidarity and communication: culture, that is, at its most basic. In the process, they draw upon and revitalize traditions at the same time as they transform them. As cultural as well as political actors, social movements reinterpret established and shared frameworks of meaning which make communication and coordinated action possible. This "common culture" comprises many levels and dimensions and takes on many specific forms, which can be broadly specified as national, regional, religious, class- and age-related, ethnic, and ideological. In this book, we have sought to show how common cultures change through the catalytic intervention of social movements.

Social movements also open spaces in which particular movement cultures – rituals, traditions, forms of artistic expression – can emerge. While such cultures are related to and dependent upon the deeper social structures from which they emerge, they are also capable of producing something new and different. Social movements produce innovative forms of understanding – what we have called exemplary action – which impact upon and are capable of transforming wider, established cultures. Even if such transformation is minimal or indirect, in the case of short-lived or violently repressed movements – or movements, like that of the 1960s, that have inspired waves of reaction and counter-movement – social movements can help to reinvent and reproduce traditions of protest and rebellion, "alternative" cultures, which live on in the collective memory and which may influence and affect the emergence of future social movements. We have used music and musical traditions to illustrate these processes. Our discussions of African-American and American folk musics, as well as the Swedish progressive music movement, were meant to illustrate how social movements have influenced and developed distinct musical genres and how music and movements together have affected the wider popular culture.

The kinds of cultural processes that we have been exploring resemble what Raymond Williams termed "structures of feeling" (see Simpson 1992). Our argument has been that those structures of feeling are more than merely emotive – that they contain a rational or logical core, a truth-bearing significance, as well. The construction of meaning through music and song is, we claim, a central aspect of collective identity formation, and our examples have been meant to illustrate and exemplify how collective structures of feeling are actually made and reorganized, in part, through song. The structures of feeling that Williams talked about are difficult to grasp by reading individual literary texts or analyzing individual artistic creations. Rather, we would contend that they can be read more easily through the songs that are sung in movements, that songs and music give us access to both feelings and thoughts that are shared by larger collectivities and that make better claim, perhaps, for cultural representativity. Structures of feeling, like emergent cultural formations, need to be conceptualized in relation to real social actors.

There is another side to our argument that is even more important. Not only are songs significant and largely untapped resources for the academic observer; they are also channels of communication for activists – within movements, but also between different movements, and, indeed, between movement generations. Music enters into what we have called the collective memory, and songs can conjure up long-lost movements from extinction as well as reawakening forgotten structures of feeling. In this respect, the songs of social movements affect the dynamics of cultural transformations, the historical relations between dominant, residual, and emergent cultural formations.

Tradition, the past in the present, is vital to our understanding and inter-pretation of who we are and what we are meant to do. As such, it is a pow-erful source of inspiration for social movements and emergent cultural formations. These include most obviously traditions of protest and rebel-lion, but also, more subtly, forms of living and underlying sensibilities, which are at a remove from those currently available, but which still exist in the residues and margins of society. Such structures of feeling can be embodied and preserved in and through music, which is partly why music is such a powerful force in social movements and in social life generally. Music in a sense *is* a structure of feeling. It creates mood – bringing it all back home, as Dylan once said – and in this way can communicate a feeling of common purpose, even amongst actors who have no previous historical connections with one another. While such a sense may be fleeting and situational, it can be recorded and reproduced, and enter into memory, individual as well as collective, to such an extent that it can be recalled or remembered at other times and places. In such a fashion, music can recall not only the shared situationally bound experiences, but also a more general commitment to common cause and to collective action. For the musician or songwriter as "movement intellectual," the spirit of his or her work can live on even when they're gone, to paraphrase an old Phil Ochs song.

In its broadest and deepest sense, culture is about meaning and identity, aspects of human life which are not instrumental, but basic and fundamental. In our understanding, social movements help articulate meaning and identity, and engender strong emotional commitment, even if they are also instrumental and strategic. Within social movements actors reinterpret their relation to the world and to others in it. They experiment with identities, individual and collective, by restating them in conscious ways, as authentic and/or traditional, for instance. By singing together at the lunch counter in Mississippi, "We shall not be moved," civil rights activists became moral witnesses, practitioners of civil disobedience. As such, they altered their identities through exemplary action. To ignore this or to see it as of secondary importance to the more strategic aspects of social movement activity is to trivialize social movements, and the motivations and understandings of activists, as well as to define far too narrowly the boundaries of culture and of collective identity. Those who would reduce social movements to instrumental actors engaged in power struggles on a battlefield called a "political opportunity structure" have made an ontological choice. They have chosen to see the world in terms of structures and processes which exist outside the meanings actors themselves attach to them. For them the world consists of causal connections between dependent and independent variables, not the struggles of real human beings meaningfully engaged in constructing their world in conflict and cooperation with others. Culture from this instrumentalist perspective must be "operationalized" as a dependent variable, as a weapon in strategic battle, which can be taken on and discarded more or less at will. In this book, we have clearly made another ontological choice, namely to view culture as the independent variable, as the seedbed of social change, supplying actors with the sources of meaning and identity out of which they collectively construct social action and interaction. In social movements, new collective meanings are consciously made and remade by creatively working with these cultural materials: this is what we have called the mobilization of tradition.

In a narrower but no less emotionally powerful sense, culture can be understood as symbolic representation and expression. Here music and art generally come into the picture as cultural expressions which represent the past in the present. We have attempted to illustrate the role social movements play in this process of tradition-making and -transforming, as well as acknowledging the more instrumental and strategic functions of art and music to social movement mobilization. Further, we have suggested ways in which the musical traditions reinterpreted within social movements have spread into and transformed the wider culture, in both the broad and the narrow understandings of the term. The musical traditions reinterpreted through social movements have helped transform popular music in the United States, as they have affected the way Americans, and others, understand themselves and their society. In making this clear we have reinstated the ancient understanding of music, and art generally, as truth-bearing cognitive forces. We have unified the two generally accepted notions of culture, as a way of life and as representation and record of that way of life in symbolic form as art. At the same time, we have brought together the two sites or repositories that have divided sociological discussions of culture: the subjective and the objective. Music as experienced and performed within social movements is at once subjective and objective, individual and collective in its forms and in its effects. Through its ritualized performance and through the memories it invokes, the music of social movements transcends the boundaries of the self and binds the individual to a collective consciousness. This is what we have identified as the "truth-bearing" message, or the rationality, of movement music, where individual and collective identity fuse and where past and future are reconnected to the present in a meaningful way.

In schematic terms our approach to social movements and culture can be thought of along lines suggested by Raymond Williams (1977). Williams spoke of culture as a formation composed of three interrelated yet distinct segments, which he labeled dominant, emergent, and residual. In our application of this model, the residual can be specified as traditions and ways of life marginal to or excluded from the mainstream society. African-American culture for a great part of its history can be considered a residual culture, which at various points in time became an alternative that could be chosen, a resource for creating an oppositional identity. Social movements, understood in cognitive terms, are constitutive of the emergent elements of culture, as Williams understood them:

by "emergent" I mean, first, that new meanings and values, new practices, new relationships and kinds of relationship are continually being created. But it is excep-
tionally difficult to distinguish those which are really elements of some new phase
of the dominant culture ... and those which are substantially alternative or oppositional to it: emergent in the strict sense, rather than merely novel. Since we are
always considering relations within a cultural process, definitions of the emergent,
as of the residual, can be made only in relation to a full sense of the dominant.

(Williams 1977: 123)

In our adaptation of Williams' model, social movements are potential sites
of emergent cultural formations. They provide spaces where aspects of
residual subcultures can be transformed into forces for social and cultural
transformation. Social movements mediate between the marginal and the
mainstream by solidifying and politicizing alternative traditions and direct-
ing them against the dominant historical blocs.

We are not the first to notice the fruitfulness of Williams' conceptualization of culture, especially when it is coupled to the ideas of Antonio
Gramsci: in particular, his concepts of hegemony, organic intellectuals, and
historical blocs (see Denning 1996). What is missing in many of these
applications, however, and what we have stressed in this book, is a sociological concern with the actions of contextually bound agents, with what we
have termed movement intellectuals and movement artists. It is here that
biography meets history. As has been the case in our previous works
(Jamison and Eyerman 1994, Eyerman 1994), the life stories of key actors
in the transformation of tradition – James Weldon Johnson, Langston
Hughes, Zora Neale Hurston, Pete Seeger, Woody Guthrie, Bob Dylan,
Phil Ochs, Janis Joplin, and Jimi Hendrix, to name a few – are central to
our approach to sociological analysis. It is through such individuals, in their
role and place as movement intellectuals, that culture and politics are creatively combined to produce social change. Social movements are the contexts, not merely the vehicles, of such change. It is within movement space
that artists, singers, and songwriters uncover a new dimension to their work
as they discover a new identity for themselves and for their art. In and
through their role as activist-artist or activist-performer such individuals
help constitute the cognitive praxis of social movements and at one and the
same time revitalize and revise tradition, creating the possibility of transforming the wider, dominant culture.

Through their exemplary actions, as movement artists and intellectuals,
they express the meaning of the movements. In another interpretation of
Raymond Williams' conception of the dynamics of culture formation one
can visualize this constructive role of the movement artist or intellectual
along three lines of tension and contention. The residual or alternative

tradition would be the bohemian, in which the artist lives out a subcultural existence, based on the principle that art is life, an end in itself. The artist rejects any involvement in politics as an intrusion and distortion of aesthetic practice. The dominant culture – the commercial, professional, or state, depending on the historical context – imposes the external standards, material conditions, and aesthetic criteria for artistic expression. The social movement, on the other hand, provides opportunities for artists to experiment and innovate and alter those standards and criteria, a context in which the artist can become a political as well as a cultural agent, and thus help shape an emergent cultural formation.

A few examples will perhaps suffice here. In the context opened by the New Negro movement, James Weldon Johnson, Paul Robeson, and Langston Hughes, each in their own way and in distinct artistic genres, explored the boundaries between culture and politics. The southern-born Johnson, journalist, high school principal, lawyer, came to Harlem to compose a new form of popular music which combined aspects of Tin Pan Alley, the concert hall, spirituals, and rural blues (Johnson [1933] 1990). Together with his brother Rosamond, he composed what has been called the Negro national anthem, "Lift Every Voice and Sing," and was, for many years, also secretary of the NAACP. Paul Robeson, an All-American football player at college, was instrumental in moving the spiritual from the church to the concert stage. While his political consciousness developed later in his life, Robeson was on the periphery of the Harlem Renaissance, but shared its central aim of redefining the cultural identity of the African-American. A member of the movement's inner core, Langston Hughes combined literary and oral traditions as he brought blues mood and rhythm into his poetry and novels. While his outspoken political awareness developed later, in the 1930s popular front, his early literary works were consciously driven by the desire to redefine the understanding and place of the African-American in American culture and society. Along with the performances of Robeson and the compositions of Johnson, Hughes' poetry and novels serve as exemplars of the New Negro movement. They objectified and expressed the visions and the meaning of that movement. As cultural artefacts, these texts make that meaning available to future others.

The Seeger family played a variety of roles in relation to American folk music. Charles and Ruth, the older generation, gave legitimacy to the songs of the people – and, for Ruth, the musical challenge of transcribing folk songs led to cultural innovations that fall between the highbrow and the lowbrow and have often been neglected as a result (Tick 1995). Pete and his younger siblings Mike and Peggy acted as midwives to the folk revival, and,

as Pete would carry the spirit of the sixties into the environmental movement of the seventies, Peggy would be one of the key contributors to a
music of women's liberation. In another kind of movement, Janis Joplin
and Jimi Hendrix helped launch the identity movements of our time, by
mixing traditions in newfangled combinations, appropriating the blues to
new historical contexts, and living their musical messages in their all-too-
short lives.

The use of punk songs in television commercials can serve as a kind of
counterexample. While it is true that punk can in some sense be thought of
as an alternative or countercultural movement, punk music was from the
very beginning commercial and the punk "style" began as a fashion which
could be bought and tried on. This is quite different from the social and
political space opened up by social movements of the 1960s. While there
were definitely "stylistic" aspects here as well, from Robert Moses' bib-
overalls to Dylan's hobo attire, the level of commitment and the motivation
are qualitatively different between these movements. That said, it is not
impossible to imagine a Dylan song being used to sell a commercial
product, even a topical song like "Blowin' In The Wind." It is much more
difficult, however, to imagine the same for "Only A Pawn in Their Game"
or "The Lonesome Death of Hattie Carroll," two of his "finger-pointing"
songs, as he described them. The difference lies in the unambiguous nature
of the lyrics and the forcefulness of their presentation. They are clearly
political songs, with an obvious message. One can choose perhaps to understand and accept that message or not, but it would be difficult to deny its
clarity. "Blowin' in the Wind," on the other hand, is a catchy tune with very
ambiguous lyrics, especially in the refrain. What is it exactly that is blowing
in the wind?

Dimensions of cognitive praxis

In earlier work we have explored the cognitive praxis of social movements
along three dimensions, the cosmological, the technical, and the organizational. The cosmological dimension is expressed through what we have
called the utopian messages that social movements stand for. In the 1920s
and 1930s, the cosmology revolved around the image of the people, brought
over from the populist movements of the nineteenth century. There was a
battle in the interwar years over what might be termed the vocabulary of
modernity. On the one hand, the communists, under the inspiration of the
Bolshevik Revolution, adopted an idiom of "laboring" (Denning 1996). It
was the worker, the working class, that came to symbolize the future: the
utopian vision was of a laboring collective, supplanting the bosses, the

capitalists, the ruling class, as the hegemonic definers of cultural meaning. The competing image of the people or the masses had vaguer but also more inclusive connotations. In the poetry of Carl Sandburg and the song lyrics of Woody Guthrie – and, in our day, Bruce Springsteen – the people are given historical agency. The people are an abstraction, but what, asks Sandburg, would you put in their place? In the songs of social movements, concepts are humanized and made less abstract, but there are visions of a better day, of a different world, of a not-yet-existent reality, be it a big rock candy mountain or that hour when the ship comes in. This utopian aspect expresses in symbolic form what a movement stands for, what it is that is to be overcome or transcended. The ideals and the meaning of the movement are thus embodied in the cultural artefacts like songs, capable of being communicated and experienced well beyond their immediate performance and reception.

The utopian and transcendent themes of a movement's cognitive praxis are expressed as exemplary action. In our examples, this was mostly presented in the messages contained and embodied in movement music. The message is one of transcendence through common struggle, of possibility, hope, and change. Yet, as we hope to have made clear, this does not mean the abandonment of tradition or a break with the past, or the rejection or transcendence of either the dominant or residual culture. On the contrary, the utopian message of a movement as expressed through music is often very traditional. Indeed, traditions provide resources for hope and become forces for change when mobilized within social movements.

The technological dimension is reflected through the performance techniques of activists as cultural producers. There is often an artisanal element to the music produced and recalled through social movements which stresses the preservation, as well as the display, of skill and virtuosity. In the context of modern industrial society, where skilled work has become another threatened species, social movements provide temporary social spaces for the preservation and display of craftsmanship. This also has exemplary aspects. As they challenge the commercialization of culture, and as they make use of this very commercialization and the technological developments that result from it, social movements encourage the rediscovery of folk rituals and performance traditions. Bluegrass is only the most obvious example. The folk revivals generally, as they converged with social movements in the 1930s and the 1960s, were the broader context in which traditional and authentic musics and instruments were revitalized.

The organizational dimension is here reflected in the notion that music should encourage active participation, both in its performance and in its creation. The music of social movements is above all else accessible, in terms of being part of a real or imagined heritage and as something which encourages the active involvement of all. The barrier between the performer and the audience is broken down, made ambiguous and fluid. This norm of active participation, a return to traditions of collective song in oral cultures, exists in tension with the stress on skilled performance and the display of virtuosity, which characterizes the technical dimension of the cognitive praxis of social movements. The two at times can coexist, however, as at folk festivals like Newport in the early 1960s, which were designed, in a generous understanding of that concept, to combine all three dimensions of cognitive praxis: the cosmological where freedom and other topical songs were sung, the technological where skilled country and blues musicians and their urban imitators performed and traded skills, and the organizational where the barrier between performer and audience was challenged, in the workshops and in the collective performance of traditional and topical songs.

Music and social movements

Despite a recent cultural turn in social theory, most scholars of social movements remain rooted in instrumentalist and behaviorist approaches to collective action. Social movements, organizations, and actors are interpreted through frameworks which at best view culture as a weapon in strategic battles over political and social power. Some social movements make better usage of their cultural arsenal than others. Some social movements are rich in cultural resources – nationalist and ethnic movements are generally pointed to – while others, environmentalism for example, are not. While we have challenged the narrow conception of culture implied in such accounts, there is a point to be taken. Social movements are at one level strategic actors and do use aspects of culture instrumentally as a resource in mobilization. There are also definite functional or instrumental aspects to singing songs while the courage of a group is being tested in a confrontation with hostile authority. But seeing this as the only or the most important aspect of culture in social movements is to exclude the most essential and vital aspects of culture.

At least two general assumptions underlie this claim. The first is that one can and should distinguish an action from its interpretation or meaning, opening the possibility of several interpretations. The second is that not any interpretation of an action – or its objectification as an artefact – is as good or as valid as any other. Embodied in an action or an artefact is a meaning, and that meaning must be respected. Songs like "Only a Pawn in Their Game" and "The Lonesome Death of Hattie Carroll," written by Bob

Dylan in the early 1960s when he was a movement artist and not just a folksinger or a commercial performer, embody in their lyrics and in the emotional force with which they were performed the values and the virtues exemplified in the civil rights movement. Heard in context, in Greenwood, Mississippi, in 1963, when Dylan joined activists on a voter registration campaign or at the March on Washington in August of that same year, "Only a Pawn in Their Game" recalls and represents the ideals of sacrifice and courage that moved the movement. There is no ambiguity here, neither in the lyrics nor in their performance. The author's own intentions are clearly sounded and recorded, there is little room for misinterpretation, and thus the range of possible readings and receptions is narrow.

Both "Only a Pawn in Their Game" and "Hattie Carroll" were written and performed in a way that expresses and helped constitute the Movement for activists and for outsiders, especially middle-class whites. Performances in the early 1960s recalled and solidified the movement by holding up a mirror to itself which reflected its aims and visions. Hearing these songs today recalls that original meaning, but also opens other possible receptions and interpretations. The original meaning is in the song, however, and, even if it cannot command the same force as it did in its original context, this original meaning and intention (even when its author later denied and withdrew it) demand to be taken into account. Such an interpretation may not be compelling or commanding, but its presence in the song itself seems undeniable.

A way of further specifying that presence is to read that song in cognitive terms. One can read the song as an exemplary movement text, as embodying the cognitive praxis of the movement containing the three dimensions we have identified, the cosmological, the technological, and the organizational. "Hattie Carroll," for example, contains the message that social inequality, race and class privilege, is wrong and should be fought against and that a world where they would be eliminated would be a better one, the basic worldview or cosmology of the civil rights movement. On the technological dimension, the song is skillfully written and forcefully performed and it is decidedly and openly non-commercial in both its form and content. It is too long to be played on the radio, and unambiguously political and thus too controversial and provocative for mass consumption and distribution. On the organizational dimension, the song breaks down the barriers between those who know and those who are kept in ignorance by taking up controversial issues in an accessible way, by breaking down in other words the barriers created in a class- and race-divided society. As part of a movement culture and an emergent, yet still unrealized cultural formation, both songs tell the movement's own story, in an accessible way that invites participation rather than excluding it. In this way they mediate culture and politics.

There are definitely strategic aspects to this process of mediating culture and politics. But that is not the only or even the most essential point, especially not if one assumes the point of view of the actor involved. Social movement actors believe in what they do and their activities are connected to how they identify and distinguish themselves. Social movement activity in this sense is intimately connected with meaning and identity: it is exemplary action. Part of the emergent culture produced within social movements represents an alternative vision and way of life to that of the dominant society. As emergent cultures, in other words, social movements present and represent alternatives. Social movements transform marginal subcultures into real alternatives by offering visions and models of alternative forms of meaning and identity which can be consciously chosen.

The emergent cultures of social movements draw upon aspects of the dominant and residual cultures in creating alternatives to both. Social movement cultures are thus innovative composites which interact with and influence the development of the dominant and alternative dimensions of culture. Our discussion of the folk music "revival" was meant to illustrate this (Eyerman and Baretta 1996). The first wave of revival of the 1930s, which actually helped constitute the folk music genre, was part of a social movement which drew upon black and white folk traditions as it reinvented and reinvigorated them. It also drew from populist and other left-wing political traditions stemming from earlier social movements which had passed over into collective memory as part of an alternative subcultural heritage. At the same time, many activists in the movement were college-educated and well-situated members of the dominant culture who turned their acquired skills into forces for cultural mediation and innovation in the emergent culture produced by the social movement. This folk music genre was turned into a form of popular music in the 1940s and 1950s as both political and commercial interests in the dominant culture were willing to accommodate them and also as activists in the movement altered their own perceptions of the dominant society. The more alternative aspects of the folk music tradition were maintained in the activities of Pete Seeger and in the summer camps organized by the Left for their children. Thus, while the Weavers made commercialized versions of folk songs like "Good Night Irene," which eliminated almost all exemplary meaning, the summer camps, which socialized the red diaper babies many of whom would be influential in the emergence of the New Left and the second folk revival in the 1960s, sang alternative versions of that song and others which were even more obviously political. Pete Seeger, as we have noted, was active in both the commercial and alternative worlds and was essential to the emergence of the topical folksingers of the 1960s and to the spread of folk music into American popular culture. In more than one sense, Seeger can be said to have mediated between the dominant and residual cultural formations.

The cognitive praxis of African-American movements offers another example. Activists like Langston Hughes and Zora Neale Hurston creatively integrated oral traditions of the black folk culture into literary traditions constitutive of the dominant culture. Duke Ellington mixed classical musical forms with blues modes and moods. Both of these cultural representations, Hughes' and Hurston's folk-inspired literature and Ellington's concert jazz, were exemplary in that they expressed the utopian images of an emergent culture which represented the demands for dignity and the self-definition contained in the notion of the New Negro which inspired, unified, and drove the movement. Their representations, objectified in books and musical scores and, especially in Ellington's case, reproduced on records and spread through the radio, objectified and diffused the central message of the New Negro movement long after its demise as a social movement.

The civil rights movement was a singing movement par excellence. It drew on the heritage of the black music tradition – from the sorrow songs to gospel and rhythm-and-blues. In the context of that social movement culture this tradition was given distinct secular and political meaning. The movement could draw on this rich musical heritage and, through it, reach into the collective memory of a repressed people, finding preexisting and deeply rooted forms of communication which for a time could bridge barriers created by class, region, gender, and even religion. This movement culture opened up to and brought together folk music traditions stemming from the residual and dominant white cultures. The civil rights movement of the 1950s and early 1960s was an integrative movement in the cultural as well as in the racial and political sense. It created a context in which the alternative, anti-commercial folk music scene could recover and recall its more directly political aspects. Within the emergent culture of the civil rights movement, folksingers like Bob Dylan, Joan Baez, and Phil Ochs became topical singer-songwriters and exemplary actors with truth-bearing musical messages. As the civil rights movement expanded (or dispersed) into the student movement and the antiwar movement, other groups and other musics were temporarily politicized. Rock and country, the one heavily commercial and the other heavily traditional, both took on political overtones as the social movement culture grew to great significance in the mid-1960s. That the popular culture seemed to be entirely transformed by the movement helped contribute to the widely shared feeling (illusion) that the United States was in the midst of a revolution.

The notion of exemplary action links social movements and culture in intimate ways. As we have pointed out, the predominant theories of aesthetics and social movements would clearly distinguish and limit the interaction between them. Viewed as strategic collective actors, social movements are seen to use art in instrumental ways, as resources in the struggle for power and domination. Movement art, including of course music, is political art, a distinct genre, which from the viewpoint of aesthetic theory is a degraded or at least suspect form of art because it involves interests above and beyond the purely aesthetic. However, if one recognizes that social movements have an exemplary dimension to their action, then culture in general and art in particular is intimately woven into its fabric. Exemplary action is a form of communicative action. It aims at communicating a vision of what the world could be like to others, as much as it provides a forum or form for reaching consensual agreement. This vision is expressed through the form and content of action and is an end or good in itself. At the same time, exemplary action is self-revelatory; through it an actor reveals her own intimate image of herself and how she would like others to see her. Such action is communicative in the sense that it must be performed in public; it requires an audience to appreciate what it exemplifies. All social movements, we would argue, contain an exemplary dimension to their activity. This is a distinguishing criterion of a social movement, separating it from interest or pressure groups, which are purely strategic in their actions. While all social movements are in some basic sense exemplary, this does not mean that all social movement activity is exemplary or that social movements can be reduced to this dimension of their cognitive praxis. However, we would assert that once the exemplary dimension disappears and action becomes primarily instrumental or strategic, we no longer are looking at a social movement.

The concept of tradition has been central to the argument of this book. As with the related notion of culture, theorists of social movements have generally viewed tradition with suspicion. This is because those concerned with social movements and for that matter social theory in general, have viewed tradition through the perspective of modernism and modern science, as a conservative and emotional heritage of an older and now transcended social order. The newest of the new social movements have forced tradition back onto the sociological agenda. A consequence of this, certainly unintended by actors in those movements, has been a new interest in the role of tradition in politics and social life generally. Not only has it become clear that modernization was at best only partially successful in rooting out superstition, myth, and ignorance through its secularization project, with the gift of hindsight we can see that tradition is part of all social life, including that form of collective action we call social movements.

Music can embody the sense of community, a type of experience and identity pointing beyond the walls of the self, which has become the central locus of modern experience and commitment. Such community may well be "imagined," but since it affects identity, it is no less real for that. As Simon Frith has written, "Music constructs our sense of identity through the experiences it offers of the body, time, and sociability, experiences which enable us to place ourselves in imaginative cultural narratives" (1996: 275). Such narratives may well be transitory and fragile, but when linked to social movements they can have lasting effects on individuals and societies. Social movements not only provide temporary spaces for the mobilization of tradition and the reconfiguration of identity, they also effect major cultural shifts, as they interact with the institutionalized practices of a dominant culture. It has been our contention here that music, as an aspect of the cognitive praxis of social movements, has been a resource in the transformation of culture at this fundamental, existential level, helping reconstitute the structures of feeling, the cognitive codes, and the collective dispositions to act, that are culture. We felt and saw and participated in that process of collective remembering at the Highlander School in 1995. Bernice Johnson Reagon, former freedom singer, continues to help us remember with her song group Sweet Honey in the Rock. The relations between music and social movements continue.

Notes

3 Making an alternative popular culture: from populism to the popular front

1. This idea of the people, and of popular culture, is, of course, not exclusively American. Bluestein discusses the writings of the German philosopher Herder, who saw in folk culture the source of national identity. The point is that, while Herder's conceptions had a certain ideological importance in Europe, and an extremely tragic distorted manifestation in Nazi Germany, it was in the United States that Herder's notions of popular culture were appropriated and assimilated most effectively (Bluestein 1994). The argument has been made, however, by Uffe Østergård and other Danish historians, that it was actually only in Denmark that the Herderian conception has had any real impact on economic and cultural development in the twentieth century (Østergård 1990). In the nineteenth century, the Danish farmers' movement developed a range of educational, industrial, and cultural organizations that remain extremely influential to this day. It has been claimed that the particular Danish style of industrialization – through processing of agricultural products – and the Danish people's high schools, the institution that provided the inspiration for the Highlander Center in Tennessee, are all based on a populism that was articulated most clearly in the writings of Frederic Grundtvig, Denmark's leading intellectual of the nineteenth century (Horton 1990). Intriguingly, many consider Grundtvig's most substantial contribution to Danish culture – and the one that continues to influence new generations of Danes – to be the hundreds of hymns that he wrote, and which became, along with the people's high schools' songbooks, a lasting representation of the message of Grundtvigianism – at one and the same time populist, mythical, and moral. Grundtvig, like Carl Sandburg, was also a popular historian, and wrote many volumes on Danish history and on Scandinavian mythology (Thaning 1972). If there ever was a movement that mobilized traditions on the road to modernity, it was the Danish peasant movement, and later the resistance movement during the Second World War, where the old songs played an important role in the collective identity that was articulated in the struggle against the Nazi occupation. This rural-based folk consciousness has

served as a source for many contemporary Danish social movements, from environmentalism to feminism (Jamison, Eyerman, and Cramer 1990). We thank Ulf Hedetoft at Aalborg University for bringing to our attention this Danish connection to our argument. It was unfortunately a bit too late in the writing process for the Danish experience to be integrated into the main text.

2. The continuity of the tradition, and the fact that it continues to develop, can be illustrated not just by Woody Guthrie's drawing inspiration from Joe Hill and, as did Hayes and Robinson, writing songs about him as well; in the 1960s Phil Ochs wrote a song about Joe Hill to the tune of Woody Guthrie's "Tom Joad" (itself written to the tune of "John Hardy"). And even today, the tradition continues to be mobilized; in the late 1980s the British "folk-rocker" Billy Bragg would rewrite the Hayes/Robinson song in order to remember Phil Ochs (Lori Taylor 1993):

> The music business killed you, Phil,
> They ignored the things you said
> And cast you out when fashions changed
> Says Phil, "But I ain't dead,"
> Says Phil, "But I ain't dead."
>   . . .
> When the song of freedom rings out loud
> From valleys and from hills
> Where people stand up for their rights
> Phil Ochs is with us still,
> Phil Ochs is with us still.
>
> (Billy Bragg, "I Dreamed I Saw Phil Ochs Last Night")

3. Just after releasing "The Times They Are A-Changin'" in 1964, Bob Dylan paid a pilgrimage to Carl Sandburg, who was an important influence on his songwriting, in North Carolina, to give him a copy of the record and to tell him, "I am a poet, too." Sandburg politely chatted with Dylan and his stoned traveling companions, and promised to listen to the record (Spitz 1989: 255).

4. Sandburg took his guitar and sang at the hospital bedside of the dying Debs in the 1920s, much like the young Dylan visited Woody Guthrie's hospital in New Jersey in the early 1960s (Niven 1991: 402).

5. Lieberman mentions that the concept of the people differed among the songwriters and folksingers, who are the subject of her study. Many of those she interviewed specifically mentioned Sandburg's *The People, Yes* as a source of inspiration (Lieberman 1995: 178).

4 The movements of black music: from the New Negro to civil rights

1. The distinction made by David Evans (1982) between "folk" and "popular" blues, which is meant to characterize the difference between a rooted oral tradition and a composed and more commercial performance which incorporated

aspects of this tradition, can be related to the difference discussed here. See also the discussion in Tracy (1988: 90ff.). Popular blues, which were first recorded in the 1920s, were a response to the growing audience demand for rural blues by the newly arrived migrants from the South into the urban areas of both North and South.

2. This is similar to the approach of A. P. Carter to country music. In another sense it is similar to that of Langston Hughes, who in using the blues tradition as a source for his poetry also made it into something "more respectable and grand." This was a conscious strategy on his part, just as it was for Carter and Handy, but different from them in that his strategic interests had more to do with racial cultural politics than commerce.

3. David Levering Lewis, author of a biography of W. E. B. DuBois (1993) is one of the leading historians of the Harlem Renaissance. In the work cited here, he offers a lively picture of the Harlem that created the Renaissance. What he describes can be understood in sociological terms as the emergence of a "Negro public sphere" in which intellectuals like Locke and DuBois and artists and writers like Langston Hughes, Aaron Douglas, and Zora Neale Hurston acted as co-producers, but whose basis lay in the city itself and social processes, such as the black migration. His description highlights the role played by promoters and organizers, the "handful of Black American notables" who secured moral and material support for the Renaissance through their "patient assemblage and management of substantial White patronage" (Lewis 1994: 61). These "notables" included "five men and one woman: Jessie Redmond Fauset at the NAACP's publication, *The Crisis*; Charles Spurgeon Johnson, sociologist and editor of the Urban League's *Opportunity*; Alain Locke, professor at Howard University; James Weldon Johnson and Walter Francis White, secretary and assistant secretary, respectively, of the NAACP; and the literate, self-effacing Caspar Holstein, Virgin Islands-born, numbers-racket king of Harlem, whose generous purse helped make possible the prestigious *Opportunity* prizes" (ibid.).

4. Lawrence Levine (1977) argues that the distinction between secular and sacred when referring to early African-American music is largely analytic. His analysis of slave songs and the later forms of music which evolved out of them shows how the distinction was a fluid one for the singers and the songs.

5. Against another of his educated, middle-class colleagues, James Weldon Johnson, who thought "the characteristic beauty of the folk song is harmonic, in distinction to the more purely rhythmic stress in the secular music of the Negro, which is the basis of 'ragtime' and 'jazz,'" and who would distinguish types of music on the basis of rhythm vs. religious message, Locke argues that the spirituals were both rhythmic and religious.

6. The terms "brush arbor," "bush harbor," "bush arbor," and "hush arbor" are all connected with secret religious meetings held by slaves in the American South. The terms were still in use in the 1920s and 1930s to refer to grass-roots prayer and religious meetings.

7. The way in which the civil rights movement reflected the southern roots out of

which it emerged can be illustrated in relation to the clothing that activists wore. Activists dressed neatly in conservative white shirts and pleated skirts and sang their religiously inspired songs with linked arms in a dignified yet unthreatening manner. John Lewis, a Nashville student leader and later SNCC chairman, described preparing for a lunch counter sit-in in 1960: "We put on our Sunday clothes and we took our books and papers to the lunch counter, and we did our homework, trying to be as dignified as possible" (Seeger and Reiser 1989: 30).

This would be in sharp contrast with later stages of the movement, especially "Black Power." But there is another contrast, extremely powerful at the time, especially as magnified through the visual media like television. It was a contrast which did not go unnoticed, even in the South. Commenting on the contrasting dress and behavior at the lunch-room confrontations, the editor of the conservative *Richmond Newsleader* wrote:

Many a Virginian must have felt a tinge of regret at the state of things as they were in reading of Saturday's "sit-downs" by Negro students in Richmond stores. Here were the colored students in coats, white shirts, ties and one of them was reading Goethe, and one of them was taking notes from a biology text. And here, on the sidewalk outside, was a gang of white boys come to heckle, a ragtail rabble, slack-jawed, black-jacketed, grinning fit to kill, and some of them, God save the mark, were waving the proud and honored flag of the Southern states in the last war fought by gentlemen. Phew! It gives one pause.

(quoted in Reagon 1975: 101)

The style of dress, like the music, reflected the meaning and the message of the early civil rights movement. Besides the conservative white shirts and blouses, the other clothing style chosen and worn to express the meaning of the movement was the bib-overalls worn by field workers and organizers in Mississippi, like Bob Moses. Born and educated in New York City, Moses was a graduate student at Harvard when he joined the voter registration drives sponsored by SNCC. To blend in, Moses affected a "country boy" look, blue workshift and overalls worn with dignity and bearing to express the goodness and courage of the "Common Negro." Martin Luther King, Jr., stated the intention behind this symbolism at one of the very first meetings in his Montgomery church at the start of the bus boycott in 1954: "If we protest courageously and with dignity . . . future generations of historians will pause and say, 'There lived a great people, a black people, who injected new meaning and dignity into the veins of civilization.' This is our challenge and our overwhelming responsibility" (quoted in Seeger and Reiser 1989: 7).

5 Politics and music in the 1960s

1. The founding father of structural functionalism, Talcott Parsons, was one of the first to speak of a distinct "youth culture." Already in 1949, Parsons referred to adolescence as a part of the life-cycle where "there first begins to develop a set

of patterns and behavior phenomena which involve a highly complex combination of age grading and sex role elements . . . [that] may be referred to together as the phenomena of the 'youth culture'" (Parsons 1949: 220). In the context of discussing emerging gender differences amongst American adolescents, Parsons characterizes "the period of youth in our society [as] one of considerable strain and insecurity" (ibid.: 229) and at the same time warns against the "tendency to the romantic idealization of youth patterns" by adults who, because of similar "strains," look back upon childhood and adolescence as periods of carefree existence which contrast greatly to their present work and family-related responsibilities.

Parsons was one of the first to notice the potential emergence of the great cultural shift which occurred in the 1960s when "youth" and youth culture, to a large extent, became the model and ideal for the rest of society (Parsons 1965). It should also be noted that in this later essay Parsons noted the differences related to social class. The youth culture he identified in the 1940s was that of the urban middle and upper classes. In the 1960s, when he returned to the theme, the idea of youth and youth culture had become more general and universal, reflecting shifts not only in American social structure but in the rest of the industrially developed world. By the late 1950s and early 1960s, the privilege of youth had spread to a much bigger part of the population.

Bibliography

Alberoni, Francesco (1984). *Movement and Institution*. New York: Columbia University Press

Alexander, Jeffrey (1990). "Analytic Debates: Understanding the Relative Autonomy of Culture," in Jeffrey Alexander and Steven Seidman, eds., *Culture and Society: Contemporary Debates*. Cambridge: Cambridge University Press

Anderson, Benedict (1991). *Imagined Communities: Reflections on the Origin and Spread of Nationalism*. London: Verso

Anderson, Paul (1995). "Ellington, Rap Music, and Cultural Difference," *Musical Quarterly*, 79:1, pp. 172–206

Aronowitz, Stanley (1993). *Roll Over Beethoven: The Return of Cultural Strife*. Hanover, N. H.: Wesleyan University Press

Baker, Houston (1987). *Modernism and the Harlem Renaissance*. Chicago: University of Chicago Press

  (1993). *Black Studies, Rap, and the Academy*. Chicago: University of Chicago Press

Beck, Ulrich (1992). *Risk Society: Towards a New Modernity*. London: Sage

Beck, Ulrich, Anthony Giddens, and Scott Lash (1994). *Reflexive Modernization: Politics, Tradition, and Aesthetics in the Modern Social Order*. Cambridge: Polity

Becker, Howard (1982). *Art Worlds*. Berkeley: University of California Press

Bernstein, J. M. (1992). *The Fate of Art: Aesthetic Alienation from Kant to Derrida and Adorno*. Cambridge: Polity

Bluestein, Gene (1972). *The Voice of the Folk: Folklore and American Literary Theory*. Amherst: University of Massachusetts Press

  (1994). *Poplore: Folk and Pop in American Culture*. Amherst: University of Massachusetts Press

Bourdieu, Pierre (1984). *Distinction*. Cambridge, Mass.: Harvard University Press

Boyes, Georgina (1993). *The Imagined Village: Culture, Ideology, and the English Folk Revival*. Manchester: Manchester University Press

Cantwell, Robert (1992). *Bluegrass Breakdown: The Making of the Old Southern Sound*. New York: De Capo Press

    (1996). *When We Were Good: The Folk Revival*. Cambridge, Mass.: Harvard University Press

Carawan, Guy, and Candie Carawan, eds. (1990). *Sing For Freedom: The Story of the Civil Rights Movement Through Its Songs*. Bethlehem, Pa.: Sing Out Publications

Carson, Clayborne (1981). *In Struggle: SNCC and the Black Awakening of the 1960s*. Cambridge, Mass.: Harvard University Press

Clarke, John, Stuart Hall, Tony Jefferson, and Brian Roberts (1975). "Subculture, Cultures and Class," in Stuart Hall and Tony Jefferson, eds., *Resistance Through Rituals*. London: Hutchinson

Cohen, Jean (1985). "Strategy or Identity: New Theoretical Paradigms and Contemporary Social Movements," *Social Research*, 52:4, pp. 663–715

Cohen, Norm (1991). *Folk Song America: A Twentieth-Century Revival*. Washington, D.C.: Smithsonian Collection of Recordings (booklet attached to CD box)

Cone, James (1991). *Martin and Malcolm and America*. New York: Orbis

Crane, Diana (1987). *The Transformation of the Avant-Garde: The New York Art World, 1940–1985*. Chicago: University of Chicago Press

Cruz, Jon David (1986). "Politics of Popular Culture: Black Popular Music as 'Public Sphere.'" Unpublished Ph.D. dissertation, University of California, Berkeley

Darnovsky, Marcy, Barbara Epstein, and Richard Flacks, eds. (1995). *Cultural Politics and Social Movements*. Philadelphia: Temple University Press

Denisoff, R. Serge (1971). *Great Day Coming: Folk Music and the American Left*. Urbana: University of Illinois Press

    (1972). *Sing a Song of Social Significance*. Bowling Green, Ohio: Bowling Green University Press

Denisoff, R. Serge, and R. Peterson, eds. (1973). *The Sounds of Social Change*. New York: Rand McNally

Denning, Michael (1996). *The Cultural Front: The Laboring of American Culture in the Twentieth Century*. London: Verso

Denselow, Robin (1989). *When the Music's Over: The Story of Political Pop*. London: Faber and Faber

DuBois, W. E. B. ([1903] 1994). *The Souls of Black Folk*. New York: Dover; orig. Chicago: A. C. McClurg
([1926] 1986). "Criteria of Negro Art," in DuBois, *Writings*. New York: Library of America
Dunaway, David (1990). *How Can I Keep From Singing: Pete Seeger*. New York: De Capo Press
Edelman, Murray (1995). *From Art to Politics*. Chicago: University of Chicago Press
Egerton, Frank (1994). *Speak Now Against the Day: The Generation Before the Civil Rights Movement in the South*. New York: Knopf
Eliot, Marc (1990). *Phil Ochs: Death of a Rebel*. London: Omnibus Press
Ellison, Curtis (1995). *Country Music Culture*. Jackson: University of Mississippi Press
Evans, David (1982). *Big Road Blues: Tradition and Creativity in the Folk Blues*. Berkeley: University of California Press
Eyerman, Ron (1981). *False Consciousness and Ideology in Marxist Theory*. Atlantic Highlands, N. J.: Humanities Press
(1994). *Between Culture and Politics*. Cambridge: Polity
Eyerman, Ron, and Scott Baretta (1996). "From the 30s to the 60s: The Folk Music Revival in the United States," *Theory and Society*, 25, pp. 501–43
Eyerman, Ron, and Andrew Jamison (1991). *Social Movements: A Cognitive Approach*. Cambridge: Polity
(1992). "On the Transatlantic Migration of Knowledge: Intellectual Exchange Between the United States and Sweden, 1930–1970," *Science Studies*, 2, pp. 79–96
(1995). "Social Movements and Cultural Transformation: Popular Music in the 1960s," *Media, Culture, and Society*, 2, pp. 449–68
Feuer, Louis (1969). *The Conflict of Generations*. London: Heinemann
Feyerabend, Paul (1978). *Science in a Free Society*. London: New Left Books
Flacks, Richard (1971). *Youth and Social Change*. Chicago: Markham
(1988). *Making History*. New York: Columbia University Press
Floyd, Samuel, ed. (1993). *Music and the Harlem Renaissance*. Knoxville: University of Tennessee Press
(1995). *The Power of Black Music*. New York: Oxford University Press
Fornäs, Johan (1985). *Tältprojektet. Musikteater som manifestation*. Stockholm and Gothenburg: Symposion
(1993). "'Play It Yourself': Swedish Music in Movement," *Social Science Information*, 1, pp. 39–65

Friedland, Roger (1995). "Interred Meanings/Meaningful Interests." Unpublished paper

Frith, Simon (1978). *The Sociology of Rock*. London: Constable

(1996). *Performing Rites: On the Value of Popular Music*. Cambridge, Mass.: Harvard University Press

Gamson, William (1995). "Hiroshima, the Holocaust, and the Politics of Exclusion," *American Sociological Review*, 60:1, pp. 1–20

Garofalo, Reebee, ed. (1992). *Rockin' the Boat: Mass Music and Mass Movements*. Boston: South End Press

Giddens, Anthony (1994). "Living in a Post-Traditional Society," in Beck, Giddens, and Lash, *Reflexive Modernization*

Gillett, Charlie (1970). *The Sound of the City*. London: Souvenir

Gilroy, Paul (1992). *There Ain't No Black in the Union Jack*. London: Routledge

(1994). *The Black Atlantic: Modernity and Double Consciousness*. London: Routledge

Gitlin, Todd (1980). *The Whole World Is Watching*. Berkeley: University of California Press

(1987). *The Sixties: Years of Hope, Days of Rage*. New York: Bantam

Goines, David Lance (1993). *The Free Speech Movement*. Berkeley: Ten Speed Press

Goodwyn, Lawrence (1978). *The Populist Moment*. Oxford: Oxford University Press

Gottesam, Stephen (1977). "Tom Dooley's Children: An Overview of the Folk Music Revival, 1958–1965," *Popular Music and Society*, 5

Greenway, John ([1953] 1971). *American Folksongs of Protest*. New York: Octagon Books

Guralnick, Peter (1986). *Sweet Soul Music*. New York: Penguin

(1988). Liner notes to "A Vision Shared: A Tribute to Woody Guthrie and Leadbelly." Folkways Records

Hall, Stuart, ed. (1989). *New Times*. London: Lawrence and Wishart

Hannerz, Ulf (1992). *Cultural Complexity: Studies in the Organization of Meaning*. New York: Columbia University Press

Harris, Michael W. (1992). *The Rise of Gospel Blues*. New York: Oxford University Press

Herf, Jeffrey (1984). *Reactionary Modernism*. Cambridge: Cambridge University Press

Heylin, Clinton (1991). *Dylan: Behind the Shades*. New York: Viking

Hobsbawm, Eric (1983). "Introduction: Inventing Traditions," in E. Hobsbawm and T. Ranger, eds., *The Invention of Tradition*. Cambridge: Cambridge University Press

Horkheimer, Max, and Theodor Adorno ([1944] 1972). *Dialectic of Enlightenment*. New York: Seabury

Horton, Myles (1990). *The Long Haul: An Autobiography*. New York: Doubleday

Hughes, Langston, and Milton Meltzer ([1967] 1990). *Black Magic: A Pictorial History of the African-American in the Performing Arts*. New York: De Capo Press

Hunt, Scott, Robert Benford, and David Snow (1994). "Identity Fields: Framing Processes and the Social Construction of Movement Identities," in Laraña, Johnston, and Gusfield, *New Social Movements*

Jamison, Andrew (1994). "Western Science in Perspective and the Search for Alternatives," in Jean-Jacques Salomon, Francisco Sagasti, and Celine Sachs, eds., *The Uncertain Quest: Science, Technology, and Development*. Tokyo: UN University Press

Jamison, Andrew, and Ron Eyerman (1994). *Seeds of the Sixties*. Berkeley and Los Angeles: University of California Press

Jamison, Andrew, Ron Eyerman, and Jacqueline Cramer (1990). *The Making of the New Environmental Consciousness*. Edinburgh: Edinburgh University Press

Johnson, James Weldon ([1925] 1944). "The History of the Spiritual," in Sylvestre Watkins, ed., *Anthology of American Negro Literature*. New York: Modern Library

([1933] 1990). *Along This Way: The Autobiography of James Weldon Johnson*. New York: Viking Penguin

Johnston, Hank (1995). "A Methodology for Frame Analysis: From Discourse to Cognitive Schema," in Johnston and Klandermans, *Social Movements and Culture*

Johnston, Hank, and Bert Klandermans, eds. (1995). *Social Movements and Culture*. Minneapolis: University of Minnesota Press

Jones, LeRoi (1963). *Blues People*. New York: Quill

Jones, Steve (1992). *Rock Formation*. London: Sage

Kaplan, Temma (1992). *Red City, Blue Period*. Berkeley: University of California Press

Karpeles, Maud, ed. (1968). *Eighty English Folk Songs from the Southern Appalachians*, collected by Cecil Sharp and Maud Karpeles. London: Faber and Faber

Kazin, Michael (1995). *The Populist Persuasion: An American History*. New York: Basic Books

Keniston, Kenneth (1965). "Social Change and Youth in America," in Erik H. Erikson, ed., *The Challenge of Youth* (reprint of *Daedalus* issue). New York: Doubleday

King, Mary (1987). *Freedom Song*. New York: Quill

Kjellström, Birgit, Jan Ling, Christina Mattsson, Mäerta Ramsten, and Gunnar Ternhage (1985). *Folkmusikvågen: The Folk Music Vogue*. Stockholm: Rikskonserter

Klein, Joe (1980). *Woody Guthrie: A Life*. New York: Knopf

Kuhn, Thomas (1970). *The Structure of Scientific Revolutions*. Chicago: University of Chicago Press

Laraña, Enrique, Hank Johnston, and Joseph Gusfield, eds. (1994). *New Social Movements: From Ideology to Identity*. Philadelphia: Temple University Press

Levine, Lawrence (1977). *Black Culture and Black Consciousness*. New York: Oxford University Press

(1988). *Highbrow Lowbrow: The Emergence of Cultural Hierarchy in America*. Cambridge, Mass.: Harvard University Press

Lewis, David (1993). *W. E. B. DuBois: The Biography of a Race*. New York: Henry Holt

(1994). "Harlem My Home," in Lewis, ed., *Harlem Renaissance: Art of Black America*. New York: Abradale Press, Harry N. Abrams Inc.

Lie, Marit (1996). "Kreativt möte eller marknadsfrieri?," *Lira*, 5/6, pp. 38–43

Lieberman, Robbie (1995). *"My Song is My Weapon": People's Songs, American Communism, and the Politics of Culture, 1930–1950*. Urbana: University of Illinois Press

Locke, Alain, ed. ([1925] 1968). *The New Negro*. New York: Athaneum

Lomax, Alan (1993). *The Land Where the Blues Began*. New York: Pantheon

Lomax, John (1947). *Adventures of a Ballad Hunter*. New York: Macmillan

Lomax, John, and Alan Lomax ([1947] 1966). *Folk Song USA*. New York: Signet

Lyotard, Jean-François (1984). *The Postmodern Condition: A Report on Knowledge*. Minneapolis: University of Minnesota Press

McAdam, Doug (1988). *Freedom Summer*. New York: Oxford University Press

(1994). "Culture and Social Movements," in Laraña, Johnston, and Gusfield, *New Social Movements*

McAdam, Doug, and Dieter Rucht (1993). "The Cross-National Diffusion of Movement Ideas," *Annals of the American Academy*, 528, pp. 56–74

Malone, Bill (1993). *Singing Cowboys and Musical Mountaineers: Southern Culture and the Roots of Country Music*. Athens, Ga.: University of Georgia Press

Marcus, Greil (1990). *Mystery Train*. New York: Plume

Marcuse, Herbert (1964). *One-Dimensional Man: Studies in the Ideology of Advanced Industrial Society*. Boston: Beacon Press

(1969). *An Essay on Liberation*. Boston: Beacon Press

Melucci, Alberto (1989). *Nomads of the Present*. Philadelphia: Temple University Press

(1996). *Challenging Codes: Collective Action in the Information Age*. Cambridge: Cambridge University Press

Mills, C. Wright (1959). *The Sociological Imagination*. New York: Oxford University Press

Moore, Allan F. (1993). *Rock: The Primary Text. Developing a Musicology of Rock*. Buckingham: Open University Press

Morgan, Edward (1991). *The Sixties Experience: Hard Lessons About Modern America*. Philadelphia: Temple University Press

Morgan, Thomas, and William Barlow (1992). *From Cakewalks to Concert Halls*. Washington, D. C.: Elliot and Clark

Mumford, Lewis (1926). *The Golden Day: A Study in American Literature and Culture*. New York: Boni and Liveright

Niven, Penelope (1991). *Carl Sandburg: A Biography*. New York: Charles Scribner's Sons

Nylén, Leif (1977). "Musikrörelsen och masskulturens politisering," in *Ord och bild*, 2–3, pp. 120–28 (English translation published as "Music power brings political strength" in a brochure, *The Rise of Alternative Music in Sweden*. Stockholm: Rikskonserter, 1978)

Ochs, Phil (1965). *The War is Over*. New York: Barricade Music

Oliver, Paul (1960). *Blues Fell This Morning*. London: Cassell and Company

Orman, John (1984). *The Politics of Rock Music*. London: Nelson-Hall

Østergård, Uffe (1990). "Peasants and Danes: Danish National Identity and Political Culture." Working paper from the Center for Cultural Studies, Aarhus University

Parsons, Talcott (1949). *Essays in Sociological Theory Pure and Applied*. New York: Free Press

(1965). "Youth in the Context of American Society," in Erik H. Erikson, ed., *The Challenge of Youth*. New York: Doubleday Anchor

Pescatello, Ann (1992). *Charles Seeger: A Life in American Music*. Pittsburgh: University of Pittsburgh Press

Pratt, Ray (1990). *Rhythm and Resistance*. New York: Praeger

Rampersad, Arnold (1986). *The Life of Langston Hughes*, Volume I, *1902–1941*. New York: Oxford University Press

ed. (1995). *The Collected Poems of Langston Hughes*. New York: Knopf

Reagon, Bernice Johnson (1975). "Songs of the Civil Rights Movement,

1955–1965: A Study in Culture History." Unpublished Ph.D. dissertation, Howard University

(1993). *We Who Believe in Freedom*. New York: Anchor

Rodnitzky, Jerome (1975). *Minstrels of the Dawn: The Folk-Protest Singer as a Cultural Hero*. Chicago: Nelson-Hall

Rönström, Owe, and Gunnar Ternhage, eds. (1994). *Texter om svensk folkmusik. Från Haeffner till Ling*. Stockholm: Kungliga Musikaliska Akademien

Rosenberg, Neil V., ed. (1993). *Transforming Tradition: Folk Music Revivals Examined*. Urbana: University of Illinois Press

Salomon, Kim (1996). *Rebeller i takt med tiden*. Stockholm: Rabén och Sjögren

Sandburg, Carl (1950). *Complete Poems*. New York: Harcourt, Brace, and World

Schechner, Richard (1993). *The Future of Ritual*. London: Routledge

Scheuer, Timothy (1991). *Born in the USA*. Oxford: University of Mississippi Press

Schribner, W. (1987). *Popular Culture and Popular Movements*. London: Hambledon

Seeger, Pete (1993). *Where Have All the Flowers Gone: A Singer's Stories, Songs, Seeds, Robberies*. Bethlehem, Pa.: Sing Out Publications

Seeger, Pete, and Bob Reiser (1989). *Everybody Says Freedom*. New York: Norton

Shils, Edward (1981). *Tradition*. London: Faber and Faber

Sidran, Ben ([1971] 1981). *Black Talk*. New York: De Capo Press

Simpson, David (1992). "Raymond Williams: Feeling for Structures, Voicing 'History,'" *Social Text*, 30, pp. 9–25

Small, Christopher (1987). *Music of the Common Tongue*. London: Calder Press

Snow, David, and Robert Benford (1988). "Ideology, Frame Resonance, and Participant Mobilization," in Bert Klandermans, Hans Kriesi, and Sidney Tarrow, eds., *From Structure to Action*. Greenwich: JAI Press

(1992). "Master Frames and Cycles of Protest," in Aldon Morris and Carol Mueller, eds., *Frontiers of Social Movement Theory*. New Haven: Yale University Press

Southern, Eileen (1983). *The Music of Black Americans: A History*. New York: W. W. Norton

Spencer, Jon (1993). *Blues and Evil*. Knoxville: University of Tennessee Press

Spitz, Bob (1989). *Dylan: A Biography*. New York: Norton

Street, John (1986). *Rebel Rock*. Oxford: Blackwell

Stuart, John, ed. ([1955] 1972). *The Education of John Reed: Selected Writings*. Berlin: Seven Seas

Sullivan, Patricia (1991). "Southern Reformers, the New Deal, and the Movement's Foundation," in A. Robinson and P. Sullivan, eds., *New Directions in Civil Rights Studies*. Charlottesville: University of Virginia Press

Susman, Warren (1984). *Culture as History: The Transformation of American Society in the Twentieth Century*. New York: Pantheon Books

Swidler, Anne (1995). "Cultural Power and Social Movements," in Johnston and Klandermans, *Social Movements and Culture*

Tallack, Douglas (1991). *Twentieth-Century America: The Intellectual and Cultural Context*. London: Longman

Tarrow, Sidney (1994). *Power in Movement*. Cambridge: Cambridge University Press

Taylor, Lori (1993). "Joe Hill Incorporated: We Own Our Past," in Archie Green, ed., *Songs About Work: Essays in Occupational Culture*. Bloomington: Indiana University Press

Taylor, Vera, and Nancy Whittier (1995). "Analytic Approaches to Social Movement Culture: The Culture of the Women's Movement," in Johnston and Klandermans, *Social Movements and Culture*

Thaning, Kaj (1972). *N. F. S. Grundtvig*. Copenhagen: Det Danske Selskab

Tick, Judith (1995). "Ruth Crawford Seeger and African-American Folk Music: The Work of a New Deal Documentor." Paper presented at the joint meetings of the American Musicological Society, the Center for Black Music Research, and the Society for Music Theory. New York, November 2–5

Tischler, Barbara (1986). *An American Music: The Search for an American Musical Identity*. New York: Oxford University Press

Tracy, Steven (1988). *Langston Hughes and the Blues*. Urbana: University of Illinois Press

Turner, Jonathan (1988). *A Theory of Social Interaction*. Cambridge: Polity

Turner, Victor (1969). *The Ritual Process*. London: Routledge and Kegan Paul

Van Deburg, William (1992). *New Day in Babylon*. Chicago: University of Chicago Press

Vincent, Ted (1995). *Keep Cool: The Black Activists Who Built the Jazz Age*. London: Pluto Press

Wallis, Roger, and Krister Malm (1984). *Big Sounds from Small Peoples: The Music Industry in Small Countries*. London: Constable

Weinstein, Deena (1992). "Rock is Youth/Youth is Rock," in Kenneth

Bindas, ed., *America's Musical Pulse: Popular Music in Twentieth-Century Society*. Westport, Conn.: Greenwood Press

Whalen, Jack, and Richard Flacks (1989). *Beyond the Barricades: The Sixties Generation Grows Up*. Philadelphia: Temple University Press

Wiehe, Mikael (1980). *Sånger 1971–1979*. Stockholm: Liber

Willens, Doris (1988). *Lonesome Traveler: The Life of Lee Hays*. New York: Norton

Williams, Raymond (1976). *Keywords*. Glasgow: Fontana

(1977). *Marxism and Literature*. Oxford: Oxford University Press

Wintz, Cary (1988). *Black Culture and the Harlem Renaissance*. Houston: Rice University Press

Wolfe, Charles, and Kip Lornell (1992). *The Life and Legend of Leadbelly*. New York: HarperCollins

Wolfe, Daniel, S. R. Crain, Clifton White, and G. David Tenenbaum (1995). *You Send Me: The Life and Times of Sam Cooke*. New York: William Morris

Index